James A. Walker, Jr.

D1502986

THE BLOSSOMING DESERT

A Concise History
of Texas Baptists

THE BLOSSOMING DESERT

A Concise History of Texas Baptists

ROBERT A. BAKER

WORD BOOKS, PUBLISHER
WACO, TEXAS

Contents

Preface

Texas Baptists have had the raw materials for growth since the Republic was born: multitudes of needy people, and a strong gospel preached by earnest men. For the most part, the people and preachers came from the older states of the South, the immigration averaging about 2,000 a month for thirty-five years after independence was secured. Most of the people came for land upon which to homestead. Although the territory stretched almost a thousand miles from the northern tip to the coast and seven hundred miles from the eastern edge to the western bulge, it was no accident that the earliest substantial growth took place between the Brazos and Colorado rivers in the fertile triangle whose top touched what is now Waco and whose base rested on Houston and San Antonio. Little did these settlers suspect that below the ground upon which they toiled was black gold and other minerals to rival the wealth of Croesus.

The story of this Baptist growth has been told many times. Formal histories probably should include Z. N. Morrell, *Flowers and Fruits in the Wilderness* (1872 and 1886); B. F. Fuller, *History of Texas Baptists* (1900); B. F. Riley, *History of the Baptists of Texas* (1907); J. M. Carroll, *A History of Texas Baptists* (1923); L. R. Elliott, ed., *Centennial Story of Texas Baptists* (1936); and J. M. Dawson, *A Century with Texas Bap-*

tists (1948). J. B. Link, ed., *Texas Historical and Biographical Magazine* (1891 and 1892, in two volumes), could almost be considered a formal history. Not only so, but there are multitudes of church, associational, and regional Baptist histories. In addition, a thousand books on secular Texas history in Fleming Library at Southwestern Seminary include some sections on Baptists and other religious history of the state.

As a matter of fact, almost any Texas Baptist could write his own state history. Except for a brief period in the earliest days of Texas, fairly accurate records are readily available in what could be termed source materials. By the turn of the century, as will be glimpsed from the dates of the histories published, the records become rather plentiful, and the problem becomes one of summary rather than research. Three Baptist histories were written within twenty-five years, the third one (by Carroll) containing over a thousand pages. Why, then, one asks, is there a need for another history of Texas Baptists? The answer will explain the character of this particular history. First, the last Texas Baptist history was published almost twenty-five years ago. Since that time, Texas Baptists have made radical organizational changes and have expanded greatly. This story has never been told, and its importance justifies more emphasis on this period than on earlier times. Second, the year 1970 represents the 150th anniversary of the first Baptist sermon in Texas. There is some uncertainty that this sermon was preached in 1820, but the preponderance of evidence points in that direction. Such an anniversary should be used as a reminder of the courage and faith of our fathers and as an occasion for us to take courage in our task.

Finally, the supervising committee of the Executive Board envisioned a concise summary, written more for the man in the street than for the scholar, one which would familiarize the average Texas Baptist with the principal movements in the Baptist history of his state.

For these reasons, the 80,000-word account presented here condenses many activities into statistics and tries to give the flavor of the work by a capsule description or a judicious sample. I have no apology for including so many statistics. Not only do these reflect the rate of growth, but they make it unnecessary for one to read this story and then seek elsewhere for specific data. Statistics compensate somewhat for the extreme condensing that was necessary. The index will show also that many names were written into the story, including the principal leaders on the state level during the contemporary period. History is made up of people, and as many as possible deserve to be enrolled in the pages of a work like this. I wish that a thousand more worthy ones could have been mentioned in the book.

Where the location of a source is evident from the context, specific documentation has not been shown. This eliminated a hundred pages of footnotes, but allows an interested reader to find the source without undue difficulty.

My special thanks to the supervising committee of James Semple, chairman, R. A. Springer, William Shamburger, and James Lindsey; and to D. D. Tidwell for reading portions of the material. Of course I assume all responsibility for the story.

Robert A. Baker

1

The Barren Land

Z. N. Morrell was not the first Baptist preacher in Texas, but he was the state's most important pioneer Baptist preacher. In his second sermon in the new land he set the theme for Texas Baptist history. He tells the story.

Having an important engagement to be at a point beyond Nacogdoches on Sunday night, that must be met "if the Lord will," and being twenty miles west of the town when the sun of Sunday morning rose, I felt compelled to violate my former custom and travel on the Lord's day. My mind was by no means at ease. Several Sundays had come and gone while we were in the wilderness, and only one sermon had been preached, and on an evening during the week. This was by no means the course I had pursued for fourteen years in Tennessee. My very soul burned within me to preach Jesus.

An election was in progress when I reached the town. This was the law and custom of the country in that day. Here was a large crowd of Americans, Mexicans, and Indians of several different tribes. My mule was soon tied, and after consultation with my great Master—for I had no one else to consult with—I decided to preach, and began looking around for a suitable place. Near by the vast crowd I saw the foundation timbers of a large framed building already laid. No floor had been laid, nor upright pieces raised. No sooner discovered than I selected one corner of this for a pulpit,—the sills and sleepers already laid and well adjusted would answer for seats. I held up my watch in my hand, and cried at the top of my voice, "O-yes! o-yes! o-yes! everybody that wants to buy, without money and without price, come this way,"—and commenced singing the old battle-song: "Am I a

11

soldier of the cross?" Before I finished my song there was around me a large crowd of all sorts and sizes and colors. A brief prayer was offered, and the two verses sung, " 'Tis religion that can give," amidst profound silence. Astonishment, rather than reverence, was stamped upon their features. Across the street was a large upper gallery, and by this time it was full of ladies and gentlemen. Just at this point some wagons and a carriage, evidently belonging to movers, drove up close to where I was standing, and I recognized brother Wm. Whitaker and family, from Hardiman County, Tennessee, three of whose daughters I had baptized in the old State. The preacher who reads this will understand the effect this produced upon the speaker. My text was announced from Isaiah XXXV. 1: "The wilderness and the solitary place shall be glad for them; and the desert shall rejoice and blossom as the rose." Never did the cane-brake preacher receive better attention. God blessed me with great liberty for one hour, amid many tears shed all around me. The congregation was dismissed in due form, and there were many hearty shakes given the strange preacher's hand. My soul was full to overflowing, and at that moment I believed the text.[1]

A generation later in his published reminiscences, Morrell related several of his experiences to illustrate how this promise—that the wilderness of Texas would blossom as a rose—gave him strength in times of personal sufferings and loss. Mrs. Sybil Leonard Armes has caught this spirit in haunting poetry.

Out of a wilderness they carved
A spiritual empire for our Lord
In blood and tears and sacrifice
They sowed his glorious, living word
And the desert blossomed as a rose
But what it cost, God only knows!

And we who follow in their wake
Mark well the price they paid.
His mantle lies upon us now,
But we are not afraid
If God be with us: This we cry,
"The light of Jesus shall not die
'Till earth's remotest corner knows
And the deserts blossom as a rose."

This Wilderness

The very first explorer to visit Texas, Cabeza de Vaca, a Spaniard, told some tall tales about his sojourn during the first half of the sixteenth century. Coronado toured Texas to see if the golden city of Quivera really existed. His failure to locate it dulled Spanish interests in further occupation. Soon thereafter Luis de Moscoso entered Texas from the east, but found nothing to warrant further interest by Spain. The Franciscan friars carrying their gospel to the Indians were the only Spanish representatives in Texas during the following century.

The explorations of LaSalle for France awakened Spain to the recognition that if she did not colonize Texas, someone else would. Between 1690 and 1693 Spain sent two missionary expeditions to the Tejas Indians, but both efforts were abandoned because of the hostility of the inhabitants. Another French effort to get a foothold in Texas spurred the Spanish to establish a line of missions from the Neches to the Red River during the seventeenth century. In the eighteenth century, Spain sent additional armies along with missionaries into western and central Texas, but no permanent colonization resulted. In the Peace of 1763 following the Seven Years' War, Spain was permitted to retain Louisiana Territory, including Texas.

Spain faced new troubles when the United States purchased "Louisiana" in 1803. The Spanish leaders denied that the territory as far west as the Rio Grande was included in this purchase, and refused to relinquish their settlement at Nacogdoches on the eastern border of the Texas territory. During the next two decades several American adventurers invaded portions of the territory, but were unsuccessful in their efforts to gain control. In the Florida Treaty of 1819, the United States formally renounced any claim she might have on Texas. Thus, by 1819, although successful in thwarting efforts of France and the Anglo-Americans, Spain had done little to colonize the land. The Indians, estimated as numbering between 15,000 and 50,000, some warlike and some friendly, had been a major deterrent to Spanish occupation. From 1819 to

1821, when Mexico successfully revolted against Spain, the Spanish seemed to feel that the only use for Texas was to provide a buffer between herself and her aggressive neighbors on the east.

The First Baptist Preacher

Joseph Bays first stood on Texas soil in the summer of 1820. This tall, powerfully built man looked more like an Indian fighter than the first Baptist preacher of record in Texas. Born in North Carolina into a non-conformist English family, he had been taken as a boy to Kentucky where he was reared in the shadow of Daniel Boone. After the death of his father, his mother taught him to read and write using the Bible as a textbook. In later years, it was noted that he would quote long passages from the Scriptures rarely looking at his open Bible, having memorized the text as a lad. The religious character of his family may be glimpsed in the names given to his brothers. His biblical name (Joseph) was matched by those of his brothers, who were called John, Peter, Isaac, Shadrack, Meshach, and Abednego.

With the first three-named brothers, he followed Daniel Boone to Missouri, where he met Moses Austin. In 1818–19 he and Austin spent many long evenings listening to exciting stories by men returning from that fabled new land called Texas, far to the south. Austin convinced Bays that the Spaniards would allow Anglo-Americans to settle in the fertile country. With thirty-three other families, Bays and his wife began the 500 mile journey, and on June 30, 1820, camp was struck on the Louisiana side of the Sabine River. It was planned that the camp would remain here until Moses Austin had secured a permit from the Spanish government allowing them to emigrate into Texas. Before long, however, without such permission Bays crossed the Sabine and soon began preaching regularly each month in the home of Joseph Hinds on the Texas side.

Doubtless Joseph Bays felt his heart leap within him as for the first time his feet touched Texas soil, the land about which he and Moses Austin had talked in low tones around the camp fire on their long trek from Missouri. His principal motive in making the journey doubtless was the establishment of a home and the opportunity of witnessing through the preaching of the gospel. Neither Bays nor any of the others could have guessed that this remote land, inhabited chiefly by wild Indian tribes and roaming buffalo, would play such a pivotal part in the history of the United States and of the Baptist people.

Just as Texas related to the major physical divisions of the North American continent—on the south with the Atlantic-Gulf coastal plain, in the north-central area with the Great Plains of North America, and in the far west, with the great Rocky Mountain system—it likewise was destined to become immediately related to the great historical developments of the continent. Already it had begun to be involved in the colonial and diplomatic patterns of France, Spain, England, Mexico, and the United States. In its rise and development it was the greatest single factor in American history that led to the fulfillment of the "manifest destiny," in that it opened the door to the far west. Both in its annexation and development it played a large part in the greatest internal struggle the United States ever experienced. It became the object of extensive missionary work by various denominations. It was the principal immediate occasion of the break between Northern and Southern Baptists over the slavery-abolitionist controversy. It became the strongest state body in the Baptist denomination.

At the very time Joseph Bays was preaching the first Baptist sermon on Texas soil, a revolutionary movement was underway that would greatly affect the history of Texas Baptists. As early as 1810 the Mexican priest Hidalgo had begun a revolt against the Spanish government. Although defeated and slain, he lighted a flame for Mexican freedom from Spain. Helped along by the Napoleonic conquests of Spain, the Council of Vienna in 1815, and other factors, Mexico was able to secure her independence from Spain in 1821 with very little bloodshed. Thus, when Moses Austin received approval from the Spanish authorities in 1820 to move 300 families into Texas, his work was wasted. The elder Austin died shortly thereafter and his son, Stephen F. Austin, after already settling some Anglo-Americans in Texas, had to journey to Mexico City to negotiate with the new Mexican government.

Meeting with success, he returned to the Texas colony to settle the "Old Three Hundred" families in this Mexican province by 1824.

Eleven of these families were definitely known to be Baptists, as follows: Elijah Allcorn and probably his wife, Mrs. J. P. Coles and probably Judge Coles, Thomas Davis, David Fitzgerald, Chester S. Gorbet, William Harvey, William Kincheloe, Abner Kuykendall, John McNeill, John W. Moore, and John Smith.

The coming of the Anglo-Americans marked a new era in the history of Texas. The slow, lethargic pace that had characterized the history of the land for three centuries had come to an end. This barren land would soon be sown with the seeds of the gospel and of independence.

2

The Baptist Witness

The successful struggle in the late eighteenth century to include the principle of religious liberty in the Constitution of the United States left a permanent deposit in the thinking of most Christians in the land, and especially the Baptists, who had been in the forefront of that struggle. Thus, when Stephen F. Austin in 1821 published his agreement with Mexico to allow Anglo-Americans to settle on the fertile lands of south Texas, there was strenuous objection to one part of the proposition—not the physical hardships, nor the fierce Indians, nor even the attempts to "Mexicanize" the newcomers—but the lack of liberty of conscience. Austin received many letters calling for religious freedom in this virgin country. Even Austin's mother urged him "to be particular on the subject of religious toleration," for, she said, to demand that every permanent settler become a Roman Catholic would "put a stop to emigration."

But Austin's hands were tied on this issue. One of the principal stipulations made by the Spanish government in response to the petition of Moses Austin in 1820 to be allowed to settle 300 families was that all colonists must either be Roman Catholics or embrace that faith before they were settled. The Mexican revolution of 1820 threw off the yoke of Spain but not the domination of the Roman Catholic Church. Austin himself was careful to distinguish between his private opinions concerning the Roman Catholic system and his conscientious fidelity to the contract he had made

17

with the Mexican authorities. In a letter of 1823, commenting on the religious situation he had just witnessed while in Mexico, he remarked,

> Friars, cannons (sic), priests, etc., literally swollen by the profusion of their food and the idleness of their corrupted lives, are supported in their sacrilegious abuses by the blindness and ignorance of a fanatic people. . . . Friends, in general, Christianity in this country exists only in name and perverted forms. . . .[1]

Publicly, however, Austin displayed his typical integrity by requiring conformance to the stipulation of the Mexican government. At almost the very time he displayed his personal repugnance for the Roman Catholic system, he wrote to his settlers reminding them that the Roman Catholic religion was the religion of the nation and that "the law will not allow of any other in this Colony."[2] He frankly said that "no public preaching or exorting (sic) will on any account be permitted, and I should feel myself compelled to silence any preacher or exorter (sic) who would attempt it, within my jurisdiction."

Baptist Immigrants Arrive

Despite this unfavorable situation, many settlers of every faith and no faith made the trek to Texas. The political and economic policies of the government of the United States provided one incentive for the move. After the War of 1812 the United States had encouraged westward emigration by offering public land at a cheap price and on easy terms. In 1820, however, the United States changed its policy and began to require cash payment for public lands. Land sales dropped from over five million acres in 1819 to less than 800,000 acres in 1821. Many Americans, unable to buy western land from the United States, simply moved across the Sabine River to homestead the rich, plentiful lands of Texas.

There were many Baptists among these immigrants. They believed that the Mexican policy of refusing to tolerate other religions than the Roman Catholic Church would be modified. They were encouraged in this belief by several factors. For one thing, there were at least eleven known Baptist families among Austin's original 300 settlers. The very presence of these Baptists in the original colony of 1821 was evidence that the legal requirement for all colonists to be Roman Catholics was really not enforced. In addition, Stephen F. Austin himself was known to hold the view that this religious intolerance would not continue indefinitely. On October 30, 1823, he wrote that "the Roman Catholic is the established religion to the absolute exclusion of all others and will so continue for a few years, but the natural operation of a republic will change that system." This same view is reflected in his dealings with the Methodists, who had been preaching south of the Red River as early as 1818 under the misapprehension that this was a part of Arkansas at that time. On December 17, 1824, Austin complained that the Methodists had publicly spoken out against him for admitting the Roman Catholic establishment. He went on to say that if the Methodists would stay out of Texas or remain quiet for a short time, "we shall succeed in getting a free toleration of all Religions," but, he commented, the government of Mexico must first be convinced that their laws are being observed. Austin believed that the passage of time would certainly bring additional privileges of religious toleration to Texas.[3]

The absence of records makes it difficult to trace all Baptist witness in Texas before 1830, but it is evident that much more house preaching took place than can be documented. One account describes the preaching of Joseph L. Bays in San Felipe in 1823. After his arrest for flaunting the Mexican laws by openly preaching a faith other than Roman Catholic, he escaped from his guard while on the way to San Antonio for trial. About this same time Freeman Smalley, a Baptist preacher from Ohio, journeyed to Texas to find his married sister, and probably preached at Old Pecan Point, not far from the present town of Clarksville. Also about this same time John Cummings and Jesse Webb, Baptist laymen, and William B. Dewees, a Baptist preacher's son from Kentucky, entered Texas. The distinguished lawyer, Judge Richard Ellis, brought his family from Alabama in 1825 and settled a large plantation on the Red River in what is now Bowie County. Later on he was unanimously chosen president of the convention which declared Texas independence on March 2, 1836. L. L. Chiles, another Baptist layman, moved to Texas about this time and settled near what is now Caldwell. In 1827 the Bowles family arrived from Kentucky, becoming some of the first members of the Houston church when it was organized. From Missouri in 1828 came Arthur Burns as one of the Dewitt colonists, and settled at Gonzales. George M. Patrick emigrated from Virginia in 1828, and although he was not a Baptist his three daughters were and each married a Baptist. About the same time Samuel Ellis Pearce and his wife settled near the present town of Pleasanton, where the Old Rock Church, probably the first Baptist church in southwest Texas, was later organized.

Two of the outstanding Baptists who came to Texas before 1830 were Thomas Hanks, a preacher from Tennessee, and Thomas J. Pilgrim, from New York, who is credited with organizing the first Baptist Sunday school in Texas in 1829. Hanks preached the first Baptist sermon west of the Brazos River in 1825 at the home of Moses Shipman, near San Felipe. Here the first public profession of faith of record was made by Mrs. Lydia Allcorn under Hanks' preaching.

In company with sixty other men, women, and children, Thomas J. Pilgrim made the perilous trip from New York to Texas in the fall of 1828, traveling in wagons, rafts, horseback, and afoot. In connection with his teaching at San Felipe he organized a Sunday school, thirty-two scholars being present on the first Sunday. Pilgrim described the situation that made it necessary to discontinue this promising movement, which people came from a distance of ten miles to attend.

> This school and these morning lectures were continued regularly, and were well attended until a difficulty occurred between some intelligent Mexicans visiting the priests from the interior and some citizens, growing out of a lawsuit which was decided against the Mexicans. The Empressario (Stephen F. Austin) deemed it prudent to discontinue them for a time, as these Mexicans could not be deceived in relation to the character of our exercises, and it was well known that we were acting in violation of the canonization law, which strictly prohibited Protestant worship and prohibited Austin from introducing any but Catholics as colonists.[4]

Later, Pilgrim continued his Sunday school work and until his death in 1877 was active in this movement. Other Baptists among the sixty New York immigrants also began a Sunday school in Matagorda in 1829. There are also references to a Sunday school organized near what is now Wharton in 1829 or 1830, perhaps in the home of William Kincheloe.

Hardening of Mexican Policy

The inevitable clash between the Anglo-American culture and that of the Mexican government began to develop. The Mexican government had encouraged the Anglos to occupy the rich lands of Texas with the hope that these settlers could be Mexicanized; instead, the Mexican culture in these areas was being American-ized. The government had nudged the colonists toward their own culture by requiring the use of the Spanish language in all public transactions, by offering more liberal land benefits to colonists marrying Mexicans, by requiring all emigrants to become Roman Catholics, and by denying all non-Mexicans the privilege of set-tling within twenty-five miles of the coast or within fifty miles of a foreign boundary without specific consent of the federal govern-ment. The Mexican Constitution of October 4, 1824, continued to name the Roman Catholic Church as the established religion of Mexico. In 1825, Texas became a part of the Mexican state of Coahuila, and the state constitution, adopted on March 11, 1827, also established the Roman Catholic Church. Obedient to the provisions of the state constitution, Stephen F. Austin endeavored to get Roman Catholic priests to come to his colony to minister to the very practical needs of his colonists; viz., christen babies, unite couples in marriage, and bury the dead. His efforts met with little success.

Meanwhile, the Mexican government became increasingly suspi-cious of the motives of the United States. Both President John Quincy Adams and Andrew Jackson were rebuffed when they made efforts in 1825 and 1829, respectively, to purchase Texas. The articles appearing in the newspapers of the United States predicting that President Jackson would soon add Texas to the

United States did little to mollify the suspicious Mexicans. The Fredonian War in 1826, when Haden Edwards and a dozen or so men incited a revolt against the Mexican government in Texas, convinced Mexico that the Anglo-Americans were trying to infiltrate Texas in order to seize it. As a result, in 1828 Mexico passed a law forbidding Anglo-Americans from settling near the eastern border, and in the following year, as a direct deterrent to Anglo-American emigration, Negro slavery was abolished in Texas. The climax came with the Colonization Law of April 6, 1830, which in effect forbade emigration from the United States into Texas, providing, as well, that Mexican convicts should be used to colonize Texas. One distinguished Texas historian judged that this Colonization Law represented for the Texas revolution what the Stamp Act was to the American revolution of 1776.[5] In the summer of 1830, implementing this law, Mexican soldiers were stationed in strategic posts in Texas, and custom houses were opened at various points to collect duties for the support of the army of occupation.

Freedom! Political and Religious

After 1830, events in Texas and Mexico moved rapidly toward the Texas war for independence. The shock of military encounter with the army of occupation was cushioned by activities connected with the Liberal political movement by Santa Anna in Mexico. By taking the side of Santa Anna in this internal struggle in Mexican politics, the Texans found an excuse to force the occupying army to leave Texas soil by August, 1834.

Additional indignation developed from the crushing of efforts by the state of Coahuila (which included Texas) to provide religious toleration. In 1833 the governor of Coahuila informed inquirers that "professors of the various sects in religion will be henceforth admitted as settlers, without any restrictions in regard to their faith." He also said that the Legislature of Coahuila, as well as representative bodies in other Mexican states, would probably soon enact laws "providing for equal toleration to Protestants and other settlers." On March 26 and on May 21, 1834, the Legislature of Coahuila enacted these laws looking toward religious toleration.

However, the Mexican central government, when informed of this action, dissolved the Coahuila Legislature by force and rendered these state laws inoperative.[6]

Another large step on the road to revolution was taken in 1834. Popular assemblies to express public opinion on government policy were held in San Felipe with the hope that some of their grievances would be rectified. However, these only served to alienate the Mexican leaders. Stephen F. Austin was summoned to Mexico City, and from February, 1834, until September, 1835, he was imprisoned as a revolutionary. This experience weaned Austin away from his long commitment to maintaining Texas as a state under Mexican rule, and after his release he began to provide responsible leadership for freeing Texas from Mexican tyranny.

In the war that followed, the Alamo and Goliad united the Texans and provided the inspiration for the victory at San Jacinto. On March 2, 1836, in the blacksmith shop of Noah Byars, a Baptist of Washington, Texas, the Texas Declaration of Independence was adopted under the presidency of Richard Ellis, a Baptist of Pecan Point. One of the injustices named by the Convention as the basis for the Declaration read as follows:

> It denies us the right of worshiping the Allmighty according to the dictates of our own conscience, by the support of a national religion calculated to promote the temporal interests of its human functionaries rather than the glory of the true and living God.

The remarkable achievement of independence from Mexico, which greatly altered the subsequent history of many nations, was a trophy to the courage of a small group of brave men. A favorite Texas tale concerns their famed Texas Rangers. It relates how the local authorities in a town were faced with a widespread riot. After appealing to the Texas Rangers for assistance, they waited at the train station for the arrival of what they supposed would be a large force of men. To their surprise, one Ranger swung off the train. He laconically remarked, "One riot requires only one Ranger." This principle was certainly involved in the major engagements of the war for Texas independence. There were only 160 Texans armed with hunting rifles at the battle of Gonzales on October 2, 1835.

Fifty volunteers took Goliad on October 9. Fannin and Bowie had about ninety men in the victory at Concepcion Mission on October 28. About 300 volunteers captured San Antonio under Ben Milam. The determinative engagement at San Jacinto on April 21, 1836, involved a Texas army under General Sam Houston numbering fewer than a thousand men. In this battle for empire, only nine Texans were killed or fatally wounded, while thirty-four received non-mortal wounds.

Baptist People, Preachers, and Churches

Settlers entered Texas in large numbers between 1830 and 1836 despite the stormy days of revolution. The wave of immigrants from the United States "had reached the Sabine and was beating against it." The white population by 1836 was approximately 30,000.

An impressive number of these settlers were Baptists. These included Aaron and Joseph Burleson, Michael Kennard and his brother William, Daniel B. Kornegay, Henry Tristan and family, Charles Covington, James and William T. Hamlett, Mrs. David Avers and Mrs. Massie Millard, G. W. Rose, Mary Waglay, George W. Slaughter, Abner Smith, and John Woodruff—the last three being preachers. These and others settled in areas which later were identified with Baptist churches, such as Washington, Nacogdoches, Independence, Round Rock, Houston, Galveston, Caldwell, and La Grange.

The first Baptist church in Texas evidently had its first meeting there on Saturday, January 20, 1834, in Austin's Colony. This church had an unusual history. Its leader was Daniel Parker. Of humble birth and practically self-taught, he was born in Culpeper County, Virginia, on April 6, 1781. He moved to Georgia where he grew to manhood, then to Tennessee, where he was pastor in Sumner County from 1807 to 1817. He was strongly anti-missionary in his views. Evidently the first indication of this came in 1815 at a meeting of the Concord Association with which his church affiliated. When that Association learned of the organization of the General Missionary Convention for foreign missions in Philadel-

phia in 1814, they were mainly favorable to the movement and
organized a missionary society to support this work. Three of the
pastors in the Association were appointed to raise money for the
foreign mission enterprise. However, at the meeting of the Association in 1816 Elder Parker "told the Association, in plain terms, that
if they did not drop the correspondence and cease their missionary
operations, he would burst the Association."[7] The Association
"knowing his influence and shrewdness, and fearing a disruption,"
dissolved their missionary society and discontinued their relationship with the general body.

In 1817 Parker moved to Illinois and in addition to his pastoral
work was twice elected to the state Senate of Illinois. In 1832 he
made a visit to Texas and was captivated by the land. He noted
that the Mexican colonization laws forbade the organization of any
non-Catholic church, but he saw nothing to keep a church from
emigrating as a body into the state. Consequently, on July 26,
1833, in Crawford County, Illinois, he organized the Pilgrim
Church of Predestinarian Regular Baptists, and was chosen as its
pastor. The seven original members of the church began their trek
toward Texas, and on October 20, 1833, while camping in Clai-
borne Parish, Louisiana, seven additional members were added to
the church. On January 20, 1834, the church held its conference in
Austin's Colony, Texas, in the home of the pastor. Eighteen months
later the church moved with Elder Parker to East Texas in what is
now Houston County.

Despite the fact that Daniel Parker vigorously opposed what he
termed the "money-getting" mission organizations, he did not do so
on the grounds set forth by some other Primitive or Hardshell
Baptists that were "anti-effort" on doctrinal grounds. Carroll says of
him:

> Daniel Parker's work is the real wonder. Entirely at his own
> expense he was ever on the go, preaching everywhere within a radius
> of a hundred miles; organizing new churches; strengthening weak
> ones, and preaching to the destitute. His life was really a direct
> contradiction to his teachings. In his own personal work and by
> riding on horseback, he covered a territory that now embraces about
> twenty counties.

The first Baptist church organized in East Texas was a church organized by Parker in 1837 in Nacogdoches or Shelby County. The name seems to have been "Hopewell," and we understand that it is still in existence. Following Hopewell, and as a direct result in nearly if not in every case of the efforts of Parker and his co-laborers, came these other churches: New Bethel in Sabine County in 1838; Mt. Pleasant, Montgomery County, in 1838; Fort Houston, in Houston County (now Anderson County), October 22, 1840; Bethel in Sabine County, February 7, 1841; Mustang Prairie (not sure what county), in 1841 or 1842; Wolf Creek (not sure of county), March or April, 1845.

There were possibly, but not probably, one or two others organized by Parker or his brethren, which we have not been able to trace. Some few of these churches afterwards co-operated with the missionaries. It is probable that, even to this day, no other preacher has ever lived in East Texas who left a deeper or a more nearly ineradicable impress on the theology of that section than was made by Daniel Parker.[8]

During the following three years about three dozen names of anti-missionary Baptists are found in the minutes of this church, including more than half-a-dozen preachers. The story of that church is given in detail in Primitive Baptist histories, and will not be continued here.

A great number of missionary Baptists continued to enter Texas between 1833 and 1836. In the former year, Gail Borden, Jr., subsequently to become famous for his condensed milk product, entered Texas and settled in Galveston. He and his wife, a daughter of Eli Mercer (a cousin of Jesse Mercer of Georgia), were baptized in the Gulf of Mexico in January, 1840, by James Huckins at the time of the organization of the church at Galveston. Also in 1833 came Captain Goldsby Childers (also spelled Childress) who located on the Little River in what is now Bell County. It was at his cabin that Z. N. Morrell preached his first sermon in Texas in 1835. Other Baptists in the large Childers party that came from Illinois in 1833 were Isaac Crouch, a Baptist minister and Orville T. Tyler, who later became the first Chief Justice of Coryell County. Crouch, unfortunately, was slain by the Indians in June, 1836.

With the Childers party from Illinois were a number of anti-missionary Baptists led by John Parker, the father of Daniel Parker. The thirty adults with the party were probably all Baptists. Their tragic story is a part of Texas legend. They did not join Daniel Parker's group, but settled in Limestone County near the present town of Groesbeck. On May 19, 1836, at their settlement, now known as Old Fort Parker, about 500 Indians led by a Mexican surrounded the fort. Through treachery, the Mexican leader gained entry into the fort, and a brutal massacre followed. Two women and three children were carried into captivity by the Indians. Cynthia Ann Parker, eight years old when seized, was recaptured in a battle with the Comanche Indians on December 18, 1860, almost a quarter of a century later.

Other Baptists who emigrated to Texas in 1834 were Hiram Little and a large family, who came from Cairo, Illinois, and settled in Fort Bend County; R. Marsh, an elderly Baptist preacher who came from Mississippi and returned there before long; another Baptist preacher, Isaac Reed, who settled north of Nacogdoches, where he later assisted in the organization of the Union Church; William Smith and his family, he being a distinguished Indian fighter and expert gunsmith who served honorably in the Texas Revolution; S. F. Sparks, one of the first converts to Baptist views in Texas; and M. G. Whitaker, who was active in the Texas Revolution.

A number of Baptists are known to have arrived in 1835. Dr. Thomas Anderson, a physician, and his wife emigrated from Virginia and settled in the area near what is now Austin. His son, Washington Anderson, was active in the Texas Revolution. James Bradberry, another soldier in the Revolution, arrived in 1835. Anderson Buffington, a South Carolinian, came by way of Nashville, Tennessee, and played a part in the Texas Revolution. He was ordained as a preacher by the Washington church in 1841. Deacon H. R. Cartmell, a Baptist leader in Tennessee, settled near Washington in 1835. George J. Glasscock of Virginia, an active missionary Baptist, made his home in Washington County. A. C. Horton with his wife was a valuable addition in 1835 also. Horton was one of the few men with Fannin at Goliad who escaped the massacre, and later became Governor of Texas. General Sam Houston also crossed the Sabine in 1835. He was not a Baptist at the time, but later on adopted Baptist views. A very active leader in Texas Baptist life was J. S. Lester, who participated in the victory at San Jacinto. George Petty, A. G. Perry, W. J. Philips, and Robert Sellers, all well known Baptists, also came to Texas in 1835.

Some of the more prominent Baptists who arrived in Texas in 1836, the year of independence, should be mentioned. Claudius Buster of Kentucky settled in Washington County. He was one of the famous Mier prisoners. J. L. Ellis and his preacher brother, B. F. Ellis, cousins of Judge Richard Ellis and sons of a Georgia Baptist preacher, settled in Liberty County and were active in Texas Baptist life. Another set of brothers, James and Ben Green, heroes in the Texas Revolution, were also active in Baptist life. James M. and George W. Harbour, James G. and Thomas S. Heard, J. S. Irvine, and William E. Kennard arrived in Texas in time to serve valiantly in the Revolution. James Sanders settled in San Augustine County, while Wilson Simpson made his home in Fayette County. Simpson escaped from the Goliad massacre and served under Houston at San Jacinto. The preacher, Thomas Spraggins, along with Henry Smith, A. M. Tandy, and Stephen Williams were other Baptists who served in the Texas Revolution.

The Coming of Z. N. Morrell

The most valuable accession to Baptist ranks in Texas in 1836 was Z. N. Morrell of Tennessee, although he was seriously ill and a cripple. Born in South Carolina in 1803, he received little formal education, but began preaching before he was twenty years old. He served for fourteen years in western Tennessee before turning toward Texas. For nine years he averaged a sermon a day. Because of Morrell's lung hemorrhages, his physician advised him to stop preaching and to seek a milder climate. With his wife and four children he moved to Mississippi in 1835, considering the possibility of living in Texas. He paused, however, because he had heard of the domination of the Roman Catholic Church in that land and reports that a political revolution was beginning in Texas. In December, 1835, he returned from a preaching tour to find his physician and several other friends from Tennessee enroute to Texas. He determined to go with them to survey the situation to see if his family could safely be taken there. Two lawyers, two Baptist deacons, the physician, and Morrell began the journey immediately. They arrived at the Falls of the Brazos, near what is now Marlin, on December 30, 1835, where a Tennessee colony was camped. On that night, with a clear voice and a stronger body than he had known for years, he preached his first sermon on Texas soil. He determined that he would bring his family to Texas and cast his lot with this turbulent empire.

This was indeed a fortunate choice for Texas. J. M. Carroll said about Morrell that to this man "is due as much, or more, than to any other man, the right beginnings and right foundations of organized Baptist work in Texas." He was just the kind of man that fitted the character of the country. He possessed his full allotment of courage and faith. He was plain-spoken, as well as outspoken. He referred to the anti-missionary group as "old iron jackets and steel buttons" because of their inflexible views. He talked about dastardly chicken-hearted politicians and tender-footed Baptist preachers. Because in the Old Testament the Levitical priests were not allowed to wear garments made partly of wool and partly of linen (they must be either all wool or all linen), he referred to preachers who included good works as a part of the requirements for salvation as "linsey-woolsey." He termed preachers who sought popularity rather than following conviction as "tin-headed"— whose heads were soft enough, like tin, to be marked by the hammer of popularity. He referred to lazy preachers as "maybe fit for something," but he could not determine what it was. He talked about his Bible as his "old Jerusalem blade," and said more than once that "my Master has a store house in the adjacent creek bottom" which took only a gun and some ammunition to open.

It has already been mentioned that Morrell provided the theme for Texas Baptist history in his sermon at Nacogdoches. This was not the only time, however, that he returned to this theme for his own strength. In the following year, while living at the Falls of the Brazos, Morrell was requested by the soldiers to make a trip to the town of Washington, one hundred miles to the south, to secure powder and lead. As he considered the perilous journey, he asked himself, "Do you believe the language of the Bible, from which you preached so earnestly to the people in the old town of Nacogdoches, just one year ago?" He said aloud, "Yes, I believe, yet, that the wilderness of Texas will blossom as the rose. . . ." A few months later, while engaged in a very severe struggle for the life of his loved ones during Indian attacks at Nashville, Texas, he received letters from Tennessee and Mississippi urging him to return to the safety of those states in his ministry. "God gave me," he said, "an inward token . . . the wilderness would yet blossom as the rose." In March, 1839, on the Colorado River about twenty miles above LaGrange, Morrell baptized his first candidate in Texas. In the following months a number of people were baptized into the newly constituted church at Plum Grove, and while observing the Lord's Supper, Morrell was greatly elevated in spirit. He later said, "My poor soul blessed God in faith that the wilderness of the Colorado would blossom as the rose. . . ." Later, in writing his recollections of the struggle to take Texas for Christ, he said, "I frequently, in 1847, held up my head and rejoiced that the wilderness was blossoming as the rose."

By 1836, therefore, the great stumbling block to Baptist witness in Texas was removed by the winning of political and religious freedom. Baptists from the South and the North were casting their fortunes with this new and exciting land, many of them Baptist preachers. Already, although Baptists in Texas were not aware of it, historical events were preparing two significant organizations that would be of great assistance in winning Texas to Christ. One had already been organized—the American Baptist Home Mission Society of New York City. American Baptists had developed a foreign mission society in 1814 which, between 1817 and 1820, performed a limited amount of home mission work. John M. Peck and James E. Welch were sent by it as missionaries to Missouri and Illinois. This society detached itself from home missions and became solely a foreign mission body in 1820. By 1832 sufficient interest had been aroused to cause the formation of a separate home mission society. Although it had not yet focused on the foreign country called Texas, its program looked to the West, including states adjacent to Texas.

The other significant organization that would greatly assist Texas was not formed until 1845—the Southern Baptist Convention. In the pioneer years before 1836 no human wisdom could have anticipated the momentous events that led to the formation of this new Baptist body in the South. Indeed, no one could have predicted the ministry of the Home Mission Society of New York to Texas. But the God of Bays, Smalley, Pilgrim, and Morrell was already at work in distant places to help meet the needs of Texas.

3

Planting Missionary Baptist Churches
(1836–40)

☆ ☆ ☆

Texas Baptists took several large strides during the first years of the new Republic. The victory at San Jacinto on April 21, 1836, insuring Texas independence, gave status to the interim government that had been established on March 17 and brought some assurance that plans for future religious activities could be made. The turbulent political, military, and economic events accompanying the founding of the new Texas government greatly affected the religious progress made in the new land. As one reads a first-hand account like that of Z. N. Morrell or R. E. B. Baylor, he can glimpse some of the difficulties that revolution and warfare brought to those striving to carry on religious activities.

After the decisive engagement at San Jacinto, many adventurers from the United States hastened to join the victorious Texas army, swelling it to about 2,500 men. They formed a restless, domineering body, even threatening the authority of the civil administration. The election of General Sam Houston as the first president of the Republic on September 1 was doubly fortunate. He was the one man that the army would respect. In addition, at the first opportunity he disbanded the relatively large standing army, thus outwitting the military leaders who were trying to renew hostilities with Mexico, and at the same time undercutting those who desired to establish a military dictatorship.

The population at this time was about 30,000 whites, about 5,000 blacks, and perhaps 10 to 20,000 Indians, some of them quite warlike. Before San Jacinto the people had fled eastward to escape the armies of the Mexicans. Now they slowly returned to build again their burned homes and plant new crops. A large number of new, stable, home-seeking families was moving into the new nation, although of course the usual parasitic groups of land speculators, confidence men, and other unscrupulous persons tagged along. It is estimated that newcomers were entering Texas at the rate of about 7,000 a year, and among these were many Baptists, some of them effective preachers and leaders. In 1837 a General Land Office was opened at Houston to survey public lands, and in 1839 the Texas Congress passed a homestead law which provided additional safeguards for the stable citizenry. Several *empresario* contracts were also granted in 1841, which distributed the settlers in more remote sections and introduced German and French families in large groups.

The Indians and Mexicans still were formidable foes. The antagonism of M. B. Lamar, the Republic's second president, contributed to the bloody Indian wars that began in this period, although it is likely that the Indian depredations would have occurred regardless of Lamar's personal feelings. The Mexicans were unwilling to accept the Texas Declaration of Independence and only awaited the right opportunity to renew hostilities.

Despite these unfavorable circumstances, the achievement of political and religious liberty and the presence of Baptist leaders in Texas presaged the establishment of Baptist churches in the new land. Between November, 1837, and the arrival of the first missionary in January, 1840, at least six small missionary Baptist churches (in contrast with the Primitive or anti-missionary Baptist churches established prior to this time by Daniel Parker and his followers) were organized in the Republic of Texas.

Old Washington Church (1837)

The first missionary Baptist church in Texas was organized at Washington, Texas, in November, 1837, under the leadership of

Z. N. Morrell, who delighted to call himself "the canebreak preacher." Morrell had settled and cultivated a crop on the Brazos River near the present town of Marlin, preaching here and there as opportunity permitted. Here was located the extreme northern fort established for protection against the Indians. The captain commanding the post informed him in early March that the supply of ammunition was almost exhausted, while stores of every other kind were very short. Morrell had shared his family stores, hauled by ox-teams about 300 miles from Louisiana, with soldiers and other citizens, and his supplies were about gone. Morrell had about $2,000 in United States currency, realized from the sale of his land in Mississippi, and he determined to drive his wagon, pulled by eight oxen and followed by two horses, to Houston, about 160 miles south, to purchase supplies. On March 18, 1837, he began the journey with his twelve-year-old son. After many hardships, he successfully returned to his home. Morrell remarked:

> When we reached the eastern bank of the Brazos, opposite our log cabin and the soldiers' fort on the west, and announced across the river that we had powder, lead, and commissary stores, hats were waved, and as loud a shout was raised as would have been during the late war on the arrival of a seventy-four gun ship in some great emergency.[1]

These supplies were exhausted by May, so Morrell arranged for a second trip to Houston. He found, however, that his United States bank currency was practically worthless. He promptly went to New Orleans and walked the streets for two weeks trying to negotiate. "I was introduced to some gentlemen in debt to the banks, and succeeded in exchanging my bills for goods at about sixty cents on the dollar. I had not come to Texas to sell goods; but, to save the little means left, I found myself unavoidably drifting into merchandise." Upon arriving at Houston he learned that the Indians and Mexicans had overwhelmed the fort near his home on the Brazos but that his wife and children had been able to flee to safety to Nashville, about forty-five miles down the river. Gone were his household furniture, farming tools, and "the best crop I ever made." Morrell promptly moved his family to Washington, the principal town between his former home and Houston. Here he opened a store and began to sell the merchandise he had purchased in New Orleans.

There had been no Baptists other than his family at his previous home, but in Washington he found kindred souls. Anderson Buffington and his wife had come to Texas from Tennessee in 1835. He had served in the Texas Revolution and fought at San Jacinto. Noah T. Byars and his wife emigrated from Georgia in 1836. In his blacksmith shop at Washington the Texas Declaration of Independence was adopted on March 2, 1836. J. R. Jenkins was a lawyer, a graduate of Mercer University in Georgia, and an active Baptist then living in Washington. H. R. Cartmell had come from Tennessee in 1835. He had been a deacon in the Baptist church at Nashville, Tennessee, and had known Morrell there. A young devout Baptist, Richard Ellis, also lived in Washington at this time, but may have moved farther west to the Colorado River before a church was organized at Washington.[1a] He is not to be confused with Judge Richard Ellis from Virginia, another Baptist, who presided at the convention of Texans on March 2, 1836, when Texas Independence was declared, and on March 17 when the first Texas Constitution was adopted.

This small group of Baptists promptly organized a weekly prayer meeting. They saw the need, however, for a Baptist church. It sprang from their concern for the lost and unenlisted in the town. Morrell described the founding of this church after the disbanding of the Texas army.

Those who had families in Texas quietly repaired to their homes, and entered upon the common avocations of life. There was another class of these soldiers, with whom we sympathized greatly, and yet they proved a terror to good society. They were principally young men of the very first families of the United States, mostly from Tennessee, on account of the popularity of Sam Houston, once the honored Governor of the old State, then President of the "Lone Star Republic." They were young men deeply imbued with that spirit of patriotism that fired the hearts of the fathers of 1776. They had now served in the Texas army for several months; there was not a dollar with which to pay them for service rendered; their clothing was worn to tatters; they had not been accustomed to labor, and were now a

great way from home, and all their available means consisted of land
certificates and bounty claims on the infant republic. Large bands of
them were among us, fit subjects for every species of dissipation. . . .

Our weekly prayer-meeting was regularly held in the town of
Washington, in a small house, the best we could secure. These young
men referred to, regularly attended; behavior was good; were very
polite, and sang elegantly all the parts of music. They had been
trained to this in other States, under pious influences. A stranger
present would have supposed that a whole church, well-organized
and drilled in some of the old States, had moved in a body and
settled at Washington. Cartmell, Buffington, Byers (sic), Ellis, and
Morrell, one after another, led in prayer, and the singing between
prayers was of the very first order, in point of time and melody. The
writer would give out an appointment for preaching every Sunday,
when at home, and after singing "Old Hundred" the congregation
would retire. After the benediction the young men would hasten
away. By the time we would pass on our way home, the grocery and
billiard-saloon would be lighted up, and a large crowd—God have
mercy on them!—would be assembled for the night. . . . It did not
require the foresight of a prophet to understand the results of this
procedure, on the part of the enemy, if continued long. Our prayers
went up to God, "O Lord, hear the prayers of thy servants, and the
prayers of mothers, in distant lands, for these wayward sons!"

We determined, let come what might, to organize a church. The
day was appointed, and eight Baptists assembled to keep house for
God. Brother H. R. Cartmell was recognized as deacon, and Z. N.
Morrell chosen as pastor. Thus sprung into existence the first church,
according to my information, that was ever organized in Texas on
strictly gospel principles, having the ordinances and officers of ancient order, and with no anti-missionary element in its body.[2]

The exact date of the founding of this church is not known. The
official date for Houston's furlough, referred to by Morrell, was
April 18, 1837. The effective date was somewhat later. On May 16,
for example, *The Telegraph and Texas Register* noted that emigrants were arriving on every vessel, "and so numerous have our
citizens already become, that we confidently believe Houston alone
could, in case of a second invasion, furnish an army of able-bodied
men, *nearly equal to that now encamped on the banks of the
LaBaca.*" The church evidently was organized sometime after the
furlough was effected. The latest possible date was November 7,
1837, since Morrell related how at its first conference the new

church wrote letters to the mission boards, and these letters bear the date of November 7, 1837. The eight Baptists referred to by Morrell as forming this first missionary Baptist church in Texas included three men who either were or would become ordained ministers (Morrell, Anderson Buffington, and Noah T. Byars); one deacon (H. R. Cartmell), one Baptist lawyer (J. R. Jenkins), and three women (Mrs. Buffington, and probably Morrell's wife and daughter). Another Washington Baptist, Richard Ellis, may already have moved westward and perhaps was not a part of this original group. Later on he became a minister, as will be seen, and served well during his brief life.

Perhaps immediately after the organization of the church, a committee consisting of Cartmell, Buffington, and Jenkins was appointed to write the mission boards to request assistance in the work. Evidently Cartmell was replaced by Morrell, since the two letters were signed by Morrell, Buffington, and Jenkins. The committee addressed letters to both the American Baptist Home Mission Society of New York and the Board of the General Missionary Convention for Foreign Missions, located at Boston. The committee was not certain which body would have jurisdiction in Texas. The appeal to the Home Mission Society was handed to Robert A. Alexander, a Methodist missionary in Texas from Natchez, Mississippi, who later delivered it to Ashley Vaughn, the Baptist pastor in Natchez. Vaughn published the appeal in his paper, the *Southwestern Religious Luminary*, and mailed the original letter to the Board of the Society in New York. The appeal to the foreign mission board evidently was sent by J. R. Jenkins of the committee to his preacher brother, S. G. Jenkins of Mississippi, who sent it to Jesse Mercer at Washington, Georgia. Mercer published it in his paper, the *Christian Index* for February 22, 1838.[3]

The two appeals, although differing slightly in wording and punctuation, expressed the same burden. The ties between the new Republic and the United States were emphasized, and the need for missionary assistance was described. It was urged that missionary posts be established in Texas at San Augustine, Nacogdoches, Washington, and San Antonio. J. M. Carroll thinks the letters sound like Morrell, although tradition ascribes them to Jenkins. It will be seen that as a result of the organization of this church at Washington, Texas, and the subsequent letter to the Home Mission Society, two valuable accessions were later received by Texas in the persons of James Huckins and William M. Tryon.

The story told by B. F. Fuller that upon receipt of this appeal Jesse Mercer at once wrote a letter to the Home Mission Society attaching a $25,000.00 remittance and offering to double it if necessary to get work started in Texas, and that the Society promptly acted on this suggestion by sending Huckins and Tryon is not correct. It was the most inflated form of a story told by Z. N. Morrell in the first edition of his reminiscences in 1872, and reproduced in the writings of Rufus C. Burleson, J. B. Link, B. F. Fuller, B. F. Riley, and J. M. Carroll, with some changes. Jesse Mercer did remember the Home Mission Society in his will with a bequest of twenty-five shares of stock in the Bank of the State of Georgia. This stock was probably worth $100 a share at the time, which totalled the $2,500.00 that seems to form the base for the original story. However, Huckins had been in Texas for over a year when Mercer died in August, 1841. Furthermore, this bequest was contested in court by Mercer's relatives, and not until 1846 did the Home Mission Society receive $1331.87 from the bequest. By that time the Society was no longer employing Huckins.[4]

This first little missionary Baptist church in Texas was dissolved early in 1839, a little more than a year later, primarily because of the moving away of the membership and the lack of regular ministerial leadership. J. M. Carroll and others mention that this church built a house of worship. Some historians have taken issue with this statement on the basis of a letter from William M. Tryon to B. N. Sanders of Georgia in July, 1841, in which Tryon mentioned he had visited Washington, where "in 1837 a Baptist Church and a Sabbath School were organized, a lot was obtained for the erection of a place of worship, and a subscription to build a house, but . . . everything fell through. . . ." However, the same writer addressed a letter to Corresponding Secretary Benjamin M. Hill of the Home Mission Society, New York, dated April 1, 1841, in which he made clear that "a lot was procured and a place of worship erected. But owing to the want of a regular ministry, the Church and school fell through; the house was sold; and the energies of the few Baptists were completely prostrated by the failure."[5]

Union Church, Nacogdoches (May, 1838)

The second missionary Baptist church in Texas seems to have been organized in a log schoolhouse four miles north of Nacogdoches. It is sometimes known as the Old North Church. This church grew out of a prayer meeting. In 1833 Mrs. Massie Sparks Millard settled in this community. Across the river from her house was a clump of trees and underbrush. This was used as a hiding place during the Indian raids, and Mrs. Millard, along with Mrs. Annette Lea Bledsoe and other devout women, hiding in this thicket for safety while their husbands were repelling Indian attacks, would mold ammunition and pray. It became a place of prayer apart from hiding and preparing for Indian inroads.

In 1834, two years prior to the Texas Revolution, Isaac Reed, along with his wife and eight or more children, moved to Texas and established a home not far from the present town of Carthage. Although he had preached in Tennessee for over twenty-five years before coming to Texas, Reed did very little of it during his first two years in the new land, commenting that it probably would have cost a man his life to have preached anything other than Catholic doctrines so near to Nacogdoches, the headquarters of Mexican land authorities in east Texas. Reed became quite prosperous, and when the severe restrictions were lifted, was active in ministerial work.

On Saturday, May 5, 1838, Reed, assisted by R. G. Green, building on the foundation laid by Mrs. Millard and her prayer group, organized the second church in Texas which came to be known as a missionary Baptist church. Seven white Baptists from the United States brought their church letters (John Eaton, Mrs. Betsy Eaton, Charles H. Whitaker, Sarah Tipps, Mary Crain, Ruth Anderson, and Emily Knight), along with two slaves (Anthony and Chancy). Reed remained as pastor of this church for nine years following its organization; C. H. Whitaker was elected clerk. Immediately after the church was formed, eight members were added by experience (Benjamin F. Whitaker, Elijah Anderson, Leander Tipps, Mary Sparks, Sybil Sparks, Elizabeth Ann Whitaker, Tera Whitaker, and Jackson, a slave). Elizabeth Whitaker was received by letter.[6] On the day the church was formed, Reed baptized Benjamin F. Whitaker, perhaps the first baptism by a misssionary Baptist church in Texas. It should be noted that Isaac Reed was one of the east Texas preachers related to the anti-missionary movement. Reed was not so much anti-missionary as what Carroll calls "omissionary." His close relationship with Lemuel Herrin, whose daughter became the wife of Reed's son, probably moved Reed toward the missionary position. Carroll remarked that all the churches Reed assisted in organizing ultimately seem to have become missionary. Z. N. Morrell mentioned that this church was greatly strengthened in the year following its organization when the pastor preached in what became a sweeping revival.[7]

Plum Grove (1839)

This was evidently the third missionary Baptist church organized in Texas. It was located on the Colorado River just south of the present town of Bastrop. As in the case of the church near Nacogdoches, the Plum Grove church was closely related to the anti-missionary Baptists, who had organized the Providence Baptist Church in that area in late March, 1834. Z. N. Morrell preached at the Providence church in 1838. His attitude was that both those who were missionary Baptists and those who were anti-missionary could cooperate together in the same church, each individual being free to engage in missionary activities or to stand aloof, as desired.

Morrell described how in the early winter of 1838 he took his little family from Washington, where the church had died because the members had moved away, and located his home on the Colorado River in Fayette County about eight miles north of the little community of La Grange. On the first Saturday after they arrived, William Scallorn, a missionary Baptist, rode into his camp and requested that Morrell preach at his house on the morrow. During the spring of 1839 this house preaching continued with good results. Morrell had cordial relations with the Providence church, and about the first of March baptized a sister into the fellowship of that church who had professed conversion at the Plum Grove meeting. On the third Sunday of March, 1839, the missionary Baptist preacher Asa Wright, along with William and Stephen Scallorn (the former a missionary Baptist and the latter anti-missionary) attended a conference at the Providence church and requested that help be given them in organizing a church at Plum Grove. In response, R. G. Green and Asael Dancer were appointed by the Providence church to assist in the organization. The church was formed in April, 1839, with the following members: Asa and Elizabeth Wright, a Brother Nelson, Asa and Susan McClure, Campbell and Sister Miller, Rebecca Spier, and Elizabeth Karnes. Asael Dancer became the pastor.

J. C. Newman, the Primitive Baptist historian, said this church belonged to their group, although Morrell referred to it as "our little church." The fact is that this church was composed both of missionary and anti-missionary members at the time it was organized. It divided in 1842 over the missionary question. Fourteen out of the twenty-two members voted missionary convictions, and as a result, the anti-missionary minority group, led by Pastor Dancer and Deacon Stephen Scallorn, voted to dissolve the church in November, 1842. This is the story of the church as related by Newman. However, the missionary-minded majority did not accede to this action. Instead, they preferred charges against the anti-missionary minority and excluded them, claiming to continue the original church. Morrell acted as moderator of the conference that took this action, and two months later he was called as pastor of the church, now totally mission-minded.

In connection with his ministry at Plum Grove, Morrell was instrumental in influencing two young men who later became influential preachers, and also "a bright star from the East." The two young men were William T. and J. V. Wright, twin sons of preacher Asa Wright, who were converted in the spring of 1839 under the preaching of Morrell.

The "bright star" was R. E. B. Baylor. He had come from Kentucky by way of Alabama. Born on May 10, 1793, his early education had been interrupted by service in the war of 1812, but thereafter he began the study of law in the office of his uncle. At the age of twenty-three he was elected to the Legislature in Kentucky, and not only was distinguished in appearance (over six feet two inches high) but was gifted in oratorical excellence. He moved to Alabama, where he served as a member of the Legislature there in 1824, and was elected to the Congress of the United States in 1828. He was commander of the Alabama Volunteers during the Creek Wars in 1836.

On July 30, 1839, while attending a protracted meeting held by his cousin, Thomas Chilton, at the Good Hope Baptist Church, now the First Baptist Church, Talladega, Alabama, Baylor made a profession of faith, and on the following day was baptized by his cousin. He was licensed to preach by the church (although their minutes do not show this action), and soon thereafter "to assist a people struggling in the great cause of humanity for religious and civil liberty" he journeyed to Texas. He never married, so had no family to bring with him. Baylor settled at La Grange. The expeditions of the Indians and the Mexicans caused the little village to be crowded with women and children, some of whom were widows and orphans while others were the wives and families of men fighting the enemies farther west. Baylor remarked that "as I had not much to do, I concluded to open a school, announcing to all it was free of charge. If the parents chose to pay me anything it was all well and good, if not it was all right the same." He soon had a crowded school, and "reluctantly went to work as a school teacher for the first and only time in my life. I toiled at this business something like six months laboring faithfully, at the end of which time I found myself nearly worn down."[8]

Morrell described his first meeting with Baylor:

On a visit to the town of LaGrange, in February, 1839, I heard of the Honorable R. E. B. Baylor, formerly a congressman from Alabama. A letter was handed to me which showed that he had professed religion, joined the Baptist church, and had been exercising his gift with great promise; so much so that the church had licensed him to preach. In this letter it was further stated that he had gone to Texas, and that the brethren were greatly exercised about his welfare as a preacher; that in consequence of his distinguished political attainments, and the inducements offered in a new country to seek promotion, fears were expressed lest he might not be active in his ministry, as there were no religious organizations to throw the mantle of protection about him. As he was then in town, I sought his acquaintance at once, and invited him to fill my appointment the following day. He declined to do this, but agreed to attend and aid me in the service. As preaching was at that time a novelty in LaGrange, the people all came out. After the sermon Brother Baylor closed the service with a very happy exhortation. He announced in the very outset that "there is a reality in religion and the Scriptures are true." This great thought was brought to bear with such power that it was easily seen that he was himself once an infidel. He contended, not only from Scriptures, but from experience, that religion was a reality and ought not to be deferred. . . . I went home from this meeting greatly strengthened, blessing God by the way for this valuable aid in time of great need.[9]

The first recorded observance of the two ordinances at the same time in Texas by a missionary Baptist church took place about a month later.

Sunday morning at ten o'clock we met at the water, and after a short discourse on the subjects and action of baptism, nine converts testified their belief in the burial and resurrection of Jesus, by allowing themselves to be buried in and raised out of the water of the Colorado River. On retiring to a small house, with an arbor of brush built in front of it for the occasion, Brother Baylor, in his usual happy manner, preached a most excellent sermon. . . . This season of refreshing from the presence of the Lord greatly revived the drooping spirit of the way-worn traveler, and as we surrounded the table, with Brother Baylor and those dear brethren, and ate the bread and drank the wine, my poor soul blessed God in faith that the waters of the Colorado would blossom as the rose, and that the solitary places along this fertile valley would one day be made glad.[10]

Some historians suggest that this was the first time the Lord's Supper was observed in Texas by Morrell, but this is not likely in view of the language of Morrell in connection with the church at Washington during 1837–38. He said that at Washington the crowd of scoffers would imitate the services of the church in mockery, and even "the bread and wine, emblems of the Saviour's love, were frequently administered by these mockers of God and religion before the public gaze."[11] Evidently the Washington church observed the Supper, and it was used as a pattern for the mockery of these unbelievers.

The language used by Morrell in connection with the Supper at Plum Grove does not indicate whether Baylor assisted in either the baptism or the observance of the Supper. This is of some moment, since only ordained ministers were permitted to engage in these ministerial functions. The question of whether or not Baylor was ordained seems to have been answered by his ministerial activity later. It is true that there is no record of his ordination, and, for that matter, no reference to it anywhere. That, however, is not unusual. The church at Talladega had no record of the licensing of Baylor, although both he and Morrell confirmed that this was done. J. M. Carroll assumed that Baylor was ordained, for in referring to Baylor's service in the Texas Congress in 1842, he remarked that since Judge Baylor was a preacher, "this was contrary to the Texas Constitution. Daniel Parker was denied a seat in the first Texas Congress because of being a preacher. An exception may have been made in Baylor's case, because of the fact that he never depended upon the ministry for a living. He was a lawyer and made his living in that way."[12] That Baylor actually was ordained after he came to Texas seems quite certain, for during the next several years he performed all ministerial functions, including the founding of Baptist churches, serving on presbyteries to ordain preachers, etc. Exactly *when* Baylor was ordained is a thorny problem. D. D. Tidwell, the Texas Baptist historian, who probably has studied this question more than anyone else, judged that Baylor was ordained by the La Grange church in 1840. His position on this stems partly from the date he fixes for the founding of the La Grange church, which is also uncertain. If the La Grange church were founded in 1839, the traditional date, this would solve some problems about Baylor's ordination and ministerial activities, as well as the date for the founding of the Travis church. This will be discussed more fully in the story of the founding of the La Grange church.

Travis Church (1839)

Little is known about the founding of the Travis Baptist Church near Brenham. Z. N. Morrell implied that it had been organized in

1839 (although his language is vague). He named R. E. B. Baylor and T. W. Cox as the ministers responsible for forming this church with seven members. If the church were formed in 1839 and Baylor actually assisted in its founding, he would have had to be ordained before this time. For that reason Professor Tidwell counts the founding date of 1839 as erroneous, since Baylor was not yet ordained, which, according to Tidwell's chronology, took place after March, 1840.

It is known definitely that at the Travis church the first missionary Baptist association in Texas was organized in 1840; that the church had a schism in 1841 when its founder and pastor, T. W. Cox, showed evidence of being a follower of Alexander Campbell; that Z. N. Morrell served as pastor for one year and was succeeded by Richard Ellis. The church was probably dissolved in 1847.

There are occasional glimpses of this church in the correspondence of the missionaries in Texas. In a letter of July 1, 1841, William M. Tryon notified Corresponding Secretary Benjamin M. Hill of the Home Mission Society that he planned to devote one Saturday and one Sunday each month to the Travis church, at which place the work of the Lord was prospering. In a letter of August 17, 1841, James Huckins wrote Secretary Hill praising the work being done at Travis, and quoted a letter which said that the church in a revival meeting in June, 1841, had received twelve new members and that many more in the neighborhood were inquiring for the truth.

Independence Church (1839)

In the little town of Independence, situated amid the beautiful, undulating valley of the Yagua Creek in Washington County, several Baptists desired a church for worship. On August 31, 1839, Thomas Spraggins, a visiting preacher from Mississippi, led in the organization of the church. The charter members were John, Ivy, Mary and Jeanette McNeese; J. J. and Biddy Davis; and Thomas and Martha Tremmier. Others were received as soon as their letters could be secured, including O. H. P. Garrett, who became one of the outstanding laymen of Texas Baptists; and a preacher, J. L.

Davis and his wife, Diadema Matson, a daughter of the renowned Jeremiah Vardaman. Most of the constituent members were from South Carolina. J. J. Davis and John McNeese were elected as deacons, and Thomas Tremmier became church clerk. Spraggins soon returned to his home in Mississippi, and T. W. Cox was called as pastor.

A noteworthy event occurred in the church before the close of 1839. James D. Allcorn and his wife, Lydia, united with this church by baptism. Lydia Allcorn was the person who in 1829, ten years before, was converted in the home of Moses Shipman while Thomas Hanks was preaching. She is thought to have been the first Christian convert west of the Brazos River under Baptist preaching.

La Grange Church (1839–40)

There is some confusion as to exactly when this old church was organized. The traditional story told by Z. N. Morrell and repeated by J. B. Link and B. F. Fuller said that in the early part of 1839 T. W. Cox and J. L. Davis organized this church with nine members, including Cox, who became the first pastor.

Several bits of evidence have cast some doubt on the accuracy of this account. On April 1, 1840, R. E. B. Baylor wrote the following letter to the *Christian Index,* the Georgia Baptist paper:

Dear Brother in the Lord: It will no doubt be gratifying to you and the friends of humanity everywhere to be informed that a Baptist church has lately been organized near this place, at a village about five miles distance. The brethren in this part of the country met on the twenty-fifth of last month and the committee who had been previously appointed to draft Articles of Faith and Church Covenant made their report, which was received and unanimously adopted. Brother James Huckins and Thomas W. Cox were appointed presbytes to superintend the organization of the church. The Articles of Faith and Church Covenant were then read, after which the members presented their letters or gave satisfactory evidence of their good standing and relationship with the several churches to which they belonged, and were all received unanimously, amounting to thirteen in number. The church being regularly constituted by the name of the United Baptist Church at Huntersville, brothers James Stephens and Joseph Shaw were unanimously chosen deacons and the Hon. J. S. Lester, clerk.[13]

No effort was made to harmonize the two accounts until Professor D. D. Tidwell thoroughly studied the founding of this church. He concluded that the traditional date was incorrect and that the account by Baylor in his letter to the *Index* actually described the first organization of the La Grange church. He based his conclusions principally on the following grounds: (1) The first definite reference to the organization of this church is found in the 1853 minutes of the Colorado Baptist Association, where it states that the La Grange church was formed in March, 1840, with thirteen members by James Huckins and T. W. Cox. This, of course, a reflection from almost the first decade of the church's history, accepts Baylor's account as the initial founding of the church. (2) There is no reference in the minutes of the Union Association to a Huntersville church. When the Association met at the La Grange church in October, 1841, it identified the church with whom it met as the Clear Creek church, La Grange. (3) The leaders mentioned by Baylor (Stephens, Shaw, and Lester) were members of the Clear Creek church when the Association met there in 1841. Professor Tidwell remarked that difference in names (Clear Creek-Huntersville) "may be due to a loose usage of sometimes applying the name of the general or immediate vicinity instead of the official name. Plum Grove or Hopewell is an example of this."

Additional evidence lends support to Professor Tidwell's hypothesis. In a letter to Secretary Hill on November 14, 1841, James Huckins mentioned that he had attended this second meeting of the Union Baptist Association at "Rutterville," and remarked that the camp was "pitched on the edge of a broad prairie in a forest of oak, close by the banks of a clear stream of water." This clear creek may have given the name to the church where they were meeting, although without doubt this was the church referred to by Baylor.[14]

Furthermore, William M. Tryon wrote Secretary Hill on July 1, 1841, saying:

> More recently we visited the town of La Grange on the Colorado River, in the neighborhood of one hundred miles from the Gulf. The

town is small, containing a population of about one hundred and fifty. . . . La Grange, until recently, has been considered a frontier country, and the inhabitants have suffered much in times past from the Indians. The Baptist church in the place is one that brother Huckins assisted to constitute, during his first visit to Texas. At its organization there were about fourteen members; it has since been under the care of brother Cox, and at present numbers upward of twenty. I was indisposed during my visit, but on the Sabbath was enabled to meet with the people, make some remarks, and assisted by brother Baylor to administer the Lord's Supper.[15]

Tryon's statement, made about one year after the church was organized by Huckins and Cox, rules out the possibility that there were two missionary Baptist churches at La Grange at that time, one organized in 1839 and one in 1840. It also links the church organized by Huckins in 1840 with the church where the Union Baptist Association met about a year later, which was called in the minutes the Clear Creek church of La Grange.

One other item of evidence suggests that the La Grange church could not have been organized before February, 1839. Z. N. Morrell said that in that month "preaching was at that time a novelty in La Grange . . . ,"[16] which would hardly have been true if a church were located there.

Despite all this evidence to the contrary, however, there are solid reasons for clinging to the traditional date of 1839 for the founding of this church. Z. N. Morrell, who gave the original story, was a contemporary of the events. Usually he is reliable in his information. Although he could have been mistaken in the date, it is hardly likely that he would not have known the names of the men organizing the church. Both Cox and Davis were in this area in 1839 and could have organized the church. Morrell undoubtedly knew about the activity of James Huckins at La Grange in 1840, for Morrell lived in that area at that time. Yet he chose to give Cox and Davis as founders of the church.

More important than this is the word of R. E. B. Baylor himself, who wrote to the *Index* in 1840 about the organization of the Clear Creek church at "Huntersville." In his reminiscences, he said that in 1839 he had arrived in Texas. He then commented:

Settling at La Grange I immediately inquired if there were any Baptists in the place and if so had they organized a church. I very soon became acquainted with brothers Shaw and Lester, noble and good brothers. They informed me there was a small Baptist church in the village. At its first meeting I applied for membership. I had no letter, simply a license from the Talledaga church to preach. But pledging myself I would get my letter they took me into the church and here I commenced my first attempts at preaching the gospel of our blessed Savior.[17]

Apart from the recollection of any date, Baylor made it clear that there was already a Baptist church "in the village" when he arrived in 1839. In this church, already established, were Shaw and Lester, who were associated in the organization of the second church in 1840. The letter of April 1 by Baylor said that the new church of 1840 was formed about five miles from La Grange, which is an exact description of the Rutersville settlement. Baylor's handwriting was misread; instead of "Huntersville" he wrote "Ruttersville." This community, near La Grange, was the site of the first Protestant denominational school in Texas, which opened in January, 1840, and named after Methodist Bishop Martin Ruter. There can be no doubt that this community about five miles from La Grange was meant by Baylor's reference, for James Huckins specifically referred to Rutersville as being the location of the church he helped organize.[18]

As one looks at all of this material, he notes that there were actually two churches involved: an earlier one in the little village of La Grange and one about five miles away in the growing Methodist community called Rutersville. Apparently neither of the two built a meeting house.[19] Probably the clue to what actually transpired at La Grange is found in Baylor's story of the first effort to organize an association in June, 1840. At that time four preachers met with a company of brethren at Independence in an effort to form a Baptist association. The preachers were R. E. B. Baylor and T. W. Cox, with strong missionary convictions; and Abner Smith and Asael Dancer, who were just as strongly anti-missionary. At that meeting Cox and Smith crossed swords over missions, and the meeting dissolved amid heated language. Baylor gives some details of what happened.

Elder Abner Smith had organized a little Baptist church, the first perhaps ever in Western Texas. Elder Smith was the first Baptist preacher west of the Colorado. He came to Texas I think in the year 1834 with the venerable Joseph Burleson and company. He was a man deeply read in the scriptures, a man of talent and of unquestionable piety, a high toned Calvinist and anti everything else except the Bible and the church of the blessed Savior. And if you did not agree with him on his platform he had no fellowship for you. Although a good man he had I think strong feelings, a narrow mind, and unnecessary prejudices. The result was the Church divided, a part adhering to brother Smith and a larger portion going with the Missionary Baptists. During this state of things the little churches in the west sent delegates to Independence to form an association. We met there and through my solicitation brother Smith was elected moderator. I thought it was due to him. He was venerable in years and the first Baptist preacher who settled in western Texas. I found, however, Elder Cox did not like the idea of his being moderator, as it turned out in the sequel. After laboring some three or four days to agree upon an abstract of principles on which the association should be formed, through the prayers and tears of myself and others, the stern old Calvinistic brother Smith softened down a little and drew up a platform of principles to which we all assented except Elder Cox. He made a warm and excited speech against them, declaring those old fellows once had the rope around his neck and that he never would again consent to be thus tied.[20]

The statement that the anti-missionary group once had the rope around his neck is significant. There is no evidence that Cox meant anyone else than the anti-missionary group at La Grange (especially his reference to "those old fellows"). Just as the Plum Grove church divided over the missionary question, it is quite likely that the original La Grange church which Baylor joined in 1839 contained both missionaries and anti-missionaries. Cox was the pastor of this mixed church, which may account for his bitterness and his statement about being "tied" by these people. If Baylor joined this mixed church in 1839, it is likely that this was the one that ordained him. This would make it possible for him to have assisted in organizing the Travis church in that year. The church organized in March, 1840, described by Baylor in his letter to the *Index*, was probably the splitting of the "mixed" church and the forming of a distinctly missionary church. Missionary James Huckins had arranged to come to the community, and a committee was appointed in advance to draft articles of faith and a church covenant. When the missionary brethren thus had a totally missionary church, Cox felt that the anti-missionary people no longer had a rope around his neck. Baylor probably refrained from assisting in the organization of the church at Rutersville because his church letter had not yet been received from the church at Talladega.[21]

This reconstruction of events is given some weight by other circumstances. In January, 1847, P. B. Chandler, missionary of the Southern Baptist Convention, wrote from La Grange that the village had a population then of about 450, but that no church of any denomination had a building for worship. Most of the Baptists, he said, were anti-missionary, and there were *two* anti-missionary Baptist churches there.[22] The only anti-missionary Baptist church of record organized at La Grange was the Friendship church in 1843 by Abner Smith, J. Harper, and Asael Dancer.[23] It is quite possible that the other anti-missionary church referred to by Chandler was the remains of the original La Grange church from which the missionary group withdrew to form a totally missionary church in March, 1840.

The real crux of the problem is the date when R. E. B. Baylor came to Texas. Both Z. N. Morrell and Baylor himself state definitely that Baylor came to Texas in 1839. Baylor and T. W. Cox were members of the church at Talladega, Alabama, and Baylor remarked on another occasion that he came to Texas shortly after Cox made the journey. The records of the Talladega church show that in the January, 1838, church conference Cox had been unanimously elected as pastor for that year. However, in the May conference the church referred to the need for another pastor, and in August, 1838, H. E. Taliaferro was chosen for the remainder of the year 1838. At the December, 1838, conference the church granted letters to Cox, his wife, and his sister. He evidently left immediately for Texas, part of his haste being his imminent arrest for some fraudulent transactions in which he was involved and which are described in detail in the records of the Talladega church.

There is no specific date given in the Talladega records to indicate when Baylor might have followed Cox to Texas, but the "short time" could quite plausibly be after July 31, 1839, the year given by Morrell. To accept this date would solve several other problems: it would verify the date given for the founding of the Travis church in which Baylor was involved; it would explain the reticence of Baylor and Morrell about Baylor's ordination (probably by the mixed missionary/anti-missionary church at La Grange before Baylor's church letter had come from Talladega); it would make clear how Baylor could describe a church already existing in La Grange when he came to Texas; and it would explain how Morrell could seemingly be ignorant of the organization by Huckins and Cox of the second church at Rutersville near La Grange.

Thus, by the time of the arrival of the first missionaries from the American Baptist Home Mission Society of New York in January, 1840, indigenous leadership had already organized half-a-dozen or more small churches since the winning of political and religious freedom in 1836. There are some references in the correspondence of Huckins and Tryon to other churches and other Baptists which are not included in subsequent history. Remarkably strong religious leadership had appeared in men like Skelton Allphine, R. E. B. Baylor, J. L. Bryant, T. W. Cox, J. L. Davis, Thomas Hanks, Z. N. Morrell, Samuel E. Pearce, George W. Slaughter, John Woodruff, and Asa Wright; while Anderson Buffington, Noah T. Byars, and Richard Ellis were active workers who would soon be ordained as preachers.

A growing multitude of gifted lay people were busy in Baptist work before the missionaries came. They cannot all be named and praised in a work like this, but God knows their names. A few outstanding ones come quickly to mind, such as Dr. Thomas Anderson and his son, Washington; Gail L. Borden; Aaron and Joseph Burleson; Deacon H. R. Cartmell; John Cummings; Judge Richard Ellis; O. H. P. Garrett; Chester Gorbet; A. C. Horton, later Governor; J. S. Lester; Eli Mercer; Mrs. Massie Millard; A. G. Perry; Thomas J. Pilgrim, who continued faithfully in Sunday school leadership for the remainder of his long life; Deacon James Pruitt; Deacon William Scallorn; Moses Shipman; Orville P. Tyler; and Deacon W. C. Veazey. These faithful workers and scores of others like them, their number increasing month by month through immigration and conversion, provided a strong foundation for the solid growth of the next decade.

4

Assaulting the Wilderness
(1840–48)

☆ ☆ ☆

The total environment in the new Republic of Texas greatly affected the work of Baptists during the period between the coming of the first missionaries to Texas and the organization of the state body. The administration of Texas President M. B. Lamar was not able to stabilize the currency, and its value dropped to about fourteen cents on the dollar. The Indians constantly harassed the settlers, so that along the frontier in particular it was most difficult to plant crops and harvest them. Early in March, 1842, Mexican troops crossed into Texas and seized Goliad, Refugio, San Antonio, and Victoria. By June the Mexicans had retreated toward the Rio Grande, but an uneasy peace ensued. On September 11, General Adrian Woll returned with 1,400 Mexican troops and captured San Antonio. This marked the beginning of tension and actual hostilities between Texans and Mexicans that continued until December 29, 1845, when Texas became the twenty-eighth state of the United States of America. War between Mexico and the United States promptly followed, ending on February 2, 1848, when Mexico recognized the independence of Texas and fixed the boundary at the Rio Grande.

It is remarkable that the tumultuous conditions of this period did not wholly stop all efforts of Texas Baptists. Morrell, Baylor, and other leaders of the Baptists engaged in the military struggle. The story in this chapter is the expanding scope of the work and the increase in the number of Baptist churches between 1840 and 1848. It will be impossible to describe accurately all that was done and by whom. The records of that day are sometimes silent or are contradictory in significant particulars. There is no doubt, however, that in addition to the distinguished R. E. B. Baylor, three great names stand out in the leadership of this period, all of them missionaries. Fortunately, a first-hand account has been preserved from each of them, giving an interesting and relatively accurate story by actors in the drama.

These three outstanding leaders were James Huckins, the first missionary to Texas appointed by the American Baptist Home Mission Society of New York; William M. Tryon, the second missionary appointed by this body; and the pioneer, Z. N. Morrell, who was appointed for a season by the Southern Baptist Convention as a missionary in Texas. The three men were as different as men could possibly be, yet each used his own gifts to make a remarkable contribution. Huckins was born in New Hampshire about 1807, and was reared as an orphan. He was schooled at Brown University and Andover seminary. He served some New England churches as pastor for a few years before his appointment by the Home Mission Society. Baylor gave a candid portrait of Huckins.

> He was tall and slender with a quick black eye, one slightly dropped, dark hair, sallow complexion, had bold and prominent features, particularly his nose. In point of intellect, we have had no man his superior in Texas. . . . He would have been a great man in almost any department of life, merchant, lawyer, or pauper. Still, with all these advantages, his ministry never came to be greatly blessed . . . If an humble individual like myself may be permitted to judge, I think his sermons were too precisely intellectual and his habit of reading them was one cause why they failed to be as impressive on the heart as they otherwise would have been.[1]

Carroll remarked that Huckins was the "balance wheel" needed to accompany the emotional preaching of Morrell and Baylor and the eloquent evangelistic preaching of Tryon.

William M. Tryon provided a perfect complement to Huckins as they worked together. Tryon was born in New York City in 1809, and like Huckins was an orphan. In 1828 he moved to Georgia, where he was licensed to preach in 1832 and attended Mercer University. He served in 1838 in Alabama as pastor before being appointed missionary to Texas. Morrell says of him:

> Brother Tryon was a man of medium size, with an erect, well-proportioned physical structure. His dark, penetrating eye, above which appeared a full, well-formed forehead, impressed every man who looked upon him, as to his intellectual powers. . . . As an orator, my profound conviction is that no preacher has ever lived in Texas who was his equal. . . . It was my fortune to hear him at many of our annual meetings, at his churches, and on missionary fields, and on all occasions he ever swayed the masses at will.[2]

Tryon was preeminently a soul-winner. While Huckins had no equal in raising funds for mission work, Tryon was without peer as a soul-winner in this pioneer period. In his regular letters to the Home Mission Society, Tryon rarely described a Sunday service or a revival meeting without reporting many converts.

In contrast with both of these was Z. N. Morrell, the oldest of the three. Born in 1803 in South Carolina, he had come to Texas by way of Tennessee. He was hampered by a crippled leg, incurred by a fall into a well as a young man, and suffered from lung hemorrhages, which ceased shortly after he came to Texas with its drier and warmer climate. He was a tall man, with a face that could show deep compassion or total condemnation in his picturesque preaching. He always wore a long, full beard which became gray before the heavy, dark mane atop his head had lost its color. He was a mixture of the practical and the visionary. Carroll remarked:

> Z. N. Morrell was in very many respects a very wonderful man. He was not what the world calls educated, and yet he was remarkably intelligent, and a vigorous and deep thinker. He was marvelously accurate in his interpretations of the Scripture, and always courageous and strong in their defense—popular and successful as a preacher and a true and uncompromising missionary. He was a hater of evil and a devout lover of God and man—a man whose strong faith was proven by his works, and whose works were constant exemplifications of his faith. He was many times pastor and mission-

ary, and nearly always at his own cost—a real pioneer of pioneers in our Texas Baptist work.[3]

Two Years with James Huckins

The inspiring story of Huckins begins with the Executive Board records of the American Baptist Home Mission Society of New York. It will be recalled that the church at Washington wrote the Society on November 7, 1837, appealing for missionaries. The Executive Committee of the New York Society read it at their meeting on December 18. At the January 8, 1838, session it was suggested that missionary Ezra Fisher, serving in Illinois, might consider going to Texas; but because he strenuously objected to slavery he chose Oregon instead. On August 20, 1838, the Committee voted that missionary David Orr, then in Arkansas, be allowed to labor in Texas during the "cold season" with the possibility that the milder climate in Texas might be beneficial for him. "For the performance of this important duty, he made his arrangements, but was nevertheless, as he believes, providentially prevented from going thither."

On January 7, 1839, the Committee received a letter from James Huckins saying that Richard Fuller, distinguished pastor at Beaufort, South Carolina, believed that Huckins should constitute a Baptist church in New Orleans. On June 20, 1839, the Committee appointed Huckins as an agent for twelve months, his field to be determined later. In their concern about Texas, the Committee voted on July 18, 1839, that the Secretary should correspond with brethren who might assist in obtaining a missionary for that Republic. The man and the Society came together soon. On September 2, the Committee learned that Huckins was willing to go to Texas as a missionary. He was sent first to Georgia to raise funds.

Meanwhile, from Texas itself other appeals came. On October 21, 1839, a letter from S. P. Andrews of Texas was read, urging that a missionary be sent to the field there. This was the man who became clerk of the Union Association when it met at La Grange in 1841. A letter from Shelbyville, Texas, dated March 25, 1838, was received by the Society, urging that Baptist missionaries come soon, for, said the writer, Baptists are reported to be more numerous in the Republic than any other denomination. Finally, the Society announced that

> A sense of the urgent necessity of early action, has at length induced the Board to dispense, for a season, with the financial services of our brother James Huckens (sic) one of the more efficient agents of the Society, and to employ him for at least four months as a missionary in the new republic. . . . Other denominations have to some extent responded to the call, but their missionaries say that a large portion of the people are Baptist in sentiment, and can be effectually reached only by members of our Church. . . .⁴

Before Huckins could reach Texas, two more letters had come to the Society. A young man from Galveston in the merchantile business, probably David R. Wright, wrote a lengthy letter in which he described the beauty of this "land of sunshine and flowers," and urged that missionaries be sent to the Italy of the American continent.⁵ About the same time David Wright of West-field, Massachusetts, probably the father of the young man in Galveston, said that his son in Galveston had been writing him for the past several months urging that a missionary be sent without delay. The son, he reported, had said that out of the population of two thousand in Galveston, there was only one clergyman, a Pres-byterian. His son also had said that in a three day period there had been twelve hundred new immigrants in Galveston alone, of whom two-thirds were from the North and East. His son's last letter concluded with the words, "I have found a great number of Bap-tists here, and if we can all unite we are as strong as any denomina-tion in this city."⁶

On January 19, 1840, Huckins arrived in New Orleans en route to Texas for the purpose of exploring the possibilities of mission work there. On the evening of January 24, the steamer Neptune with seventy-one passengers sailed into Galveston Bay. Huckins described how between fifteen and twenty boats were floating at the wharf, and a large crowd was awaiting the docking of the vessel. Huckins left the boat the following morning and met an old friend with whom he took breakfast, during which time he met several Baptist families. On Sunday, January 26, he attended an interdenominational Sabbath school, after which he preached to a congregation numbering about two hundred. At the close of the service he invited all members of Baptist churches or those interested in Baptist work being begun in Galveston to tarry. In response, a dozen Baptists met with him and urged him to organize them into a church before proceeding to spy out the land. On the following Thursday, the group met to examine candidates for organizing a church. At this time Gail Borden, Jr. and his wife presented themselves as candidates for baptism. It was voted that on the following Sunday, February 3, the church should be constituted.

On that day, according to a letter from David R. Wright, the new church clerk of the Galveston church, addressed to S. H. Cone of New York, "Brother Huckins preached to us all day."[7] Six Baptists from New England and New York were present with letters in hand. Mrs. Louisa R. Borden and Lewis Graves were from the First Baptist Church, Seneca Falls, New York; Mrs. Abigail W. Bartlett and David R. Wright were from the Central Baptist Church, Westfield, Massachusetts; George Fellows was from the First Baptist Church, Deerfield, New Hampshire; and Francis W. Pettigrove was from the First Baptist Church, Calais, Maine. The following then united on promise of their letter: Barnabas Haskell, Norwich, Connecticut, and his wife Mrs. Abigail Haskell from the same church; and Mrs. Sarah A. Burnet, Clinton, Louisiana. Gail Borden, Jr. and his wife were received upon their profession of faith. On the following Tuesday at 3:00 P.M., Borden, his wife, and his wife's sister were baptized in Galveston Bay. Huckins wrote in his Journal:

> This day has been one of the happiest in my life. God has given me the privilege of baptizing three individuals. Never before since the creation of man have the waters of the great gulf this side of the Mississippi been visited for the performance of a rite so sacred. As long as life shall last I will cherish that scene, and it seems to me that my spirit in eternity will love to linger around its portraiture.[8]

The next day Huckins wrote Jesse Mercer of Georgia, whom he knew well, and told him of baptizing Borden's wife, who was a

Mercer. The Lord's Supper was observed on the next Sunday, and a weekly prayer meeting was inaugurated. Subscriptions were begun for erecting a church building.

Huckins had expected to spend one day in Galveston, but he was there almost a month. On February 19, he rode to Houston, eighty miles away. He spent about a week here, finding over a dozen Baptists in the population estimated at 3,000. On February 29, he began his first mission tour, evidently traveling north on the Brazos River and returning by way of the Colorado. The beauty of the prairie constantly amazed him, reminding him at times of the green hills of Vermont. He returned by way of La Grange, where he met T. W. Cox and R. E. B. Baylor and assisted in the organization (or reorganization) of the La Grange church. In a letter to S. H. Cone of New York, published in June, Huckins remarked that he had visited Richmond, about thirty miles from Houston on the Brazos, and Matagorda on this trip. "If we had the services of a few good missionaries," said Huckins in his letter, "in whom the public could confide, we might have twenty-two Baptist churches in Texas, as soon as the work of collecting an organization could be entered upon."[9] The Society said later that they had made seven appointments in Texas during 1840, but that only two had taken up the work.

Soon after his return from this tour, Huckins journeyed back to the headquarters of the Society in New York City, spending the remainder of the summer and the fall speaking to churches and conventions about the needs of Texas. The reports of the Society show offerings from Georgia and Louisiana; from Utica and Albany, New York; from Wilmington, Delaware; and from two churches in Baltimore and two in Texas. The "farewell" meeting for Huckins in New York took place, not before his first exploratory journey of about two months, as J. M. Carroll indicated, but on his second departure.[10] On January 18, 1841, he wrote from Galveston that he had arrived there on December 29 after a rough passage of twenty-one days. He had since been in bed, too ill to minister.[11] On March 28, 1841, he wrote to the Society that William M. Tryon had arrived during January.

On May 24, 1841, Huckins wrote the Society that he had

assisted in constituting the First Baptist Church in Houston on April 10, 1841. Evidently Barnabas Haskell and his wife Abigail accompanied him or preceded him to Houston from Galveston, for they were two of the original sixteen members of the new church. A number of Baptists soon joined on promise of letter. The records do not show the places from which the members of this church came, which would be of interest for history. On August 17, 1841, Huckins wrote the Society that the Houston church was increasing in strength and building a house of worship. He praised the work of Tryon and Baylor at Washington, where a sweeping revival was taking place. Revivals were also occurring at the Independence and Travis churches, where Tryon was now pastor. Reference was made by Huckins to new churches at Mount Vernon and Comanche, the latter located twelve miles below Austin. Huckins reported that he was still fighting disabling illness, but had managed to continue his work.[12]

On November 14, 1841, Huckins wrote that he had been confined with a fever and ulcerated throat for two weeks. "My house," he said, "has been like a hospital ever since the eighteenth of August," but things were now looking up. On September 29 he had begun a missionary tour, attending the meeting of the Union Baptist Association "near Rutterville." He described the exclusion of T. W. Cox, pastor of the host church, and rejoiced in the organization of a Home Mission Society and an Education Society. Upon returning to his home, he was called to Washington County on October 19 to assist in the ordination of Anderson Buffington, who had been a charter member of the old Washington church. Buffington served as a missionary in Montgomery County during 1842 under the new Texas Home Mission Society.

On December 10, 1841,[13] Huckins reported to the Society that God's hand was evident in the work in Washington and Milam counties, and especially at the Mount Gilead church, where a revival had begun in June and had spread through the entire area. Huckins was traveling extensively at this time. In the summary of the Society for 1842, their minutes reported that Huckins had preached 139 sermons, had made fifty pastoral visits, had traveled 2550 miles, had baptized five, had 120 scholars in Sunday school in

Galveston and Houston, and had secured 150 volumes for the libraries of the churches.

These were two busy years for Huckins, who labored steadily despite severe illness. His correspondence with the Society reflected a constant solicitude for the needs of Texas, and he made repeated appeals for additional missionaries.

A Year With William Tryon

The colorless minutes of the Home Mission Society of New York for 1842 simply report that William M. Tryon was a missionary in Texas at Independence and Washington for fifty-two weeks, and that he had preached 141 sermons, traveled 1250 miles, and baptized 137 people. Fortunately, a rather detailed record of his early strenuous service in Texas is available from his correspondence. Originally, it had been planned that he should spend four months of the first year raising funds for Texas in the United States, but his immediate fruitfulness and active service prevented his leaving the Republic during this first year.

Departing from Alabama on January 4, 1841, by way of Mobile and New Orleans, he traversed the stormy sea route to Galveston, arriving on January 18. He promptly began his first missionary tour in Texas. On horseback, accompanied by his wife, he took a circuitous route up the Brazos River, arriving late Saturday afternoon near Washington where the first missionary Baptist church had been founded in 1837. This first church had died, he reported, their house was sold, and the Baptists remaining there were discouraged. He preached at Washington on the following day. He must have been persuasive, for he soon baptized his wife, who had been a Methodist before coming with Tryon to Texas.

On March 14, 1841, "after consultation with Brethren Cox and Baylor," Tryon led in the organization of a church of twelve members. He remarked that "a deacon who had held this office in the United States" would serve similiarly at Washington. This probably was H. R. Cartmell, who had been a deacon in Nashville and had served the old Washington church in this office. Cartmell was not one of the original twelve members of this reorganization, but soon came with his letter. Meanwhile, Tryon took charge of the church at Independence at the request of T. W. Cox, its pastor, who lived at La Grange about sixty miles away. At this time "the congregation is the largest in the republic."[14] By April 1, Tryon reported that he was preaching in a "thickly settled neighborhood" about twenty miles from Washington, where he expected to organize a church. Probably he was referring to the vicinity of Chapel Hill. He also reported preaching monthly at "Brazos Ferry," forty miles from Houston, where "we have a large and respectable congregation."

On July 1, Tryon reported to the Society that he was preaching one Saturday and Sunday at Independence, one "at a newly constituted Church in this county" (probably the Providence church at Chapel Hill), and one Saturday and Sunday at the Travis church in Austin County. He described how in May he had ridden to Matagorda, near the mouth of the Colorado River, where he had preached the first Baptist sermon ever heard in the little town of six hundred which was notable for its "refinement and intelligence." The only Baptists here were "Col. Albert C. Horton" and wife. Horton had distinguished himself in the Texas Revolution. From Matagorda he rode north to LaGrange, about one hundred miles from the Gulf on the Colorado River, where, although ill, he met with the people on Sunday and assisted by R. E. B. Baylor, administered the Lord's Supper.[15]

In July Tryon assisted in a sweeping revival at the Washington church and administered the first baptism known by him to have been performed in the Brazos River. Immediately thereafter he and Baylor preached a revival meeting in a settlement twenty-seven miles west of Washington. Fourteen of the twenty-two who professed conversion were baptized into the Independence Church. On August 21 he and Baylor began a meeting at the Mount Gilead church, situated on Mill Creek in Washington County. A stirring revival took place, with thirty-nine being baptized at the close of it and the whole area stirred. This church, Tryon said, had been constituted in November, 1840, and although only ten months had elapsed since it was organized with thirteen members, it was now the largest Baptist church in Texas, numbering 130 members, between eighty and ninety of whom had been added by baptism.[16]

In September he rode to Milam County, constituted the Providence Church with the assistance of Baylor, and baptized forty converts. This church, Tryon said, numbered thirteen when it was organized, but in less than three months it had grown to between sixty and seventy members.

This was a typical year in the energetic service of Tryon. Multiplied by seven, it became a widespread ministry of strenuous service by this dedicated man before his untimely death in 1847.

A Month With Z. N. Morrell

This limping giant among Texas Baptist pioneers was remarkably active in the period between 1840 and 1848. It did not at first seem that this would be true. At the beginning of 1844, with the health of his wife rapidly declining and himself weary of frontier life, Morrell moved to Houston to begin again.

My way was by no means clear. The church I first organized at Washington failed, and now the frontier church at Gonzales were scattered; my farming and financial operations all had failed, and in the midst of my distresses, like Jacob, after the loss of Joseph and Simeon, and the demand for Benjamin also, I could but cry out, "All these things are against me;" and faith revealed no reason why these things should fail to "bring down my gray hairs with sorrow to the grave."[17]

But it was not in the nature of this man to be discouraged for very long. He described his resurgence.

The waters had not overflowed me, and the fires had not consumed me, and with a heart full of gratitude to Him who walked in the presence of Nebuchadnezzar with Shadrach, Meshach, and Abednego, in the midst of the fiery furnace, and who, walking upon the water himself, caught the hand of the sinking Peter and restored him to his place, I buckled my armor on, and, with a fixed determination to fight his battles while I lived, went forth in what I supposed to be the line of duty. With a full realization of the fact, that the sparse settlements would very soon be populous neighborhoods, in need of churches and a regular ministry, I sold out my little estate at the mouth of the Trinity, and gave myself exclusively to the work, commencing at the Providence church, Washington County.[18]

He revisited the valley of the Colorado and preached in the neighborhood of La Grange with R. E. B. Baylor. Then he visited a number of important points in what was then Montgomery County, extending from the Brazos to the Trinity River, and found that widespread immigration had provided a great challenge for new churches. "Outside of Galveston and Houston there was not, at this time, a single Baptist church between the Trinity and the Brazos Rivers, from their springs in the mountains to the Gulf of Mexico. . . ."[19] After laboring in the vicinity of Danville and assisting in the organization of a little church (which later dissolved), he gave his attention to the area around Huntsville. On September 16, 1844, along with Thomas Horseley, he constituted the Huntsville church. Anti-missionary and unsavory Baptist preachers made the task difficult there.

During this time he also preached regularly each month at a little school house, resulting in the organization on November 11, 1844, of the church at Anderson. Horseley and Morrell constituted the presbytery.

Still another monthly preaching service during the year resulted in the organization on November 25, 1844, by Morrell and Tryon, of the Post Oak Grove church, seven miles west of the town of Montgomery.

Morrell himself described a typical month of his work in early 1846. He had resigned as pastor of the churches he had helped to constitute, and became a missionary under the Domestic Mission Board of the Southern Baptist Convention. His field was the area north of the old San Antonio road, between the Brazos and Trinity rivers, which included that part of Texas where he had first lived. His salary was $250.00 a year to be paid quarterly. A month of his life presents an amazing picture.

During the spring of 1846 I encountered many difficulties in traversing the broad field assigned me. The Little Brazos and Navasota Rivers both had to be crossed on every trip, and there was no ferry on either stream. They were frequently swollen for weeks together, and many a time I was compelled not only to swim the main streams, but also in the low grounds adjacent. It was sixty miles to Leona, where I filled an appointment the first Sunday in every month, with both these rivers to cross. It was then, the way I travelled, fifty miles to Springfield, with several streams between, without bridges, where I preached on every second Sunday. It was forty miles to my next appointment for the third Sunday, in Navarro County, with Richland and Chambers Creeks on the way. It was one hundred miles on a direct route to my own neighborhood where I preached in Milam County, on the fourth Sunday. With extra rides, in visiting among the scattered settlements, over three hundred miles were travelled monthly, during the entire year. High waters never prevented me from filling a single appointment. . . .

On this same trip, in the month of March, passing from Leona to Springfield, with only one house on the road, I found a creek swimming, about midway between these points. About two hours were lost in my efforts to head the swimming water. It was very cold and I dreaded it. Finally, my horse was plunged into the swollen stream. He swam with me to the opposite bank without any difficulty; but as he struggled amid obstructions on the Springfield side, I was compelled to dismount in the water and give the animal my assistance.

Morrell then related how his boots were full of water and his clothing thoroughly saturated, while a "blue Texas norther whistled around my ears." It was four o'clock in the evening, and he had to ride twenty-five miles toward the north to reach Springfield. However, about eight miles farther, his clothes now freezing, he found a new camp by the roadside, where he spent the night with Christian friends. He was dismayed to find, upon opening his saddlebags, that "my old Jerusalem blade (his Bible) and the old Concordance that I carried for twenty-five years" were soaking wet. He was forced to spend the next day waiting for the creeks to fall, but was still able to make Springfield in time for his preaching.

We now crossed Richland creek, and passing preached at Corsicana. Only a few small houses there then. Chambers' creek was crossed and an appointment filled in a settlement beyond, where the Providence church was organized in July, 1846, without any minister present but myself, with fourteen members. People from a long distance off met us there in March and afterwards, and we had a large congregation for that day, which met us regularly.

As I retraced my steps homeward, I turned up Richland creek, and visited brother N. T. Byars, preaching in his community. According to my recollection, he had some time previous to this organized the church known as Society Hill. Sometimes on my return I preached at Springfield. On my arrival at the little Brazos the weather was quite cold, the canoe on the opposite side, and nobody in sight or hearing. Here was another large swollen stream to swim. Reaching home, I filled my appointment where the Little River church was organized in 1847, with six white and one colored member, by Z. N. Morrell.

You now have the history of one month's work performed by a pioneer missionary. A change of horses was required every trip, and these trips were made in succession, monthly, for two years, making over seven thousand miles. My salary each year was two hundred and fifty dollars, and the last year I spent three hundred dollars to keep myself in horses.[20]

The Southern Baptist Convention Helps

Northern and Southern Baptists cooperated together in carrying on foreign mission work beginning with the organization of the General Missionary Convention in 1814, in the publication and circulation of religious tracts with the organization of the Baptist Tract Society in 1824, and in home mission work with the founding of the American Baptist Home Mission Society in 1832. It was this last-named body that received the appeal from the Washington church and sent James Huckins and William M. Tryon as its missionaries. As a matter of fact, the Society also sent Benjamin B. Baxter under their commission to work in Texas in 1842, and the minutes for 1844 show that he worked at "Senter Hill" for fifty-two weeks in 1842–1843.

However, since about 1835 the slavery-abolitionist controversy, trumpeted across the Atlantic from English Baptist life, had brought tension between Northern and Southern Baptists. The issue had become critical by 1841, and it is quite likely that a "Compromise Article" agreed to at Baltimore by the principal northern and southern leaders prevented the break in that year.

One of the objections of New England to the admission of Texas as a state in the Union was the fact that she was a slave state.

Curiously enough, the two missionaries in Texas from the Baptist home mission body became the occasion for the organizational break between Northern and Southern Baptists in 1845. On December 27, 1843, an anonymous inquiry was published in the *Baptist Record,* Concord, New Hampshire, asking if it were true that James Huckins and William Tryon, missionaries of the Baptist Mission Society in Texas, were slaveholders. This aroused the ire of Editor Thomas Meredith of the *Biblical Recorder* of North Carolina, who answered sharply. During the next four months this question was heatedly discussed by the *Christian Reflector* of Boston, *Zion's Advocate* of Maine, the *Christian Index* of Georgia, and other Baptist papers.

On April 11, the *Christian Reflector* of Boston published a letter by a former member of Huckins' church stating emphatically that both Huckins and Tryon were slaveholders. As a matter of fact, Huckins owned one household servant, while Tryon had come into possession of some slaves when he married Mrs. Louisa J. Higgins of Montgomery, Alabama, on April 26, 1840, before he had even begun work with the Home Mission Society. When the Home Mission Society met in late April, it was this newspaper controversy that brought a resolution to dissolve the body, which, however, became unnecessary when the Southern Baptist Convention was organized on May 8–10, 1845, in Augusta, Georgia.

In 1846, the Domestic Mission Board of the new Southern body issued commissions to Huckins and Tryon, both of whom promptly toured southern churches soliciting funds for the erection of houses of worship in Galveston and Houston, where they were serving as missionary pastors. In August, 1846, the Board appointed J. W. D. Creath of Virginia, Plesant B. Chandler of Georgia, and Noah Hill of Georgia to the Texas field. The contribution of these men to Texas can hardly be estimated. By coincidence, on the same ship that brought these three men to Texas was another man of destiny —Henry L. Graves, the president-elect of the newly formed Baylor University at Independence, Texas. Huckins wrote to the Board in 1846 to say:

In the month of December, our hearts were gladened by the arrival of the missionaries of your Board. Such a freight was never before landed in our city. Four Baptist ministers and their families, and in the same company, some six or seven other Baptist families. It was a glorious day to my own soul, and which opens a new era for the denomination in Texas. The spirit of these missionaries, the profound sense of the nature and responsibility of their work, the hours of agonizing prayer during their passage, made me feel, during my interview with them, that I was in the company of holy men; men called of God to come to Texas. . . .[21]

Morrell later remarked that "no ship that ever ploughed the waves between New Orleans and Galveston, I suppose, ever brought at one time a more valuable cargo for Texas. . . ."[22] Morrell was named as missionary in 1846 and 1847, but was then forced to resign because of ill-health. Jesse Witt of Virginia was appointed and began service in 1847. Robert H. Taliaferro arrived in Austin in 1847 under the auspices of the Home Mission Society of New York, but in the following year he was appointed by the southern Board. However, he soon resigned to carry on an itinerant but effective ministry, principally around Austin and near the Colorado River. Also in 1848 the Domestic Board appointed J. F. Hillyer as mission pastor at Galveston. Rufus C. Burleson, a distinguished and familiar name in Texas Baptist history, was appointed to succeed the lamented William C. Tryon as mission pastor of the church at Houston, effective January 1, 1848. Apparently Willis M. Pickett also was appointed to serve in the vicinity of Clarksville during this period, for he regularly reported to the Domestic Mission Board.

The Old Guard

As important as the new missionaries were to Texas, their contribution would have been diminished greatly without the faithful service of God-called men already in the land. Three outstanding men were ordained in the older section of the state within one year of one another. On October 16, 1841, Noah T. Byars, the blacksmith for General Houston in 1836, in whose shop at Washington the Texas Declaration of Independence was signed, was ordained, evidently the second missionary Baptist ordination in Texas. He had been a member of the first missionary church at Washington in 1837, and in the fall of 1841 resigned his position as associate county judge under the conviction that he was called to preach. He was ordained by the Macedonia church below Austin in the presence of President Lamar of the Republic and several of his cabinet. Z. N. Morrell and John Woodruff constituted the presbytery. Most of the remainder of his life was spent on the frontier in Texas, although from 1868 to 1871 he served in Mississippi. Link remarked that Byars assisted in the organization of three associations and sixty churches, among them the First Baptist Church in Waco.

Three days later (October 19, 1841) Anderson Buffington, another charter member of the Washington church, was ordained by the Washington church with the assistance of James Huckins and others. Buffington was immediately appointed as a missionary of the Texas Baptist Home Mission Society (mainly paying his own expenses). He served principally in what was then Montgomery County.[23] In later years he was well known for his labors among the black population at his own expense.

The third man ordained during this year was Richard Ellis, who may have left Washington just before the first church was organized in 1837, although this is not certain. He was a member of the Macedonia church below Austin, which requested the Plum Grove church to ordain him. This was done in August, 1842, with Z. N. Morrell and R. E. B. Baylor as presbytery. He served faithfully, dying prematurely in 1852. For the insight that it gives both into the life of Ellis and the spirit of R. E. B. Baylor, an excerpt from Baylor's description of Ellis is given.

As I started on (a) trip up the Colorado a brother said to me, "If you meet with a brother Ellis at your meetings cherish him, he will do. I have seen him tried on our border campaign and amid the wildest scenes of the soldiers he never lost sight of his religion." At our first meeting brother Ellis was present. He sang beautifully and was wonderfully gifted in prayer. I called on him to pray at the close of the service. He did so with much feeling and pathos, and I immediately left the pulpit, went to him and taking him by the hand with tears in my eyes I said, "Why do you not preach?" He immediately commenced weeping and said, "I ran away from Virginia to keep from preaching." I replied, "You have been a runaway long enough from the Master: obey the divine impression you have, take up the cross and preach Jesus to a lost and ruined world." The next thing I heard of brother Ellis he had been licensed by the little church we organized to preach. At first he was greatly embarrassed and would sometimes be so overcome as to sink down in the pulpit. I was however much with him. Often we preached together and by encouragement and kind advice his embarrassment gradually wore off. He was apt to learn. Tell him of a fault and he rarely ever committed it again. He had but a plain education and was emphatically a self-made man. Ultimately he became one of our greatest preachers. I recollect the last time I ever heard him preach at Chappell Hill, he delivered a series of sermons that would have done credit to any man in the ministry. His piety and sincerity in religion none ever doubted. He literally killed himself in the cause of the master. By incessantly singing, preaching, exhorting, and praying, he finally took the consumption, of which disease he ultimately died. He now sleeps on the banks of the Colorado and there let him sleep until the morning of the resurrection, when I have no doubt he will awake in the beautiful likeness of our blessed Saviour. None who were present at our last interview in Chappell Hill will ever forget it. Far gone in consumption, as soon as he saw me in the congregation he came trembling and weeping, threw his arms around my neck and as we embraced each other in silence and tears, many in the congregation mingled their tears with ours. Peace to thy ashes, my dear brother, God only and you know how we loved each other in undying love which can only be fully developed in eternity. . . . Once more, farewell, my dear brother, it will not be long before we will meet I hope where consumption, sickness and sorrow can never come and where the weary are at rest. . . . In his ministry under God he was wonderfully successful in winning souls to the dear Redeemer. He often wept whilst preaching and his sermons always had a telling effect on the congregation. Once more, farewell my dear brother.[24]

Many more men and women served faithfully in the period before the organization of the state body on September 8, 1848. Over half a hundred names of missionary Baptist preachers are found in the various accounts of the scattered Texas fields. It is not possible to mention all of them, but it is equally difficult to leave out any of them, for who knows which work was more important? Reference has been made to the appointment of Willis M. Pickett, a Kentuckian, who had come to Texas in 1843 and settled near Clarksville in Red River County. He had been licensed in Kentucky and after his arrival in Texas was ordained by a presbytery headed by Noah T. Byars. John Briscoe, who came to Texas in 1846, worked by the side of Pickett, as did Benjamin Clark, a veteran preacher of Missouri, and M. Piland.

One of the outstanding leaders of this period was Hosea Garrett. He preached and farmed in South Carolina before coming to Texas with his nephew, O. H. P. Garrett, in February, 1842. With Baylor, Tryon, and Elias Rogers, he formed the presbytery to organize the Providence church at Chapel Hill, where he kept his membership until his death forty-five years later. He was pastor of the church several times and preached also in Washington, Austin, Lee, and other adjacent counties.

Another outstanding name was that of Lemuel Herrin, who came to Texas in 1841 and located in Harrison County. He was one of the early east Texas preachers who was a missionary. With others he helped organize the Border church in 1843 and the Sabine Association in the same year, and led in withdrawing from the latter in 1847 because it was anti-missionary. He also helped organize the Eight Mile church in 1845 and the Macedonia church in Panola County in 1844.

The principal name farther north was that of David Myers, who moved from Illinois in 1845 and settled in Dallas County. He is reported to have preached the first Baptist sermon in Dallas in June, 1846. He led in organizing the Union church, Rowlett's Creek church, the Bethel church, the Liberty church, and perhaps others.

James H. Stribling came with his family to Texas in 1841. As a young man he joined the Texas army in 1842 to repel the Mexican invasion. In September, 1843, he was baptized by William M. Tryon and about a year later was licensed to preach. Feeling a need for further education, he became the first ministerial student at Baylor in May, 1846. After his ordination in 1849 he entered into an active and influential ministry in some of the strongest churches in Texas.

A close companion of Stribling at Baylor was David B. Morrill, whose untimely death in 1868 cut short his zealous and dedicated service. When he surrendered to the ministry in Galveston, one of his associates remarked that his entering into Christian service had "spoiled the finest young businessman in Galveston," but his effective ministry was better than stocks and bonds.

An example of one of the many preachers in Texas, limited in education but faithful in earnest zeal, was Thomas Horseley, who helped Z. N. Morrell organize the Anderson church in 1844. Horseley farmed near Huntsville and preached to many small churches without remuneration.

Along with these ministerial servants were many strong lay leaders that moved into Texas during this period. Space will not permit the inspiring stories that could be told of faithful people like General J. W. Barnes, Willett Holmes, A. G. Haynes, Terrell Jackson, and the continuing service of Annette Lea Bledsoe, whose sister married Sam Houston.

A Great Thrust

The several years immediately following statehood in 1845 brought unusual expansion in missionary activity and organization, so much so that it becomes impossible to identify the founding of individual churches and describe the faithful service of many leaders. There were reasons for this accelerated progress. (1) New confidence developed when all of the resources of the United States were thrown behind the relatively small band of Texans in their struggle against the Mexicans and the Indians. The rapid defeat of Mexico in the lightning war of 1847 and the reduction of the Indian menace encouraged many new Baptists to move into Texas, and those within the state to launch challenging programs. (2) The missionaries of the Southern Baptist Convention, described earlier in this chapter, gave additional stability and talent. (3) New preachers began to flood into Texas after statehood and served faithfully and well. (4) The old guard was particularly effective. Z. N. Morrell seemed to find new strength for a season after 1845, and was quite active in his preaching and organizing. Noah T. Byars served in an adjacent field, and the two formed a congenial team, inspiring one another to good works. Not only so, but in 1846 R. E. B. Baylor was given a new court assignment in the very area where Morrell and Byars were serving. Morrell deliberately planned his preaching engagements so that he could utilize the distinguished jurist to preach at night in every term of court Baylor held. (5) The establishment of the new university at Independence gave impetus to Baptist growth.

Most of all, as Morrell expressed it in his own jubilant language, the hand of God was with Texas Baptists.

> The events recorded in 1848 show that progress was written upon the banner that the Baptists carried in those days. Far up the Trinity and Brazos Rivers, in the direction of the Indian country, they pressed their way, and God smiled upon their work. . . . As the number of associations was rapidly multiplying, and as the Baptists of Texas saw the clearest indications that "the Captain of their salvation" and their glorified Leader intended that they should occupy the vast field and combat error and sin at the very outposts of civilization, north and west, they were now busily engaged in the centre of their operations laying the foundation of the Baptist State Convention.[25]

The First Associations

(1840–48)

In the previous chapter a glimpse was given of the missionary and educational efforts of Texas Baptists between the coming of James Huckins, first missionary of the Home Mission Society in January, 1840, and the organization of the first state body in September, 1848. This chapter will sketch the development of organizational life beyond the local churches during the same period.

Union Baptist Association (1840)

The first attempt to organize a missionary Baptist association in Texas took place at Independence in June, 1840. It cannot be determined who took the initiative in this movement. Z. N. Morrell remarked,

> There were so many different opinions on doctrine, that a conference of the whole, to consider the common interests of our great Master, was a pressing necessity. This necessity had profoundly impressed the mind of the writer during the whole of 1839 and the early part of 1840.[1]

The Christian maturity and experience of Morrell, exceeding any of the other early leaders, might suggest that he had a voice in discussing the need for an associational body, although he was not involved in the organization of it.

At the June meeting about twenty-five Baptists, including four preachers, met at Independence to discuss the organization of an association. Two of the preachers were missionary Baptists (R. E. B. Baylor and T. W. Cox) while the other two (Abner Smith and Asael Dancer) were anti-missionary. Abner Smith was elected moderator, principally through the efforts of Baylor. Although Smith was anti-missionary, Baylor thought that this position of honor was due him as the oldest preacher among them and the first Baptist preacher settling in western Texas. Baylor related how the preachers labored three or four days to agree on an abstract of principles on which the association could be formed, and that finally, "through the prayers and tears of myself and others, the stern old Calvinistic brother Smith softened down a little and drew up a platform of principles to which we all assented except Elder Cox. . . ." Cox, however, made "a warm and excited speech against them" and "broke up the convention."

The missionary-minded group promptly arranged for another convention to meet on October 8, 1840, at Travis, about ten miles south of Brenham in Washington County, for the purpose of perfecting an associational organization. Messengers from three churches responded. The Independence church sent three of their seventeen members as messengers (J. J. Davis, John McNeese, and Thomas Tremmier). The Travis church sent three of its thirteen members (William H. Cleveland, J. W. Collins, and James Hall). The La Grange church sent four of its fifteen members, three of whom were preachers. T. W. Cox, R. E. B. Baylor, and J. L. Davis were the preacher representatives, while J. S. Lester was the fourth messenger from this church.

T. W. Cox was pastor of all three of these churches, so it is not surprising that he was called to the chair to moderate the initial meeting. Z. N. Morrell was ill and could not attend, although he had planned to do so. Consequently, the Plum Grove church was not represented, although its membership was larger than any of the three churches that responded. Missionary James Huckins was not at the June meeting nor at the organizational meeting in

October. As pointed out previously, he came to Texas in January, 1840, and after organizing the Galveston church, spent several months on a missionary tour. He then journeyed to the headquarters of the American Baptist Home Mission Society in New York, and did not return to Texas until January, 1841.

All preliminary arrangements were made on the first day of the meeting, and on the next day (October 9, 1840), the association was organized. Cox was elected moderator; J. W. Collins, clerk; and R. E. B. Baylor, corresponding secretary. The name, Union Baptist Association, was selected with the hope that it might prove prophetic in the harmonizing of the various types of Baptists in Texas. A constitution and articles of faith, already approved by the three churches sending messengers, were adopted. Also approved was an interesting document known as a "Bill of Inalienable Rights," in which the authority and autonomy of each local church were asserted, as well as the right of each member to exercise his discretion "in contributing to the support of missions, general benevolence, etc., ..." The first Executive Committee for the association was Cox, Baylor, and Collins, plus Z. N. Morrell (who was ill at home), William H. Cleveland, James S. Davis, a Brother Yeamen of Montgomery County, and a Brother Andrews of Houston, probably S. P. Andrews.[2]

The articles of faith modified the harsh Calvinism of the antimissionary group. The sixth article read:

We believe that Christ died for sinners, and that the sacrifice which He made has so honored the divine law that the way of salvation is consistently opened up to every sinner to whom the gospel is sent, and that nothing but their own voluntary rejection of the gospel prevents their salvation.

Baylor offered a resolution, which was adopted, urging the formation of a temperance society, and he was requested to prepare a Circular Letter, the writing of which was a common practice in early associational life. This letter asked the prayers and assistance of Baptists in the United States and urged

sister churches and brethren in western Texas who have not joined with us in the common union, ... (to) come and unite with us.

. . . It could not be expected, my dear brethren, that thrown together as we have been from the various Baptist churches throughout the United Sates, we at once harmonize upon all points of doctrine.

This may have been another appeal to the anti-missionary Baptist churches on the Colorado to form a part of the new body.

In the next seven years, until some of the churches withdrew to form a new association, this body showed an increase yearly in its constituency and in the number of churches cooperating with it. In the second session, held at La Grange, messengers from six new churches were admitted: Mount Gilead in Washington County, Macedonia and Providence in Milam County, Galveston, Houston, and the reorganized church at Washington. The regular meeting of the third session in 1842 was disrupted by the Mexican invasion under General Woll, but the association met in called session beginning November 26, 1842, at Mount Gilead. Messengers from newly organized churches were seated from Providence at Chapel Hill (the later spelling will be used hereafter), Plum Grove, and Gonzales. This brought the number of churches to twelve and the membership to 433.

At the fourth session two new churches sent representatives, Caldwell and Ebenezer in Robertson County. At the fifth session, messengers from two additional churches were added: Bethany in Fayette County, and the Dove church replacing the former church at Caldwell. At the sixth session, messengers from new churches at Antioch, San Jacinto, Post Oak Grove in Montgomery County and the Huntsville church were recognized. At the seventh session in 1846, two new churches sent messengers, Rocky Creek and Bethel in Washington County. This brought the number of affiliating churches to twenty-one, who reported 515 members.

In the eighth session in 1847, messengers from the Concord church in Liberty County and the New Year's Creek church near Brenham were recognized. At this meeting, with the approval of the association, affiliation of the churches at La Grange, Macedonia, Plum Grove, Bethel, and Rocky Creek was discontinued to allow representatives from these churches to assist in the formation of a new association. Also at this session a resolution was passed inviting Baptist churches in Texas to send messengers for the purpose of organizing a state body. Before the meeting of the ninth session in October, 1848, at which representatives from new churches at Olivet, Bedias, and Laurel Hill at Cold Springs were recognized, the new state convention had been inaugurated at Anderson.

During these eight formative years, the Union Association wisely and systematically laid foundations for the future in three decisive actions. One of these was the prompt expulsion from their midst of the so-called Reform movement associated with the name of Alexander Campbell. The second was the organization of the Texas Baptist Home Mission Society. The third was the formation of the Texas Baptist Education Society, which led to the founding of Baylor University in 1845.

Expelling the Followers of Campbell

In March, 1841, William M. Tryon, associated with T. W. Cox as pastor of the Independence church, held a church conference at which the issue of the views of Alexander Campbell arose. Campbell and his father, Thomas, were of Scottish Presbyterian background when they came to America in the opening decade of the nineteenth century. They moved into Baptist life about 1812, but after about ten years Alexander Campbell began to attack Baptist doctrines in his paper called the *Christian Baptist*. Churches and associations in the South began condemning his doctrines and withdrawing fellowship from his followers. In 1830 the Appomattox Association of Virginia condemned a number of his views, including the assertion that there is no promise of salvation without baptism; that baptism should be administered to all who state that they believe that Jesus Christ is the Son of God, without examination on any other point; that baptism produces the remission of sins and the gifts of the Holy Spirit; and that all baptized persons have a right to administer the ordinance of baptism.[3]

Some members of the Independence church were followers of Campbell's doctrines, and claimed the support of Cox in their efforts to practice them. When one of the lay members of the Independence church, with the approval of Cox, baptized a convert into the church, the issue came to a head. Tryon was able to lead the church to discountenance the baptism, but the majority of the church at this time sustained Cox in this and other views of Campbell.

Meanwhile, Cox was having other difficulties. He and R. E. B. Baylor had belonged to the Talladega church in Alabama, and Cox had left for Texas shortly before Baylor made the journey. However, before Baylor left the Talladega church he learned that Cox had been accused of dishonest dealings there. In Texas, Baylor went to Cox privately and told him about the charges at Talladega, urging him to make the matter right in Alabama. Cox was unmoved, indicating he would do nothing further about this. Since at this time Baylor and Cox were co-pastors of the La Grange church, Baylor confidentially discussed the matter with Deacon Joseph Shaw, who urged him to write to Talladega to see if this matter were serious enough to pursue further. Baylor later said,

> I did so, and God knows I penned the kindest letter I was capable of writing. I stated that Brother Cox was here preaching to the church and seemed to be doing much good. He had a large family dependent on him and if the church could consistent with duty throw the mantle of charity over his past conduct I wished them to do so. I heard nothing from this letter for something like twelve months. . . . To my surprise after this long delay in answering my letter I received a newspaper containing a letter from the Talladega church addressed to me and through me to all the Baptists of Texas stating all the facts and that Brother Cox had been expelled as a member from that church, ...[4]

While the association was meeting at the La Grange church beginning on October 7, 1841, Cox preached on the subject of faith and, Morrell said, ". . . clearly taught the errors embraced in the system commonly known as Campbellism."[5] At the close of his sermon, Cox offered an opportunity for members to join. His views expressed in the sermon and the method of admitting members caused James Huckins and William M. Tryon to make a public protest, and the reception of members was postponed.[6] At the request of the other ministers Morrell remained for the next church conference. Cox ignored him entirely and preached another sermon that Morrell judged also followed the teachings of Campbell. Several persons, apparently of this disposition of mind, were preparing to join the La Grange church at the close of the sermon, which would have given Cox the majority in the church and have enabled him to turn out the minority. At the close of the sermon, Morrell arose and entered a protest against the heresy of the pastor. Formal charges of following the doctrines of Campbell had been written out and were read at this time. Just before going into this conference, Baylor had given Morrell the paper published in Alabama which described the revocation of the church letter granted Cox by the Tallageda church on the grounds that Cox had committed fraud about the time he left for Texas. Both of these charges were then presented to the church. Morrell described the conflict that followed:

> He was a man of extra-ordinary ability, especially in defence of himself, and in consequence of his commanding manner and pleasant address, taking right hold of the sympathies of his hearers, it was with great difficulty that the church could be made to see his guilt under the charges. Three times during the trial he was charged with false statements, and the proof clearly brought to bear. After a full investigation, the church was called to a vote, and he was excluded. Of course, under such circumstances, the ill will and hard sayings heaped upon his accusers, by those who still sympathized with him, were very bitter.[7]

Baylor wrote again to the Talladega church and reported what had been done, saying that Cox had denied the charges emphatically. In the February conference, 1843, a committee was appointed by the Talladega church to make a full study of the affair, and in the May term, 1843, with considerable heat the committee reported the fraud of Cox in detail.[8]

In consequence of this confrontation early in the history of Texas Baptists, their tiny churches were spared the widespread internal wrenching and loss of membership that this movement brought in states like Alabama and Georgia. While Cox was excluded at the Independence church, he was able to obtain a majority of the members to follow his views at the Travis church, of which he was also pastor. This majority voted themselves letters, organized another church, and erected a building on Kentucky Ridge not far from town. Cox was their pastor, but later drifted away from an active ministry. The strong minority of the followers of Cox at the Independence church did not organize another church body. The La Grange church, split almost in half by the schism, reported only ten members to the association in 1842, and after a few years its name does not appear in the minutes.[9] In 1847, P. B. Chandler, missionary of the Southern Baptist Convention at La Grange, wrote that when he reached his field on January 12 of that year he found that the few scattered members of the church had not met together for about two years, but that they would make another effort to rebuild the church.[10]

Texas Baptist Home Mission Society

A Texas Baptist Home Mission Society was also organized in 1841 at the second session of the Union Association. The records of this society have been lost, if they were kept at that time. J. M. Carroll said that it lived only until 1848, when its work was taken over by the Union Association and the new state convention, but that during its short life this society had put Z. N. Morrell and Noah T. Byars on the field as missionaries. J. B. Link added the name of Anderson Buffington as another of the missionaries of this body. This is confirmed by the letter of November 14, 1841, from James Huckins to the Home Mission Society of New York, in which, after describing the ordination of Buffington, Huckins said, "(he) is now in our Home Missionary field, laboring under the direction of our board."[11] As Morrell later remarked, it is likely that this Texas society paid very little salary to any of its missionaries, but that they served under the same salary situation as the "army of Texas during the Revolution."

Texas Baptist Education Society

At the second meeting of the Union Association in 1841, it was voted that an Education Society be formed. Z. N. Morrell said that this Society was formed on the spot under the leadership of William M. Tryon. J. B. Link and others questioned the accuracy of this statement by Morrell, written over thirty years after the event took place, because in 1846 Tryon delivered a sermon mentioning that the Texas Baptist Education Society was organized in 1843. These historians felt that Tryon, who was present in 1841 and the succeeding meetings of the Association, would have a better recollection in 1846 than Morrell would in 1872. No minutes of this Society are extant until 1847, when they appeared with the minutes of the Union Association. In 1852 Recording Secretary Horace Clark numbered the annual meetings of the Society for the first time, and called that session the eleventh annual meeting. This would suggest the year 1841 as the time of founding, but Link still felt that Tryon's statement outweighed both Morrell and Clark.

However, on November 14, 1841, James Huckins wrote to the Society in New York and expressed jubilation at the progress being made in Texas. He said, among other things:

> Thus you will perceive that we are making some headway. We have now an Association of nine churches. We have a Home Missionary Society, an Education Society, one missionary in the field sustained wholly by our funds, and arrangements made to supply our denomination with books.[12]

This statement, written within a few weeks of the event, makes it clear that some sort of Education Society was organized. It is likely that the word of Rufus C. Burleson represents what actually happened.

> Owing to the disturbance thus created (political and military relations with Mexico), only informal meetings of the Educational Society were held in 1841, 1842, 1843, and 1844 at which little was accomplished, or even attempted, in the way of executing the great purpose for which it was formed.[13]

Morrell says that the first officers of this Society were R. E. B. Baylor, president; S. P. Andrews, recording secretary; William M. Tryon, corresponding secretary; B. Collins, treasurer; and a Board of Managers made up of James Huckins, Z. N. Morrell, J. L.

Farquhar, Gail Borden, Stephen Williams, William H. Ewing, and J. S. Lester.[14] There is no reference in the minutes of the Union Association to the Education Society during the first four years of its existence. A private memorandum of Richard Ellis named the officers in 1844 as R. E. B. Baylor, president; Tryon, vice-president; Benjamin Baxter, recording secretary; J. G. Thomas, corresponding secretary; and J. L. Farquhar, treasurer. The Board of Managers consisted of Hosea Garrett, Noah T. Byars, Richard Ellis, Stephen Williams, and Z. N. Morrell.[15]

It is evident that the initiative in organizing this Education Society was taken by William M. Tryon in order to provide a Baptist University for the new land. Baylor later wrote,

It is (due) to Brother Tryon to say that the thought originated with him to establish a Baptist University in this country. He suggested the idea to me. . . . We sent a memorial to the then Congress of the Republic of Texas for a charter. . . . I was most familiar with such things (and) I dictated the memorial. He wrote a suggestion in it found in these words: "We wished it to be distinctly understood that we asked no donations from the Government." We expected none and never would receive any. At that early day some of the other literary institutions under the control of the various religious denominations had applied to the Government (for) lands and obtained them, but it seemed to me if the government gave to some and withheld from others, it would be giving one religious sect a preference by law over another, and this you know was at war with our principles, ...[16]

The well-known incident of how the school got its name is succinctly told by J. B. Link:

When the charter was presented the place for the name was vacant; Baylor suggested that it should be filled with the name Tryon, but Elder Tryon demurred, saying he had so much to do with bringing the enterprise forward, that he feared that it might be thought he was working for his own honor, and so it might injure the prospects of the school. He filled in the blank with the name of Baylor. The charter was passed by the Congress of the Republic and approved by the President, February 1st, 1845.[17]

Baylor himself said:

A word as to its name. When the bill passed chartering the Institution, I protested against the name. I did not think I was worthy of such distinction. My humble donations might not be understood and the motive that prompted them misconstrued; but Brother Tryon and Vice-President Anderson were inflexible. They were determined upon it and this may account for the name of Baylor University. How well or how wisely they acted it is not for me to say but I leave others to judge.[18]

The feeling of Tryon for this school can be glimpsed in the last letter he wrote before his death to the Domestic Mission Board of the Southern Baptist Convention. He said:

During the past quarter I visited Independence, attended a meeting of the Board of Trustees of the Baylor College. During a residence of nearly seven years in this western country I have traveled extensively in different parts of it, and visited those portions most celebrated for richness of soil, noted for excellent pasturage, having the greatest reputation for health and highly cultivated society; as a result my observation is, that Washington County, the location of our Baptist College, in point of health, society, fertile soil, and picturesque scenery, combines more advantages than any other portion of our State. It may justly be denominated the garden spot of Texas. I consider our Literary Institution calculated with God's blessing, to do more securing permanency to our denomination than any other movement with which I have been connected since my removal from Alabama. It is a nucleus around which the denomination will rally; there will become a school of the Prophets, from which, in years to come, their children will go forth as missionaries to various parts of the world.[19]

The first trustees named in the charter were Baylor, Tryon, J. G. Thomas, James Huckins, A. G. Haynes, A. C. Horton, James L. Lester, R. B. Jarman, Nelson Kavanaugh, O. Drake, Eli Mercer, Aaron Shannon, James L. Farquhar, Robert S. Armistead, and E. W. Taylor.[20]

The Board organized at Brenham on May 15, 1845, and on October 13, 1845, at the Mount Gilead church, four bids for the location of the school were received: from Travis, Huntsville,

Shannon's Prairie (east of Navasota), and Independence. Each bid offered a bonus, consisting of land (generally valued at seventy-five cents an acre), oxen, cattle, horses, cotton, some cash, and even a certain number days of manual labor for helping to locate the school. All but one of the trustees voted for Independence, which had offered the largest bonus, estimated to be the equivalent of $7,925. The Board then organized permanently, electing Tryon as president, E. W. Taylor as secretary, and A. G. Haynes as treasurer.

At a meeting in December, 1845, the Board agreed to use a two-story frame building which was included in the Independence bonus as the first home of the school. On January 12, 1846, they elected Henry L. Graves of North Carolina as president; and Henry F. Gillette, who had been teaching in Houston Academy for several years, as principal of the preparatory department. Pending the arrival of Graves from Georgia, where he had been teaching, the school was opened on May 18, 1846, by Professor Gillette, with twenty-four pupils. Thus, curiously enough, Baylor's first teacher was a devout Episcopal layman, thirty years of age, and "unquestionably among the best educators then to be found in this infant State." Since Tryon was president of the Board of Trustees when Gillette was appointed, it is likely that the uniting in marriage of Gillette and spouse by Tryon on March 3, 1842, had acquainted the missionary with this young scholar's gifts.[21] Graves arrived at Independence on February 4, 1847, to take up his work. In addition to these two, the teaching staff was augumented before the close of this period in 1848 by J. H. Finch, who served as tutor beginning in 1848; Warren Cowlls as professor of mathematics, probably having served at first as a tutor in that same year; and Daniel Witt, (son of the preacher Jesse Witt), who began teaching Spanish and ancient languages in 1848.

The little school struggled with finances from the very beginning. At a meeting on January 12, 1846, the Board appointed Richard Ellis to seek funds within Texas, while R. E. B. Baylor and William Tryon were asked to solicit funds both in Texas and in other states. In the following year, Rufus C. Burleson was requested to act as agent to collect funds in Kentucky, Ohio, Mississippi, and Alabama. As a matter of fact, as J. M. Carroll pointed out, a score of Baptist preachers regularly acted as unpaid agents to solicit funds. In 1847, Baylor, Huckins, Tryon (before his death), J. W. D. Creath, Hosea Garrett, Noah Hill, Richard Ellis, Z. N. Morrell, James H. Stribling, P. B. Chandler, and G. W. Rogers all served in this capacity. Effective January 1, 1848, Huckins resigned his Galveston pastorate, and was employed at a salary of $1,000 a year and expenses to raise money for the school. J. M. Carroll judged that it was the service of this talented agent that preserved the very existence of the institution. Huckins traveled, mainly on horseback, in all parts of the United States, and in his five years of service he secured between $30,000.00 and $40,000.00 for the school. He was a very dedicated man.

At the end of 1848 the school was in debt to President Graves in the sum of $1,200.00 and to Gillette in the sum of $800.00. On this debt Eli Mercer paid $150.00, while ten other men paid $20.00 each. The untimely death of Tryon on November 16, 1847, removed one of the tireless and talented supporters of the school. At the Board meeting of June 1, 1848, it was voted that the entire management of the school, including the selection of the faculty (subject to the approval of the Board), would be the responsibility of President Graves, and the tuition fees of the students should serve as compensation for the president. The school did not grow as rapidly as had been hoped. The student body numbered twenty-four when it opened in 1845, but closed that year with seventy. However, the number of students in 1848 at the close of this period probably was not over one hundred.

At the Board meeting in 1847 at Houston, James Huckins offered a resolution calling attention to the need of ministers for the churches and urging that "a vigorous and systematic effort be made to assist young men of piety and promise in their preparation for the ministry." Already James H. Stribling had been admitted to Baylor as a ministerial student without tuition at the request of the Society on February 4, 1846. In 1848, another ministerial student was admitted on these terms, David B. Morrill. Both became faithful Texas ministers while in school and after graduation.

Thus, by 1848 the Union Association had embarked upon an

active and ambitious program in Texas, including the formation of a home mission society and an education society, both of which performed significant services.

Other Associations

The missionary forces of Texas had only one association from 1840 until 1847. In 1847 and 1848, three additional associations were organized.

Colorado Association. The second missionary association in Texas was the Colorado, representing a westward thrust. In September, 1847, Mexico City surrendered to General Winfield Scott, ending the war between the United States and Mexico. The final removal of the fear of invasion again by Mexico and the increasing strength of the churches in the western part of the state doubtless encouraged the organization of this second association. On Thursday, November 18, 1847, seven preachers and messengers from nine Baptist churches, whose membership totaled 119, gathered at the Rocky Creek church in LaVaca County. Z. N. Morrell preached the sermon and Hosea Garrett was elected provisional chairman. The Union Association had appointed six of its members as a committee to assist in the organization; namely, O. H. P. Garrett, Hosea Garrett, James Huckins, Z. N. Morrell, J. M. Hume, and William M. Tryon. Tryon was felled by yellow fever at Houston at almost the very time the Colorado Association was being formed. Five churches from the Union Association were given letters of commendation to affiliate with the proposed new body. These were the churches at La Grange, Macedonia, Plum Grove, Bethany, and Rocky Creek. Although the records are incomplete, it is believed that the other four churches involved in the initial organization were Wharton, Matagorda, Gonzales, and Austin.

Letters from the churches were read to the convention, and the body was organized provisionally by electing Noah Hill as the presiding officer and Thomas J. Pilgrim as secretary. The convention then adopted articles of faith and a constitution. The association was organized under the constitution by electing Richard Ellis as moderator and Pilgrim as clerk. At that time these nine churches represented six counties in a territory reaching from Austin south to the Gulf and west to the Guadalupe River.

Soda Lake Baptist Association. The third missionary association emerged in east Texas in the midst of great hardships. That section had been in turmoil over a decade, initially because of the anti-missionary churches which dominated the area, and then from the struggle between the Moderators and the Regulators, self-styled champions of justice in east Texas. In November, 1843, at the Old Union church in Nacogdoches County, messengers from the Union and Mount Zion churches in Nacogdoches County, the Border and Bethel churches in Harrison County, and the Bethel church in Sabine County met and organized the Sabine Association under the leadership of Isaac Reed, Lemuel Herrin, and Asa Wright.

It will be recalled that Reed, while missionary in spirit and purpose, was strongly opposed to the organization of any societies or other "man-made" methods for spreading the gospel, while Herrin championed mission boards, Sunday schools, Bible societies, and similar organizations. The disagreement at this point brought the dissolution of the Sabine Association in 1847, and on Friday, December 3, 1847, representatives of churches from Macedonia, Henderson, Eight-Mile, and Border met at the last named church and organized the Eastern Missionary Baptist Association. A resolution was passed explaining that this action was being taken because the Sabine Association had displayed the anti-missionary spirit. Lemuel Herrin was its first moderator, and J. B. Webster, its clerk. This body adopted the name Soda Lake Baptist Association in the following year.

Trinity River Baptist Association. On Friday, July 14, 1848, messengers from the churches at Leona, Society Hill, Springfield, Union Hill, Corsicana, and Providence (Navarro County) met at the last named church for the purpose of organizing an association. These churches represented a membership of about forty Baptists. Z. N. Morrell preached the usual opening sermon, then acted as moderator, while Alexander Patrick was named secretary. On the following afternoon the group adopted articles of faith and a constitution. Morrell and Patrick were named moderator and secretary, while Noah Byars and C. B. Roberts were elected corresponding secretary and treasurer, respectively.

Thus, between 1840 and September, 1848 (when the state body was formed), Texas organized four associations—Union (1840), Colorado (1847), Soda Lake (organized in 1847 as the Eastern Missionary Association, then renamed the following year), and Trinity River (1848). The total number of missionary Baptists in Texas in 1848 is uncertain. Morrell estimated that in 1849 there were about 2,000 Baptists and seventy-five churches. B. F. Fuller supposed that there were about thirty-five churches when the state body was organized in 1848. However, it appears that there were more churches than this at the time of the organization of the state body. Twenty-three churches appointed messengers to the organizational meeting of the state body at Anderson on September 8, 1848. In addition, it is known that from the Colorado Association, the churches at Plum Grove, Macedonia, and Austin sent no messengers. The churches from the Soda Lake Association that apparently were not represented were Border, Macedonia, Henderson, Eight-Mile, and perhaps others. Churches from Trinity River Association not represented were Leona, Society Hill, Springfield, Union Hill, Corsicana, and Providence (Navarro County).

Furthermore, just one month after the organization of the state body, a number of ministers and brethren representing eight churches met at Honey Grove in Fannin County to form the Red River Baptist Association. It is definitely known that the Concord church, which was not represented in this meeting but was added in the following year, was organized before 1848. The church at Honey Grove also was in existence in 1848. It seems unlikely that the other seven churches at this organizational meeting were founded in a period of less than thirty days, so some of them must have been in existence before the organization of the state body. Willis M. Pickett had come to Texas in 1844, and the minutes of 1849 show him as pastor of five of the churches out of the eight represented.

Other churches that were known to exist before the organization of the state body were those at Tyler, Rowlett Creek in Collin

County, and Lonesome Dove. This casual calculation makes a total of at least forty missionary Baptist churches definitely known to exist, plus perhaps a dozen more that may have existed in September, 1848.

At any rate, the years between the coming of the first missionary in 1840 and the organization of the first state body in 1848 were most significant ones for Texas Baptists, and laid the foundation for the rapid growth that took place betwen 1848 and 1865.

6

Open Doors . . . . Many Adversaries

(1848–60)

☆ ☆ ☆

On October 13, 1854, Noah Hill wrote to his brother-in-law, saying,

> On the 18th of September we had a hurricane in Matagorda that lasted about thirty-six hours. There never has been the like heard of in the annals of history. It prostrated the town. Almost every house in the place was blown down or greatly torn to pieces.[1]

This hurricane was symbolic of the numerous and diverse storms that buffeted Texas Baptists from every direction during this thirteen-year period. On April 16, 1849, a heavy frost almost destroyed the corn, cotton, and sugar cane. It gave that year the name "the black year," for the freeze was followed by a lengthy drouth that permitted no further planting. Inclement cold weather and drouth alternated during the remainder of the period. In 1857 the severe drouth was most painful. B. F. Riley described it vividly.

> Only the slightest rains fell from one end of the year to the other. The attendant consequences were terrible, the water ceasing from the streams, then from the springs, and finally from the wells. Animals wild and domestic, died in great numbers and the air was laden with the most unsavory stench. Sickness among the people ensued, and to the horrors of the general situation was added that of much personal suffering. The grass refused to grow and the trees in many places

91

were leafless. The earth was so dry and scorched that crops were a total failure, and the commodities of life had to be brought from distant ports, at great expense. The limy earth was rent in great fissures, wide and deep, which rendered overland travel perilous. A dearth so phenomenal brought matters to a standstill, and imposed fearful privations on the people.[2]

In one of his notable sermons, B. H. Carroll has a classic description of the thirsty earth and the burning sky in Texas, and it is likely that either the drouth of 1857 or the one in 1859–60 constituted the background of this picture.

Not only so, but Indian depredations became almost unbearable during these years. After unusually severe raids by the Indians in 1846–47, the United States in 1849 established eight outposts from what is now Fort Worth in a diagonal line to Eagle Pass on the Rio Grande River. Soon, however, new settlements began to pass the original line, and a new series of forts about one hundred miles farther west was established in an effort to provide protection for the frontier. Two Indian reservations were created in 1855, but the Indians preferred not to remain in these. The year 1857 marked increasingly severe Indian raids. Despite active efforts to control them, the Indians continued to harrass the frontier until the Civil War. The severity of these attacks may be measured by the fact that the line of western frontier settlements in 1855 retreated eastward at least one hundred miles by 1865.

The political struggles of the new state and the secession of Texas from the Union in 1861 added to the storms faced by Texas Baptists. The war, in particular, disrupted all religious work.

However, Texas Baptists found inspiration in the spirit of the apostle Paul who wrote of the many adversaries that confronted him, but in a single sentence matched these with open doors for witnessing in the midst of the difficulties (1 Corinthians 16:9). Despite their arduous trials, Texas Baptists found that their opportunities overshadowed their adversaries. One of the open doors that beckoned was the large immigration of people from older states. On one day in December, 1848, the ferry across the Brazos at Washington transported three hundred immigrants into the new land. The population, estimated at 35,000 in 1836, had reached 142,000 by

1847, 213,000 by 1850, over 613,000 by 1860 (although 182,566 of these were slaves), and by 1870, a total of 819,000, of whom 253,475 were Negroes. Almost 90% of this immigration came from the South. The census of 1860 also showed 20,553 Germans and 12,443 Mexicans.

This vast company came to Texas to find homes, not to prospect for gold or other valuable minerals. In 1860, more than half of the 105,491 replies listed in the census showed farming as the principal occupation. Improved farm land increased from about 600,000 acres in 1850 to about 2,650,000 acres in 1860. Cotton was the most important money crop, while corn and sweet potatoes were the indispensable food crops. It is interesting to notice that in 1860 there were over 2500 carpenters, over 800 lawyers, over 1400 physicians, 65 dentists, and more than 750 clergymen in Texas.[3]

Another favorable factor during this time was the considerable improvement in the financial situation of the state. At the time of annexation in 1845 it was provided that Texas should retain its vacant and unappropriated lands, the revenue from which could be used for reducing the state's immediate liabilities, or to be disposed of in any other fashion the state might desire. The public domain consisted of almost 182,000,000 acres unappropriated, together with many millions more acres claimed by individuals and grants under illegal titles. The debts of Texas in 1845 amounted to almost $12,000,000.00. In 1850, the United States proposed to pay Texas $10,000,000.00 to relinquish about one-third of the area that Texas claimed (principally what is now the western section of New Mexico). In addition, in 1855 Congress paid Texas $2,750,000.00 to reimburse the state for money expended in defending against the Indians. As a result of securing these funds, all of the debts of Texas were paid and the treasury had a balance of about $3,000,000.00, along with millions of acres in public lands. This improved fiscal situation made it possible for Texas to secure quickly a financial stability that both attracted substantial immigration and made the development of the young state a much more rapid process.

Added to these favorable factors was the evidence of interest by the state in public welfare, as seen in the encouragement of transportation and the making of provision for public education. Although the bandit Cortinas briefly raided Texas settlers in 1859 from across the border, the threat of Mexican invasion had been eliminated.

In this context, Texas Baptists made good progress in the years between the organization of the state body in 1848 and the outbreak of the Civil War. The remainder of this chapter will trace the direction taken by Texas Baptists and indicate some areas of progress.

The First State Body

It will be recalled that at the eighth session of the Union Baptist Association meeting in 1847 at Houston, a resolution was passed instructing the secretary to correspond with associations and churches in the state to ascertain their views relative to the formation of a state body. A special committee consisting of preachers Graves, Garrett, Ellis, Chancellor, Tryon, and Creath, along with laymen Haynes, Farquhar, and Thomas was appointed to study the replies by the churches and the associations, and should a majority favor forming a state body, this committee was authorized to appoint a time and place of meeting and to invite the churches to send messengers for the purpose of organizing a state convention.[4]

The majority of the correspondents favored the formation of a state convention, so the committee set September 8, 1848, for the messengers of the churches to meet at Anderson to organize.

The Organization of the Texas Baptist State Convention. Although there were four associations and probably more than fifty Baptist churches in Texas at the time, fifty-five messengers from twenty-one of the churches gathered at Anderson for the formation of the new body. Seventy-five messengers had been elected by twenty-three churches, but twenty did not attend. The messengers participating in the organization were from Independence, Washington, Providence (Washington County), Dove, Houston, Rocky Creek, Post Oak Grove, Antioch (Anderson), Concord, New Year's Creek, Matagorda, Gonzales, Austin, Cuero, Bedias, Mount Gilead, Galveston, Hamilton, La Grange, Bethany, and Wharton.

None of the messengers from Plum Grove and Providence (Burleson County) was present.

Although Henry L. Graves of Baylor University had been appointed to preach the sermon, and Noah Hill of Matagorda had been named as his alternate, each refused to preach the opening sermon, and others approached for this chore likewise declined. Z. N. Morrell commented on such "tenderfooted" Baptist preachers, and when he was asked to preach he promptly accepted, remarking later, "I had no reputation to uphold." He chose Isaiah 9:7 for his text, as applicable as though he had pondered the subject for months, for it read: "Of the increase of his government there shall be no end."

After the sermon R. E. B. Baylor was called to preside and J. G. Thomas was chosen as recording secretary. Letters from the churches were read. Although not sent by churches, Z. N. Morrell and Z. Worley were seated as visiting brethren. A committee to prepare a proposed constitution was named, and the document brought by Chairman Hosea Garrett was discussed and approved *seriatem.* This constitution named missions, and education, fellowship and concert of action, and the promotion of the Redeemer's Kingdom in the state as the objects of the new body. It was to be composed of members of Baptist churches in good standing who would pay $5.00 for an annual membership. An association, church, or society could send a messenger for every $5.00 contributed to the convention, while any church belonging to an association was permitted one representative without a contribution. Like the first association in Texas, this new state body in its first meeting disclaimed any power "absolutely and forever" over a church or an association.

The constitution adopted, an election of officers was held. Henry L. Graves was named president; J. W. D. Creath, Hosea Garrett, and James Huckins, vice-presidents; Rufus C. Burleson, corresponding secretary; J. G. Thomas, recording secretary; and J. W. Barnes, treasurer. The appointment of special committees to report to the body reflects the areas of particular interest. They involved education, publication of a Baptist paper, foreign missions, home missions, finances, distribution of Bibles, and the religious condition of the black population. In discussing the reports of these various committees, the convention voted that they would not incur any financial responsibility in the publication of a paper, but urged that such a paper be inaugurated and sustained by their constituency.

Two of the committees made very strong appeals. Jesse Witt, a home missionary of the Southern Baptist Convention, had ridden 200 miles to attend this meeting, and made a fervent plea for the support of state missions. More missionaries are sustained by the Domestic Mission Board of the Southern Baptist Convention in Texas, he said, than the Board has in any other state.

> And yet, when we take a survey of our State, in its wide extent, ... we are . . . . deeply impressed with the fact that the great work which devolves on the Baptists is barely begun. . . . Your committee, in its enquiries, have ascertained that in those portions of our State, where churches and ministers are most numerous, there is at best but a very inadequate supply of the means of grace; and the east, the west, the north, present extensive regions where the voice of our ministers is never heard. In two sections it is asserted that in ten or fifteen counties in a body, not a Baptist preacher is to be found, ...

Noah Hill, whose entire ministry was directed primarily toward the black population, urged the messengers to send missionaries among the Negroes, as well as to develop a program by which the white churches in cities and villages would give a part of their attention to the spiritual welfare of the Negroes.

A word should be said about the character of this new body. A dual type of representation caused some discussion. Copying similar organizations both North and South, it was agreed that Baptist church members could purchase an annual membership in the Convention by the payment of $5.00 or a lifetime membership by the payment of $25.00. This financial emphasis was displeasing to some. In 1859 a resolution was introduced to change the constitution at this point, and in 1860 the article on membership stated that the body

> shall be composed of delegates of regular Baptist churches and associations in proportion to the numbers as follows: each Association

shall be entitled to five delegates, and one additional delegate for every five hundred members after the first five hundred; and each church shall be entitled to one delegate, and one additional delegate for every twenty members.

Another controverted point concerned the power of the Board of Directors who, under the original instrument could appropriate whatever money they chose, appoint missionaries as they would, and create any indebtedness for the body, all without further authority from the convention. Although discussed, this provision of the constitution was not changed during the period ending in 1860.

The Baptist State Convention had only modest attendance during the thirteen years before the Civil War. Representation at the annual meetings varied from year to year, depending upon the location of the meeting and the circumstances that prevailed at the time of the meeting. For example, at the second session in 1849 at Houston, there were only twenty-seven messengers and two visitors. Houston was centrally located, but the cholera epidemic raging in the city diminished the attendance. In 1850 the Convention met in the court house at Huntsville with only fourteen churches reporting. The one appointed to preach the opening sermon was not present, so after a prayer meeting the convention adjourned until the afternoon. It was then learned that the corresponding secretary and the treasurer were absent with no reports available, and that the Board of Directors had no report. This represented the low point in the meetings of the convention. It required a controversy to bring a full attendance. The number of churches sending messengers varied from twenty-nine in 1851 to forty churches and three associations in 1856 to thirty-eight churches and nine associations in 1860. The number of messengers probably never exceeded the one hundred and fifty who attended in 1859.

In the thirteen years of the convention before the war, Henry L. Graves was named president six times, James Huckins three times, Rufus C. Burleson two times, and R. E. B. Baylor and J. W. D. Creath one time each. Rufus C. Burleson was corresponding secretary during the first seven years. The office of recording secretary was first held by J. G. Thomas, followed by R. S. Blount, then for three years George W. Baines, Sr., filled the office. Baines served again in 1854, Horace Clark served for three years beginning with 1856, and O. H. P. Garrett followed him for the next two years. Several names are included for one year as recording secretary or corresponding secretary.

Missionary Activity of the State Convention. These years naturally fall into two sections: from 1848 to 1855 (when a rival state body was organized in east Texas), and from 1855 to 1860, when each of the two state bodies carried on its own program. To provide unity in the story, the account of the original state body (the State Convention) from 1848 to 1860 will be given, followed by the story of the schism in 1855 and the work of the new state body (the Eastern Texas Convention) from 1855 to 1860.

State missions, in particular, were of great concern at every meeting of the Baptist State Convention, due to the large number of new settlers constantly enlarging the dimensions of the task. Efforts were made to win the unchurched and to enlist church members scattered in the new areas regularly opening in Texas by appointing missionaries and appealing to preachers to give voluntary service. A survey by the state convention in 1849 reported that only twenty-nine missionary Baptist preachers were at work in the state, twenty of whom were regular pastors. Those named were John F. Hillyer, Richard Ellis, J. J. Wells, Noah Hill, P. B. Chandler, A. S. Mercer, James T. Powell, J. N. Joiner, W. H. Vardeman, Hosea Garrett, H. L. Graves, R. E. B. Baylor, J. H. Stribling, D. B. Morrill, David Fisher, Luther Seaward, B. B. Baxter, A. Buffington, J. Pearce, J. W. D. Creath, Z. N. Morrell, N. T. Byars, James Huckins, R. H. Taliaferro, Rufus C. Burleson, A. E. Clemmons, Willis M. Pickett, Jesse Witt, and J. M. Perry. However, this list is undoubtedly incomplete, for reference is made to other ministers in the minutes of that meeting.

The freeze, drouth, and emigration to California caused the meeting at Huntsville in 1850 to be quite disorganized and evidently unreported. However, the minutes of 1851 show that N. T. Byars had been appointed in October, 1849, to work in Navarro County; Luther Seaward in October, 1849, to work in Burleson County; David Lewis in October, 1850, to work in Houston and

Anderson counties; A. Ledbetter on January 1, 1851, to work in Dallas, Ellis, Navarro, and Tarrant counties; and Noah Hill to spend a part of his ministry with the colored people in Wharton, Matagorda, and Brazoria counties. The death of H. P. Mayes in the following year left the counties of Limestone and Freestone entirely destitute. The Convention called attention to other needy fields, like San Antonio, Seguin, Bastrop, Brownsville, and counties in northern Texas near the Red River. In 1852 J. W. D. Creath was reappointed missionary agent. Anderson Buffington was asked to work with the Negroes in Grimes County beginning in June, 1853, while Hill, Lewis, and Ledbetter were reappointed. David Fisher was appointed to work on the Brazos and Little rivers. In addition, in that year, $100.00 each was given to Elm Fork Association, Red River Association, and Cherokee Association to aid them to secure missionaries in their areas.

In 1853 Baptists from east Texas complained vigorously that needy areas in their section of the state should be receiving missionaries, but that they were being neglected. The convention instructed their Board to give this attention. In the following year it was reported that every effort had been made to secure two evangelists for east Texas, as well as two for west Texas, but that it had not been possible to find two evangelists for east Texas. Two pastors had served briefly in the West, but were forced to return to their churches for support during the year.

During the next several years after the withdrawal of Baptists in east Texas to form their own state body, the Baptist State Convention appointed preachers (mostly to serve part time) for the western and central areas of the state. David Fisher and Anderson Buffington were reappointed to continue their service, while Benjamin Clark was named for Robertson County. With the $100.00 appropriated by the State Convention, Bethleham Association secured the service of E. A. Phelps for a part of his time. Appropriations formerly made to associations in east Texas were discontinued because of the work of the new body organized there in 1855. Huckins was appointed to the Galveston church in cooperation with the Southern Baptist Convention.

Between 1855 and 1860 the State Convention kept about a

dozen missionaries on the several fields, including new names such as John Clabaugh, A. W. Elledge, J. M. B. Haynie, W. B. Eaves, J. G. Thomas, J. J. Haggard, J. H. Thurmond, Richard Howard, and R. E. Brown. Most of these missionaries worked only part time for the state. The indefatigable J. W. D. Creath gave part of his time as financial agent for the convention.

During this period the Domestic Mission Board of the Southern Baptist Convention assisted in the support of many missionaries serving in Texas, both with reference to the State Convention and with the second state body after 1855. The *Missionary Journal* of the southwide body is filled with letters addressed to it by Z. N. Morrell, Noah Hill, R. H. Taliaferro, J. W. D. Creath, P. B. Chandler, Rufus C. Burleson, and Jesse Witt. These letters give stark examples of the heroism involved in being a missionary on the Texas frontier. Practically all of the missionaries at one time or another suffered with malaria or yellow fever. The habit of fording or swimming icy creeks during the freezing weather was not conducive to good health. In October, 1849, W. M. Pickett wrote that there had been almost a continuous flood on his field at Clarksville, and said that he rarely made a preaching tour without swimming creeks.[5] In the same Journal in May, 1849, Creath described the death of a missionary at Clarksville.

> He was found dead in an old house by the roadside frozen. He attempted to swim the creek in a buggy. In the effort his horse was drowned, and he fatigued by his exertions to extricate himself from the flood, wet and chilled, turned into this old house, being unable to go further.[6]

From the location of the assignments of the missionaries in the northern and western counties, it can be seen that the State Convention was trying to keep up with the frontier as the settlers constantly moved further west. There were many discouraging factors mentioned in the reports to the state and the southwide bodies year by year, but Z. N. Morrell sounded the keynote of the spirit of these indomitable missionaries when he wrote:

> Our population is sparse; but our fertile lands, fine water, extensive rain, and other local advantages, hold out such inducements to the

emigrating population, that we must have a densely settled community at no distant period. Though Jacob is now small, he will arise in the strength of Jehovah. It will be some time before self-supporting churches will be reared up; but these small interests will, by proper culture, and divine blessing, increase with our increasing population, and exert a happy and controlling influence upon our growing country.[7]

Educational Activity of the State Convention. The second principal program carried on by the State Convention was that of education. At the beginning of this period in 1848 the infant school at Independence under the presidency of Henry L. Graves was struggling to maintain itself financially in the midst of very difficult years. Freezes and drouths cut sharply into the resources of the few supporters of the school. James Huckins resigned as pastor of the Galveston church effective January 1, 1848, and actually saved the school by using his genius as a financial agent to keep funds coming. On April 4, 1849, a committee examining his accounts reported that subscriptions of every sort had amounted to over $9,600.00, much of this sum from states outside of Texas where Huckins had made some of his appeals.

At the April trustee meeting in 1849 a contract was let to erect a stone building for the school, while arrangements were made with A. S. Lipscomb to deliver a series of law lectures. A Department of Law was established at the June meeting, 1849, and bi-weekly lectures were arranged for May 1 through December 1, using Lipscomb and R. E. B. Baylor. Despite the fact that vigorous efforts had been made to sell scholarships to endow the presidency in the sum of $10,000.00, the prospects were gloomy. At the June meeting, 1851, Graves resigned as president. This was accepted with regret and expressions of appreciation for his service.

Two brilliant young men were yoked together to lead Baylor in 1851. Rufus C. Burleson, the gifted pastor of the Houston church, was unanimously elected president; Horace Clark, an experienced educator who had recently moved to Texas, was named principal of the female department.

Burleson was born on August 7, 1823, near Decatur, Alabama. In 1839 he was converted and felt a call to preach, but his health gave way in 1841 under the strain of hard study. He taught school in Mississippi for three years, at the same time serving as pastor for four churches. In 1846 he entered Western Baptist Theological Seminary, Covington, Kentucky, and was appointed missionary to Texas by the Southern Baptist Convention after his graduation. In January, 1848, he succeeded the lamented William M. Tryon as pastor of the church at Houston.

Horace Clark was born on July 7, 1819, at Charlestown, Massachusetts. His family moved to Illinois where he attended Shurtleff College. For four years he was principal of an academy at Newcastle, Kentucky, and moved to Texas in 1850.

An unfortunate clash between Burleson and Clark was caused partly by the negligence of the Board in failing to clarify administrative responsibility in the operation of the school. Burleson felt that as president he should have supervision over both the male department and the female department, while Clark understood that as principal of the female department he was answerable only to the Board and not to Burleson. The clash between the two men occurred in 1854, although as early as 1852 the two departments were separated and had different faculties. The ladies remained in the old frame building from 1851 to 1857, while the young men moved to the new two story rock building completed in 1851. Between 1855 and 1860 the controversy between the two men became notorious. In December, 1857, the trustees of the school warned Burleson and Clark that their patience had been exhausted, and said that "We will promptly apply the remedy even if it should sever the ties that connect us together, from the President to the last professor, if they shall merit it by their conduct. Co-operation and peace we must have between our departments." This was the situation in 1860 at the very close of this period.

Baylor, of course, was not the only school operated by Baptists in Texas. There was a rapid multiplying of small Baptist schools before 1860. Most of them lived for but a short time. There were good reasons for the development of many schools of this sort. For one thing, most of the schools were for girls. The pioneers were not willing for their daughters to grow up without some type of intellectual training, and the distance a girl had to go to attend school was very important. Settlements were miles apart, there were few roads and fewer bridges over creeks and rivers, and many dangers lurked along the frontier. The expense of boarding a daughter away from home probably also was an item. Many of the teachers were preachers, and in some instances the school consisted of one teacher meeting in a small room. There were no educational requirements, and the ease with which a literate person could begin a school made it inevitable that schools of this sort would spring up everywhere.

J. M. Carroll identified over a dozen of these: the Austin Female Academy sponsored by the Colorado Association; the Tyler Baptist University, founded in 1852 by the Cherokee Association; Mound Prairie Institute, operated by James R. Malone and J. S. Hanks after 1853 near Palestine, Texas; Anna Judson Female Institute, located between Tyler and Marshall; Eastern Texas Female College, located at Tyler under the direction of J. T. Hand and others; the school of Otis Smith at Marshall; the school of J. R. Clarke at Cussita in Cass County; Margaret E. Houston Female College at Daingerfield in Titus County, sponsored by the Rehoboth Association; Luther Rice Baptist Female College, Marshall, sponsored by the Eastern Texas Baptist Education Society which was organized in 1856; the school of J. V. E. Covey at Halletsville, known as Alma Institute; Cold Springs Female School, under the patronage of Tryon Association; and Ladonia Institute, a coeducational school established by the Sister Grove Association in 1859.

A word should be said concerning two other schools that were founded before the close of this period in 1860. The first of these was the Waco Classical School. At a meeting of the Trinity River Association in 1855, a resolution called for establishing a school within the limits of that body. The following year S. G. O'Bryan, pastor of the Waco church and corresponding secretary of the Trinity River Association, wrote an article indicating that a flourishing female school had already been located at Waco, and that they desired a male school. A male school was begun at Waco and in 1857 reported good prospects with O'Bryan as president. O'Bryan resigned in 1859, and John C. West was named president. On November 10, 1860, Waco Association was organized, and this school was adopted as the project of this new body.

The other school founded during this period was a male college sponsored by the Eastern Texas Baptist Convention and located at Tyler. This meant that there were two schools at Tyler, one sponsored by the Cherokee Association and the other by the Eastern Texas Baptist Convention.

Whether this list includes all of the early schools operated by Baptists in Texas cannot be determined. There are hints of other schools, but the records are sparse.

Another State Body

There are numerous instances in Baptist history illustrating the divisive nature of state sectional interests. Texas Baptists also experienced this. At the meeting of the Baptist State Convention at Marshall in 1852, the church at Tyler in east Texas proposed that a female school be established at Tyler and that the Convention provide for it the same kind of support that Baylor was receiving. Almost overwhelmed by unmet needs of Baylor, the Convention did not look favorably upon this suggestion, replying to the request as follows:

> As we deem it incompatible with the constitutional province and design of this Convention to solicit and raise funds for the establishment of any literary Institution, our educational efforts extending only to the aid of the ministers of the Gospel, and as we have under our patronage the Baylor University, designed especially for this purpose, we cannot consistently promise aid to any other institution, nor extend to such a fostering or controlling influence. We would therefore recommend the proposed Institution to the patronage of the Baptist church in Tyler and the Educational Boards of those Associations that may think proper to favor and engage in the enterprise.[8]

Those favoring the Tyler institution could not accept this reply, since they interpreted the purpose of the Convention to include "educational" as well as missionary objects. Furthermore, everyone knew that Baylor had a female department and that the male department had very few ministerial students.

In June the following year the Baptist State Convention met at Huntsville. An unusually large group attended, evidently expecting controversy. At once it was demanded that a committee be appointed to determine how much money was contributed to the work from the churches east of the Trinity River and how much from those west of it; also, how much was disbursed east of the Trinity and how much west of it. The committee was appointed and reported that east Texas had contributed $735.85 with disbursements amounting to $700.00, while west Texas had contributed $2,315.70, with disbursements of $800.00. Still unsatisfied by the attitude and answers of "the Convention in the West," as they called it, a group of messengers from churches in east Texas met at Larissa in Cherokee County in November, 1853, under the leadership of G. G. Baggerly, and organized the Texas Baptist General Association. The name and purpose of the body clearly revealed that it was intended to become a rival to the State Convention. Not only so, but serious charges of misappropriation of funds were made against some of the leadership of the older body. Both of these moves—involving rivalry and the claims of misappropriation —alienated some of the strongest pastors in east Texas.

The Organization of the Eastern Texas Baptist Convention. On May 24, 1855, at Tyler, this new General Association was dissolved, and the Eastern Texas Baptist Convention was formed by messengers from twenty-four churches and one association. The first move of the new convention was to act as committee of the whole to investigate the charges of misappropriation against the agents of the State Convention. After thorough study, it was agreed that the charges were not true, but that the agents of the State Convention had been "careless" in preparing their published financial records. Whereupon, the Eastern Texas body declared themselves satisfied with the integrity of the accused brethren and called upon all persons in both bodies to retract "all unkind and unchristian words or articles" that had been spoken or written. Arrangements were made by the Eastern body to cooperate with the State Convention at several points. The first officers were William H.

Stokes, president; Garlington C. Dial, treasurer; William Daven-
port, secretary, and J. S. Bledsoe, assistant secretary.

Missionary and Educational Activity of the Eastern Convention.
The first report of missionary work was made in 1858. Jesse Witt
and George Tucker were financial agents. George W. Butler served
as missionary in the Central Association, David D. Myers in the
Elm Fork Association, James Isaacs in the Rehoboth Association,
W. H. Gorman in the Soda Lake Association, and Willis M.
Pickett in the Red River Association.

The constitution was amended in 1859 to allow additional representation based upon a larger membership. A. E. Clemmons and D.
B. Morrill had served as agents for the body during part of the year,
while T. W. Anderson, A. T. Calahan, J. R. Briscoe, James Isaacs,
Willis M. Pickett, J. M. Carter, and F. S. Wall had served as
missionaries for part of the year. A committee was appointed to
locate a "denominational school" to meet the needs of eastern
Texas. In 1860, at the close of this period, the convention voted to
locate the college at Tyler and call it the Texas Baptist College.
W. B. Featherstone and J. R. Clarke were named as teachers, while
J. S. Bledsoe was appointed agent to collect funds.

Other Activities of Texas Baptists

A Denominational Newspaper. Quite early in Texas Baptist
history it was felt that a denominational newspaper was a necessity
for unifying the people and propagating information. In the earliest
general body (the Union Association in 1840) attention was called
to the need for a periodical publication. It was the practice in that
day for frontier states to insert a news column in an established
paper of a state nearby. This would make it possible for a paper in
Louisiana or Tennessee, for example, to have subscriptions from
Baptists in Texas, and a column of information from Texas itself
could be included in the paper as a matter of interest to readers in
other states and to keep Baptists in Texas informed about their
work. At the 1840 meeting of the Union Association, T. W. Cox
offered a recommendation that the *Baptist Banner and Western
Pioneer,* published at Louisville, Kentucky, should be considered

favorably as a denominational paper, with the probability that articles on Texas and from Texas would occupy some of its space. This was accomplished in the following year, when the Kentucky paper offered one column of its paper for Texas matters. The Union Association accepted this proposition and James Huckins was chosen as editor of that column. A few years later both Union and Colorado Associations suggested that the *Southwestern Baptist Chronicle* of New Orleans should be considered as a denominational paper for Texas Baptists.

In 1848, however, when the state convention was organized, a vigorous report was made on the importance of securing a denominational paper in Texas. A paper for Texas itself was urged as a unifying factor, an invaluable promoter of the interests of Baylor, and a medium of communication to disseminate the principles of the denomination. The drouth and crop loss of 1849 discouraged beginning such a new project in 1849, 1850, and 1851, although in these years the committee on publications recommended the *Southern Baptist Missionary Journal,* the *Baptist Chronicle* (Louisiana), the *Southwestern Baptist* (Alabama), the *Tennessee Baptist* (Tennessee), and publications of the Southern Baptist Convention from Richmond, Virginia.

In 1852 Rufus C. Burleson reported for a committee that it was imperative for Texas Baptists to publish their own paper. It was needed, Burleson said, (1) to advocate the claims and explain the objects and proceedings of our Convention; (2) to sound the Macedonian cry for preachers for destitute towns and neighborhoods; (3) to press the claims of the schools; (4) to explain the doctrines and practices of Texas Baptists; and (5) to unify the Texas Baptists who have come from many older states and maintain various little peculiarities that ought to be resolved into a Texas Baptist practice. A committee of seven was established to look into the matter. A favorable report, written also by Burleson, was unanimously adopted and a collection of $13.50 was taken "to pay for publishing a prospectus."

Many obstacles prevented anything from being done in 1854. However, at the 1855 convention it was reported that the *Texas Baptist* had published its first issue in January and had continued as a weekly paper thereafter. It was being edited by George W. Baines, assisted by J. B. Stiteler. Its subscription list numbered about one thousand, but the paper was not nearly self-sustaining. The associations across the state commended the publication of this paper, and the Baptist Convention of Eastern Texas in 1855 adopted the paper as a denominational organ, electing William H. Stokes as Corresponding Editor from their Convention. When Stokes resigned in 1860, D. B. Morrill continued this service.

The subscription list reached 2,600, but the paper was not free from financial woes. There was practically no advertising; many subscriptions were not paid promptly and some not at all. In 1860 Baines resigned as editor. The beginning of the Civil War made it impossible to secure printing paper to continue, and the paper died.

Circulation of Baptist Books and Tracts. A committee at the State Convention in 1850 recommended that Baptist books like Howell on *Communion,* Jewett on *Baptism,* and Benedict's *History of the Baptists* should be read by Texas people. In 1851 the Convention jubilantly reported that Virginia Baptists through their state body had made a donation of $500.00 to provide religious books for Texas. A depository for books was established at Independence, and John Clabaugh was employed by the Convention as a colporteur. It was remarked that within six weeks he had sold over $300.00 worth of books.

The books most frequently recommended in the *Texas Baptist* are significant. J. R. Graves, editor of the *Tennessee Baptist* was just introducing his Landmark movement, and his books were frequently mentioned. *The Old Landmark Reset,* the primer of the movement, was quite popular. Other books by Graves, Howell on *Communion,* and Dayton's books, *Theodosia Earnest* and *Grace Truman* were very popular. J. M. Pendleton's *Three Reasons,* Orchard's *History of the Baptists,* and similar popular books suggest that Texas was being nourished on a great deal of the Landmark literature. When it is remembered that the *Tennessee Baptist* was probably the most widely circulated paper in Texas and that the books of Graves, Pendleton, and Dayton (the Landmark triumvirate) were quite popular, it is no wonder that a work like Morrell's *Flowers and Fruits in the Wilderness* shows a distinct Landmark tendency in several places. So do writings of R. E. B. Baylor and others.

Sunday Schools. During this period Texas Baptists encouraged the organization of Sunday schools. One of the nagging problems of early Texas Baptists was to find buildings in which to meet. The fact that many Baptists did not have their own church buildings greatly affected the character of the Sunday schools that developed. Generally the school house in a community was used for all religious services, each denomination having an appointed time to meet. As a result, the Sunday school was usually a union school composed of several denominations. For example, in 1851, Thomas J. Pilgrim reported to the Colorado Association concerning Sunday schools within the bounds of that Association. He said that there were twenty-four union schools and five Methodist schools. The union schools in which Baptists cooperated included those at such villages as Austin, Matagorda, Gonzales, and San Antonio. Pilgrim praised these union schools when he made his report to the Colorado Association in 1853, as he remarked:

> Scaling the barriers of sectarian prejudices and sectional opposition, it penetrates where the missionary himself cannot go, and converging to one point all the combined talent and piety and Christian influence of that community which it enters, forms a center from which again diverges the rays of light, and truth, and heavenly wisdom, to benefit and to bless mankind. The Christian missionary now enters: the sanctuary is reared; the churchgoing bell proclaims the approach of a Sabbath morn; the wilderness and the solitary places are made glad, and the desert begins to bud and blossom like the rose.[9]

Even at that time the importance of the Sunday school was recognized as an agency of evangelism and enlistment.

> More than three-fourths of the members of our churches are now received from the Sabbath schools, and nineteen-twentieths of our missionaries to foreign fields receive here their first serious impressions. Here they learned to feel that they were sinners, here they learned the great and glorious truths of the everlasting Gospel, and here, too, they learned to feel for the miseries of their fellow-creatures.[10]

The reports of Pilgrim over a century ago have a surprisingly modern ring. He wrote:

> The time was when, in New England at least, one day in each week in their day school was spent in giving instruction from the Bible. Now that practice is discontinued, and the Bible as a classbook, is banished from our schools; and if our children are not instructed in the Sunday school, in most cases they receive no religious instruction whatever; and, as faith cometh by hearing, and hearing by the Word of God, can we expect our children, as they grow up, to embrace the sublime truths of the gospel and become active and efficient members of our churches, when they have never been taught the very elementary principles of Christianity?[11]

By the close of this period, there was widespread feeling among the Baptist leaders that the union schools were not accomplishing what was desired. In 1858, for example, at the Colorado Association, W. P. Hatchett reported for the committee on Sabbath schools that children could not be indoctrinated with Baptist teachings in a union school. It was hoped that more distinctly Baptist literature could be secured. He concluded:

> But your committee doubts the applicability of the present plan of conducting Sabbath schools to our sparsely settled country and it is of the opinion that if we ever have efficient Sabbath schools in the country, some other plan must be adopted.

In the animated discussion that followed, hope was expressed that help might come from the Southern Baptist Publication Society which had been formed in South Carolina in 1847, as well as the Baptist Sunday School Union, just organized at Nashville, Tennessee. However, at the close of the period Texas Baptists had not settled the problem of denominational Sunday schools for Baptist children alone, literature to teach Baptist doctrine, and teacher training of some sort.

Work With Other Groups. Texas Baptists also confronted the problem of working with other races, particularly the Negroes and Mexicans. The census of 1850, two years after the beginning of this period, revealed a total of 58,161 Negro slaves, which increased by 1855 to 105,704, and over 150,000 at the beginning of Civil War. Part of the rapid increase in the number of slaves in Texas occurred because many of the people in the older South, recognizing that hostilities might soon begin, sent their Negro slaves to Texas for safekeeping.

During the period from 1848 to 1860, the pastors, the associations, and the state bodies gave attention to trying to win Negroes to Christ. Noah Hill reported on the condition of the Negroes at the first meeting of the Baptist State Convention. He said that there were many Negroes in Texas who had not heard the sound of the gospel for years, and recommended that one of the leading objects of the Convention be to take the gospel to the black people. He urged pastors in every village to make this a part of their regular work week by week. In the period before the war Hill was employed to give a part of his time to this work alone, and Anderson Buffington, although appointed by the State Board, always gave his services without remuneration. Both the State Convention and the General Association after its organization reported regularly on efforts to evangelize the Negroes. Most of the associational bodies also gave encouragement to this task.

It is interesting to notice that in 1854 a colored church in Matagorda county petitioned for membership in the Colorado Association and was received. There was disagreement among the several associations over the best policy to pursue at this point. Union Association, for example, did not feel that the Negroes should establish independent churches,[12] but in the same year Colorado Association recommended just the opposite—that there be separate churches for the colored people. It was reported in 1857 that there were some separate colored churches presided over by white ministers and some by colored ministers. Most of the Negroes, however, remained as members of the white churches until the war.

German immigrants had been settling in remote southwest Texas as early as 1838. There were Germans among the early *impressarios*. Many immigrants from Germany came in 1842 as a result of the organization of a society near Mayence on the Rhine. New Braunfels was founded in 1845. Fredericksburg was settled in 1846, about eighty miles north of New Braunfels, and by 1860 the

Germans constituted a majority of the population in the counties between Austin and San Antonio. In 1860 foreign born Germans made up nearly five percent of the white population, and there were probably half as many more Germans who had been born in Texas. When it is noted that only slightly more than ten percent of the white population in Texas was foreign born in 1860, it will be seen that Germans formed a large part of this group.[13] There were two or three newspapers in the German language in 1857.

The State Convention, as well as the Domestic Mission Board of the Southern Baptist Convention, recognized the need of working among the Germans. In the June issue of the *Southern Baptist Missionary Journal* for 1848, it was reported that J. W. D. Creath had baptized a young German convert, who had enrolled at Baylor University, and it was hoped that this young man and others like him would be instruments of the Lord for converting the Germans in Texas.[14]

But the principal name in winning the Germans was Frank Kiefer. He was born on August 13, 1833, at Muelheim in the Rhineland, Germany. As a boy of seventeen, he made the trip to Galveston, arriving on November 2, 1850, and providentially, it seemed, settled at Independence. Here, under the preaching of President Burleson of Baylor he was converted in the fall of 1854. He entered Baylor University as a ministerial student, then went to Galveston for medical training, and after his marriage in 1858, became very active both as a physician and a preacher.

At the state convention in 1855 this twenty-two-year-old was put on a committee with President Burleson and J. B. Stiteler to spend an appropriation made for Germans in Texas to buy books and periodicals. In the following year Kiefer reported to the convention on work among the Germans, noting that there were more than 30,000 of them in Texas, and that a German speaking missionary was needed among them. In 1860 Kiefer was appointed to this post just at the close of this period. J. M. Carroll said, "It is probable that more people were converted under his ministry than under that of any other Texas preacher, except, possibly, Major W. E. Penn, our greatest Texas evangelist." More of his work will be traced in later periods.

The period of Civil War from 1861 to 1865 marked the only regression in the forward progress of Texas Baptist work. Not only was there division in the nation over the propriety of secession, but within Texas itself good men took each side. The dreary story of war and reconstruction will be told in the following chapter.

7

War and Reconstruction

(1861-74)

The melancholy story of the Civil War and reconstruction in Texas, "the hardest years in all our history," was prefaced by the humiliation of one of its noblest sons, Governor Sam Houston, who was baptized into the Baptist church at Independence by Rufus C. Burleson on November 19, 1854. Houston was elected Governor of Texas in 1859 despite his feeling that secession was "unjustifiable, unconstitutional, and revolutionary." The election of Lincoln aroused the radical pro-Southern faction in Texas. A state convention voted almost unanimously to secede, annulling the annexation ordinance of 1845, and the voters sustained this action by 46,129 to 14,697. When Houston was called upon to swear allegiance to the new Confederate government at Montgomery, Alabama, he refused to do so and was removed from office by the convention. His health rapidly declined and he died July 26, 1863.

It was a foregone conclusion that Texas would take the side of the Confederacy. Ninety percent of the white immigrants had come from the old South. It had entered the Union as a slave state in 1845, and the number of slaves had increased from 38,753 in 1846 to 180,682 in 1860. Many of the slaves had been sent from sections of the older South for safekeeping. On March 23, 1861, Texas officially joined the Confederate States of America.

The Dreary War Years (1861–1865)

Despite some harsh internal conflicts between Union and Confederate sympathizers, military operations were not particularly hurtful in Texas. From a religious standpoint, however, the total effect of the war was disastrous. Radical pro-Southerners had seized the leadership at the beginning of the secession agitation, and radical pro-Unionists succeeded them at the close of the war. There were few moderates. Animosity and hatred were widespread.

During the war the work of Baptists suffered greatly from the loss of manpower. At the commencement service of Waco University in 1866, it was mentioned that one hundred of the students taught by President Burleson at Independence and Waco had died in the conflict. Texas rapidly furnished between 50,000 and 65,000 men for the Confederacy, among them such distinguished leaders as a full General (Albert Sidney Johnston), a Lieutenant General, three Major Generals, thirty-two Brigadier Generals, and ninety-seven Colonels. Before the conflict ended, men between the ages of sixteen and sixty were drafted. In 1863 Governor Francis R. Lubbock estimated that not more than 23,000 men in this age bracket remained in the state. Practically every able-bodied man was in military service at least a part of the four years. Despite general prosperity in Texas during the war, the economic privations suffered by the people are illustrated by the fact that in 1864, when the state undertook to support destitute families of the soldiers, there were 74,000 persons receiving such aid. Crops were planted and harvested by women and children. The armies in the field received a major share of all Texas agricultural and mineral products they could use.

The minutes of the two general bodies in Texas reflect the near collapse of organized religious work. The Eastern Texas convention probably met in June, 1861, but there are no extant minutes. Evidently it did not meet in 1862 and 1863. Little was done at the 1864 meeting, and there was no meeting in 1865. At the Tyler meeting in 1866, where the work of 1865 was described, it was reported that all educational enterprises had been abandoned, few Sunday schools existed and few attended; and practically nothing had been done in mission work. The spirit of the closing scene of this convention, however, promised brighter tomorrows. Link described it in these words:

> A general coldness pervaded the churches everywhere, and a fearful responsibility was felt to rest upon the body at this time. The Convention had no means at command, no efficient organization and but little character or credit; but few of those who had been previously active were present. . . . It was finally agreed to select some one and ask him to go out on the field and commit the matter of his support to God, and try to stir up the brethren and churches to the great work that was lying neglected. A small amount was raised to meet the present necessities of whoever might go. Tenderness and sympathy now pervaded all present. Elder D. B. Morrill was chosen. His heart and thoughts had been previously directed to such a work, and although he had a large family looking to him for support, he felt that the voice of the brethren was the voice of the Master in deciding the path of duty and he agreed to go. Elder D. D. Swindall also volunteered to go in the same way, and Bro. W. G. Caperton, now of Albany in this state, volunteered to spend about half his time in this sort of field service. It was a deeply affecting scene when the brethren came forward to give these volunteer missionaries the pledge of their sympathy and their prayers, and we all bowed down to commend them to God and to the word of His grace, and their wives and little ones to His care and protection. Some doubted the propriety of trusting God's grace so far, but it was suggested that if we cannot trust God's promises for this life, how can we trust them in regard to that life which is to come? But before we left the ground we had some evidence that our Father in heaven, who watches the sparrow's fall and hears the young raven's cry, will also care for his trusting children.[1]

The Baptist State Convention fared a little better during the war. Baylor University at Independence was hard hit. The continuous quarrel between President Rufus C. Burleson and Principal Horace Clark of the female department came to a head in the first year of the war. Feeling that his office as president entitled him to supervise both the male and female departments of Baylor, and smarting from the sharp words of the trustees, on May 15, 1861,

Burleson, along with the faculty of the male department—Richard B. Burleson, David R. Wallace, Oscar H. Leland, and George W. Wilrick—announced their intention of resigning their positions with the school effective at the end of the 1861 session. Promptly Burleson was named president of Waco University and the others joined the Waco faculty. Whereupon, the entire senior class at Baylor, consisting of M. M. Vanderhurst, Willis P. Darby, Boling Eldridge, John C. Watson, Mark A. Kelton, James L. Bowers, and Henry F. Pahl addressed a letter to the trustees asking that the class be allowed to transfer to Waco University. B. H. Carroll was a member of this class, but on April 15, 1861, after the secession convention had successfully united Texas with the Confederate States of America, he volunteered for army service and left school. The remainder graduated from Waco University in a few months.

To replace Burleson, the trustees elected George W. Baines, Sr. as president on an interim basis, while Clark continued to head the female department. William Carey Crane succeeded Baines in the following year, reporting sixty students in 1863 in the male department and 140 in the female department. In 1864 the State Convention was informed that 101 students had patronized the male department during the previous year and 160 attended the female department. A chair of theology had been established at the school.

At the 1861 meeting of the State Convention it was reported that no missionary work of any kind had been performed officially. The Convention appointed fourteen unpaid agents to present the financial situation to the pastors, churches, and associations, urging that funds for missionaries be provided. It will be recalled that some of the founders of this body in 1848 remonstrated when the Constitution allowed its Board full freedom to create debts in behalf of the body in the missionary and educational work. In 1861 the Constitution was amended to forbid the Board from appropriating money which they did not have or was not pledged. This promptly curtailed the work, but also stopped reports of indebtedness which had been made at previous meetings of the convention. It came at an appropriate time, for the beginning of the war could have ballooned indebtedness without this provision. Another operating principle was adopted in 1861, which encouraged the associations to name destitute fields, suggest missionaries, and estimate how much they could raise for missionary support. The war and poor communications killed this plan.

Little was done in 1862 and 1863 except army missions. Not only the state conventions, but strong associations like Union, Trinity River, and Cherokee were ministering to the soldiers in the army. In 1864 five state missionaries reported working part-time during the year. In 1865 Corresponding Secretary Horace Clark said that little mission work had been done, but that several of the strongest Baptist preachers of Texas, including William T. Wright, J. S. Allen, J. W. D. Creath, and J. G. Thomas had been working with the soldiers in the southern army with gratifying results.

Needless to say, the Domestic Mission Board of the Southern Baptist Convention was unable to do any kind of work in Texas during the war.

Rebuilding Zion's Walls

In speaking of the gloomy situation at the end of the war, D. B. Morrill outlined the collapse of most of the religious work in Texas and the "spiritual torpor which everywhere characterized our churches. Yet, there were a few like Nehemiah, who came up to survey the extent of Zion's desolations and commence the work of rebuilding the walls."

His description was not overdrawn. Governor Pendleton Murrah was unable to stop the lawlessness and violence in the state, particularly along the frontier, during the exhausting days when everyone knew that the South was defeated. The public debt was about eight million dollars in 1865, and after the surrender of Lee at Appomattox, the Governor and other state officials fled to Mexico, leaving complete chaos in government until the end of July, when A. J. Hamilton became the provisional governor by the appointment of President Johnson.

> The confusion already existent in Texas had been increased by the freeing of the slaves on the eve of the cotton-picking season, by inevitable conflicts between loyal Confederates and returning Union-

ists who had been forced to flee the state, and by the general economic paralysis that followed the close of the war.[2]

Normalcy appeared to be returning when J. W. Throckmorton defeated E. M. Pease for Governor, and on August 20, 1866, President Andrew Johnson declared that Texas was no longer in a state of insurrection. However, Congress began its radical political reconstruction. General Phillip H. Sheridan removed Throckmorton and appointed Pease as Governor, a new state convention was convened in 1868, and a new constitution was adopted in 1869. Governor Pease resigned in disgust in October, 1869, and the military controlled the state until Unionist General E. J. Davis was elected Governor in November, 1869. Congress then voted to readmit Texas to the Union in March, 1870. Davis promptly inaugurated a despotic rule. He controlled the legislature, the state militia, and a state police force; he appointed judges, sheriffs, and city officials. Bribery and mismanagement brought sky-rocketing government costs. At this time Texas had 564,700 white and 253,487 black citizens. Misguided efforts by outsiders to aid the blacks and by some to coerce them, through such groups as the Freedmen's Bureau, Union League, and the Ku Klux Klan brought conflict and confusion.

The people of Texas began a systematic effort to secure control of their state government. At the election in November, 1872, they captured both houses of the legislature. In December, 1873, after a bitter campaign, Richard Coke defeated Davis at the polls. Davis tried to prevent Coke from taking office, but his effort collapsed when President U. S. Grant refused to send Federal troops for that purpose. As a result, the hated reconstruction era was ended by the inauguration of Governor Coke on January 15, 1874.

In the midst of this turmoil, Texas Baptists set forth a four-fold program: to reinstitute the missionary work which had been interrupted by the war; to carry on a program of education, including ministerial training; to publish a Texas Baptist newspaper; and to encourage other benevolent activities, such as Sunday schools and the circulation of religious literature.

Mission Work

Baptist State Convention. The paralyzing effects of the war, as well as the continuing confusion and violence of reconstruction, retarded Texas Baptists during this period. In 1865 Secretary Horace Clark reported to the State Convention:

> The year commenced under the pressure of a war unsurpassed in its magnitude, and involving in its issue the independence of our people, their wealth, and in a great measure, their dignity and happiness. The anxiety of the public mind while these issues were pending; its agitation, when the probability of an adverse decision grew into a terrible certainty, and the doubt and distress necessarily accompanying the upturning of the foundation of our social system, have paralyzed to a great degree all our benevolent enterprizes, and suspended mid-way our best matured schemes for the promotion of the objects for which the Convention was organized.[3]

In the same report Clark gave a valuable summary of the Convention's work since its organization on September 8, 1848. He said:

> In reviewing the financial history of the Convention from its organization to the present time, we find the aggregate of receipts to be about $35,000, or an average of nearly $2,000 a year. The smallest amount was $94 contributed at the organization of the Convention in 1848; the largest amount in specie funds was $3,353.59, contributed in 1858. . . .

> The missionaries, who since the organization of the Convention, have been supported in whole or in part by its funds, have left a record of their labors that should cheer the heart and nerve the arm of every friend of the Convention and every lover of Zion.

> They have been instrumental in the organization of five or six associations and between forty and fifty churches, and in the erection of from twenty-five to thirty meeting houses. They have ordained from twelve to fifteen ministers of the gospel, and from twenty-five to thirty deacons; six hundred converts were baptized in one year by them, and about 2,500 in all.

The State Convention appointed J. W. D. Creath as general agent and George W. Baines, Sr. as a "general missionary." Baines was the first and only general missionary appointed, and he served for only one year. Most of the leadership of the mission work in the State Convention was done by Creath, who served from 1867 to 1873. He received practically no salary and paid most of his own expenses. In 1873 and 1874, young preachers from Baylor used their summer vacation period to preach in missionary areas.

When Creath resigned in 1873 to give his remaining years to the work in San Antonio, it was an end of an era in Texas Baptist life. He had served for eighteen years as financial agent, traveling on horseback over almost every part of southwest Texas. His expense accounts many times amounted to less than $10.00 a year, and were never over $25.00 a year. J. M. Carroll told a story that typifies the spirit of this man who in 1846 left his home state of Virginia to work in Texas. Carroll said that during his college days he and several friends were getting ready to go for a one night and day camping and fishing expedition when they happened to meet Brother Creath.

He asked: "Where are you young brethren going?"
"Fishing," was the answer.
He soberly responded: "Well, since the Lord called me to preach, all the fish I have caught I caught on dry land, and then put them in the water."
He passed on. We understood him.

R. E. B. Baylor remarked concerning Creath:

As a preacher he has never been ranked as he deserves. At the last Baptist Convention I heard all the gifted men of our denomination who had been appointed to deliver sermons on this occasion. Most of the big guns had been loaded too long. They fired clear, but they wanted hot shot to reach the heart. Brother Creath preached during the sitting of the Convention. His sermon was in the old-fashion style, full of religion, and I, with many others who sat around him, were in tears. We felt that there was a living reality in the religion of Jesus. May God give us many such preachers and fewer arctic and professional ones!

In 1874, Joseph Mitchell was appointed general agent to succeed Creath.

Texas Baptist General Association. The second general body in the state, the Eastern Texas Baptist Convention, changed its name in 1868 to the Baptist General Association of Texas. D. B. Morrill mourned that little had been done in a field of great destitution, but said that plans were being laid to enlarge the work. R. C. Buckner reported on home missions at the 1868 meeting and said that the territory occupied by the body extended 300 miles east and west and about 250 miles north and south, embracing a large number of extensive and populous counties, but that he knew of only two churches within this vast region that had preaching every Sabbath. Buckner was chosen general agent, serving also as missionary, working entirely without salary. Considerable progress was made, but in the following year Buckner had to resign because of his health. The report to the General Association in 1870 expressed concern at the destitution and urged that funds be secured to carry on the work of state missions as the principal work of the body.

With T. B. McComb as general agent in 1871, a new thrust was made in the midst of great difficulty. However, in 1872 there was discouragement. No general agent was under appointment, and the Board said, "We deprecate the fact that we have not been able to accomplish more for the cause of Christ. We find a general apathy and indifference throughout the bounds of the General Association on the subject of missions." The following two years were also discouraging years. The General Association, despite the appointment of J. B. Daniel as financial agent, reported that "no means have been at our disposal to aid feeble churches, or to send missionaries to important fields entirely destitute of gospel preaching." It was reported in 1874 that yellow fever, panic, quarantine regulations, and a general financial depression were all working against the missionary enterprise.

In addition to the two state bodies, several associations engaged in state missions during the reconstruction period. Each year between 1867 and 1874 from five to eight associations regularly employed one or more missionaries to carry on the state program in their field. The theme in general was set in the report of the Union

Association in 1868, when they said that the destitution was great and that the "preachers are tent-making." It is likely that Union Association did about as much work as all of the other associations put together during this period. Acting at times with the Baptist State Convention and at times with other associations, the old Union Association carried on an intermittent program among a large number of German immigrants in the area through the ministry of Frank Kiefer and another German convert, F. J. Gleiss. The Association reported in 1870 that there were five German Baptist preachers active in the Association.

Neither the Domestic Mission Board of the Southern Baptist Convention nor the American Baptist Home Mission Society of New York was able to assist Texas Baptists to any extent during this period. The former sent William Howard in 1866, but he soon accepted the pastorate of the First Baptist Church in Galveston. The Southern Board also sent J. B. Link in 1865 to direct army missions, but the surrender of Lee at Appomattox ended that work. Link became editor of the *Texas Baptist Herald* for the next twenty years.

A New Relationship

Texas Baptists expressed interest in the religious condition of the black population from the earliest days of their history. The question of the formation of separate Negro Baptist churches probably began at least a decade before emancipation was accomplished on June 19, 1865. At the September, 1854, meeting of the Colorado Baptist Association a petitionary letter was received from the "Colored Church on J. H. Jones' plantation, Matagorda County, Texas, by her delegates, Elder N. Hill, and J. I. Loudermilk, ..."[4] The messengers were seated, but it should be noted that Hill and Loudermilk were white Baptist preachers. In the following year the Union Association rejected a petitionary letter to seat messengers from the African Baptist Church at Anderson. This was consonant with the action of the Colorado Association, for in this instance the petitioning church was evidently a completely separate Negro Baptist congregation. In support of their action the Union Association said that even though "separate meetings and special preaching," "their own Deacons," and encouragement "to maintain a correct discipline among themselves" were permitted to Negro churches, still they must be "aided in this work by the presence and counsel of some judicious white members."[5] In 1857 the Baptist State Convention meeting at Anderson noted that there were "a few places in our state where our colored brethren have a separate organization, presided over by a white minister. . . . In other places they have their own colored minister . . ." but a committee of white brethren in the latter case was delegated to meet with them "in all their meetings."[6]

The new relationship with the Negro after emancipation was accomplished brought a difference of opinion among Texas Baptists as to the proper connection Negroes should have with white churches. A strong committee reported at the Baptist State Convention in 1865, calling their hearers to the duty as good loyal citizens and as good Christians to recognize the new relationship to the Negroes. The report closed:

> Your committee would be pleased to recommend some definite plan for the churches to adopt regarding the colored population of their respective communities, but on account of the frequent change of military orders and their uncertain and future action, together with the various conditions and dispositions of the blacks in the several localities of the churches—we cannot say more than to strongly recommend that ministering brethren at churches furnish them with preaching and the use of houses as heretofore, in order that the "poor may have the gospel preached unto them,"—and leave the subject of separate church organization to the circumstances surrounding each church; manifesting and proving at all times, and on all occasions, our desire for their spiritual improvement and moral elevation.[7]

It is probable that the noble F. M. Law did as much as any Texas Baptist to engender the proper attitude toward the freed Negroes. In a report to the Union Association in 1865, he said concerning them:

> Since the last meeting of our body a radical change has taken place in reference to the relative position of the Negroes of the South.

They are no longer our property, but have been placed in a state of freedom. With this change our responsibilities as masters cease. Not so, however, with the obligations of philanthropy and Christianity. While it is our duty to labor for the general good of the human family, and especially for the salvation of souls, we should feel that this population here in our midst is entitled to our sympathy and labor. The slaves of the South are not prepared for the change that has taken place. They are not in a condition, it is feared, to be profited by freedom. Their general course will probably not be a wise one. They will naturally be indolent, idle, and unreliable. This we may expect as a natural consequence, and should be prepared to make new allowances and exercise charity towards them. Let none of these things move us in bestowing upon them the free and elevating principles of Christianity. No changes that have been made will relieve us of these obligations. Let us, as Christians and ministers, do our duty—our whole duty—in this regard. If the Negroes have friends on earth they are among the Christians of the South. Where else should they expect as true and faithful friends as among us? We should not now forget their past faithful services to us, and to our fathers, and let us remember their present necessities, doing what we can for their relief and improvement.[8]

The divided opinion about the best manner of handling the question is seen in the action of the associations. At the Union Association in 1866 there came a petitionary letter from the First Colored Baptist Church of Houston, applying for admission to the Association. A strong committee of F. M. Law, J. W. D. Creath, J. B. Link, and C. R. Breedlove reported on its application by saying that they did not

"deem it prudent, under existing circumstances, for our African membership to dissolve their connections with white churches; still, in view of the facts in this case, we recommend the admission of said African church upon condition that they will confine their annual delegates to this body to white members in good standing from the First (white) Baptist Church of Houston, and that they promptly and at once adopt the Articles of Faith of the said First Baptist Church."[9]

The Association also recommended that the African Baptist Church select its moderator and clerk from the membership of the white Baptist church of Houston.

In the same year the Colorado Association faced the question, and a committee appointed to discuss it was divided in opinion. The majority of the Committee said that the colored people were not yet able without assistance from the whites to keep the doctrines and ordinances in God's work pure, and that even colored ministers had not been sufficiently educated and trained to carry out these responsibilities. Consequently, the committee urged that the Negroes remain within the white churches for the present. It did recommend, however, that wherever practicable, the Negroes should have separate meetings and preaching, at which a committee of whites should attend to assist them in problems that might arise. It also suggested that in every case the Negro churches should have a white preacher whom they themselves should call, and that it was the duty of the Association to safeguard the ministry by overseeing the ordination of colored ministers.

This majority report was subsequently adopted, but the minority report indicated the direction that was to be taken. It recommended that the Negroes, if they wished to do so, form their own separate organizations where their population and number of members justified it and where they could secure competent ministers to preach to them. "Thus with their own pastors, their own deacons, and meeting-houses of their own, and under their own exclusive control, a much greater number would hear the gospel and be saved than under the present system."

During the remainder of the reconstruction era, when there was much resentment against the Negro because of the manipulations of Northern selfish interests, the general bodies and associations in Texas showed a gracious interest in the welfare of the freedmen and provided missionaries to assist them in their work. In 1872 the General Association recommended that pastors and evangelists visit and observe the Negro congregations in all meekness and humility and assist them at whatever point they could.

It is further recommended that these pastors and evangelists do raise from their respective churches and areas of labor, funds to purchase Testaments, books, papers, and Sunday school literature for gratuitous distribution among them. That they especially place a church manual in the hands of every Negro minister. It is also especially recommended that no charge at present be made for literature or labor furnished them.[10]

In 1874, at the very close of the reconstruction era, the Baptist State Convention was encouraged by the progress of the Negro Baptists. It was reported that they had organized a state body, the constitution of which did not differ materially from the State Convention constitution. They had invited Brethren Law, Link, Smith, Johnston, and other white brethren to assist them in the organization, and prospects were bright for progress in this area.

One of the factors that greatly blessed the newly organized Negro Baptist churches was the movement known as Ministers' Institute. E. W. Warren of Atlanta, Georgia, apparently was the one who developed this program in 1872 or 1873. These institutes aimed to gather uneducated ministers and deacons for a week or ten days and teach them the basic Christian doctrines. Warren, for example, first would secure a faculty of white leaders who would give their services without charge, then would personally solicit the Negro ministers and deacons in the entire area around the town where the institute was to be held. He would provide transportation for them to the institute, find homes for them in case distance forbade daily travel, keep them happy during the period of study, and then see to it that they were returned to their homes.

His programs were so effective that the Southern Baptist Convention officially endorsed them in 1875, and a similar project was begun by the Home Mission Board in the following year. The Home Mission Society of New York soon adopted this program in dealing with the leadership of the new Negro churches in the South. In Texas, F. M. Law, J. B. Link, W. H. Robert, W. C. Crane, R. C. and R. B. Burleson, William Howard, B. H. Carroll, R. C. Buckner, and many others of the white Texas Baptist leaders, gave themselves freely to this ministry.

The minutes of the Austin Association in 1875 complimented the Negro churches for their large congregations and liberality in giving. The Neches River Association in the same year reported that at the Negro Baptist Associational meeting there were seventeen ordained ministers, representing thirty-seven churches and 2,299 members.

The Avenue L Baptist Church of Galveston is generally counted the first completely separate Negro Baptist Church in Texas after emancipation. In 1865, I. S. Campbell, an educated Negro minister from Richmond, Virginia, arrived in Galveston to become pastor of this church. In July, 1866, the Lincoln Missionary Baptist Association, the first Negro association in Texas, was organized, and it covered the entire state. In 1875, the first state body was formed, when the Western Baptist State Convention was organized at Corsicana, Texas.[11]

The inspiring story of the progress of Negro Baptists in Texas will not be continued in this account. It should be the subject of an entire volume.

The German Ministry

One of the bright spots during the war and reconstruction was the winning of many Germans. Reference has been made to the conversion and ministry of Frank Kiefer in the previous period. In 1860 he held a revival in the Greenvine community near Brenham and organized the non-English speaking German Greenvine Baptist Church, which historians call the mother of German Baptist churches in Texas. This church was also called Ebenezer. In 1868 Kiefer won another German, F. J. Gleiss, to Baptist views, and these two served the Baptist State Convention as missionaries to the Germans. In November, 1869, Gleiss held a revival in the Cedar Hill community, not far from Brenham, and, along with some members of the Ebenezer or Greenvine church, Gleiss united the new converts on November 21, 1869, to form the second German Baptist church in Texas. This became a precedent in the multiplying of German Baptist churches: wherever members of the Greenvine church moved, they called for their preachers to hold a revival in that community and help organize a new German Baptist church. In this way the Greenvine church became the mother of a number of closely knit German Baptist churches. Before the end of the century the German speaking Baptist churches related themselves to the German Baptist Conference of North America.

The Educational Task (1866–74)

Baylor at Independence. The friction that led to the resignation of Rufus C. Burleson in 1861 and his removal to Waco University with his faculty and senior class was not settled with the coming to the Independence presidency of William Carey Crane. His title was that of president, but he had no jurisdiction at all over the female department under Horace Clark. In 1866, as a consequence, steps were taken to separate the male department from the female department. The boys were being taught in classes separate from the girls in buildings nearly one mile apart and with separate faculties. On September 28, 1866, the Texas Legislature officially established Baylor Female College as a distinct institution with its own Board of Trustees. The resignation of Clark, who had been principal of the female department for fifteen years, was accepted by the new Board of Trustees, and B. S. Fitzgerald was named as the president of this new school. However, in the following year Clark became its president and served during most of the reconstruction period.

Baylor University (now consisting simply of the male department) began its work after the war with considerable encouragement, but yellow fever disrupted the work. During the next several years there were ominous suggestions by some that the school should be moved from Independence because of its inaccessibility. The two railroads that had been built had by-passed Independence, and the roads leading to the school were often almost impassable. The attendance at the school during the remaining years of reconstruction generally was far below one hundred, and the financial panic of the early 1870's brought considerable distress to the institution.

Some advance was made during this time in ministerial education. At the meeting of the Baptist State Convention in 1866, funds were raised to assist one ministerial student at Baylor. Two preachers enrolled in 1867, A. F. Perry and Reddin Andrews, Jr. On October 4, 1872, it was decided to reorganize the Texas Baptist Education Society, which "has been reposing since the late war," in order to assist in the education of young ministers. The membership numbered a few less than fifty (both individuals and churches) and raised in that year $781.00 to assist young ministers. One year later Corresponding Secretary William Carey Crane of the Society reported that eight young preachers were beneficiaries of the Society in Baylor, and that three other young men were also studying "under other auspices" at the University. Prospects were not bright for Baylor when the installation of Governor Coke brought an end to reconstruction.

Considerable friction continued in the relationship of the Female College with the Baptist State Convention during the period of reconstruction. In 1869 the trustees complained to the Convention that this school had not received the patronage from the denomination to which it was justly entitled. "This, we apprehend has arisen not so much from a preference for other schools as from the lack of interest for a high degree of intellectual cultivation for our daughters." In 1870, the trustees passed a resolution sharply critical of the State Convention's neglect of their school. At the same time, there was considerable agitation to remove Baylor Female College from Independence.

Perhaps caused by the depression in the early 1870's, Clark announced in 1871 that he would no longer serve as president. Henry L. Graves was elected and served one year (1871–72), and W. W. Fontaine succeeded him. In 1874 Fontaine resigned and William Royall of North Carolina accepted the post at the close of the Texas reconstruction period.

Waco University. During its first five years under President Burleson, Waco University was simply a male school. The war restricted its student body to those in the primary and preparatory departments, and the collegiate course was dropped for the time. In 1866 the trustees reported ninety-five in the male department, thirty-five in the female department, the restoration of the collegiate course, and the operation of a theological department. In 1867 there were 172 matriculated in the male department and 81 in the female department. The school evidently maintained approximately this enrollment during the remainder of the reconstruction period and was in a flourishing condition when reconstruction ended.

Other Baptist Schools. It will be recalled that Tyler had two Baptist schools at the opening of the war—one operated by Cherokee Association and one by the East Texas Convention. A disastrous fire destroyed the male building of the former school and it was never replaced. The female department survived for about twenty-five years. The Convention's school closed when most of its student body volunteered for army service during the war.

A very influential school known as Concrete College was founded about 1865 at Concrete in DeWitt County by J. V. E. Covey, an experienced and dedicated educator. It was never under the auspices of any Baptist body, but was operated by outstanding Baptists. The opening of free public schools forced its demise in 1880. The war and the public school movement also brought a slow erosion and death about 1873 to the Ladonia Institute, fostered by the Sister Grove Association.

There were other private Baptist schools about which little is known. Most of them died during this period or shortly thereafter. In this category should be mentioned the Bosqueville Male and Female College, Sabine Baptist College, Mt. Calvary Seminary in Elm Fork Association, Cleburne Institute, Davilla Institute, and other lesser efforts. They played their part and moved on.

Baptist Newspapers

In 1865 the Baptist State Convention requested William Carey Crane to make an effort to begin the publication of a Baptist newspaper. There had been none for Texas Baptists since the death of the *Texas Baptist* in 1862. A new paper known as the *Texas Christian Herald,* edited by Crane and Horace Clark, was begun. One issue of the paper had been published when the collapse of the Confederacy undermined the enterprise.

On December 13, 1865, the resources of the *Herald* were transferred to a newcomer, J. B. Link from Virginia by way of Missouri and Mississippi, who became one of the principal figures in Texas Baptist newspaper history for the next half-century. He was born May 7, 1825, in Virginia, as John Bodkin Link. He graduated from Georgetown College in Kentucky in 1853 and completed the theological course at Rochester Theological Seminary, New York, in 1855. From Missouri he entered the Confederate army as a Division Chaplain. In 1864 he became an agent for the Domestic Mission Board, Marion, Alabama, which brought him to Texas. On December 13, 1865, he published the first issue of the paper he renamed the *Texas Baptist Herald*. Through grit and determination he edited this paper throughout the remainder of the reconstruction era. It should be kept in mind that J. R. Graves' *Tennessee Baptist*, however, continued to be a very popular rival to the indigenous Texas paper.

Sunday School and Colportage Ministry

The Sunday school movement was not particularly strong in Texas before the war. J. M. Carroll remarked that when the war ended in 1865 there was no organized effort by any association or state body to forward this interest.

At the meeting of the Union Association in August, 1865, a committee recommended that a Sunday school convention be called to meet at Independence on October 28, 1865, in an effort to awaken interest in Sunday school work. At Independence there were 115 messengers from twenty churches and seven Sunday schools in attendance. The Texas Baptist Sabbath School and Colportage Union was organized with Judge A. S. Broaddus, president; R. E. B. Baylor and F. M. Law, vice-presidents; S. S. Cross, corresponding secretary; B. S. Fitzgerald, recording secretary; and Isaac Parks, treasurer. In the following year S. S. Cross was named general superintendent for half his time. He was succeeded by T. S. Allen in 1869, M. V. Smith in 1872, and W. H. Robert in 1873. As a reflection of the increased interest in Sunday school work, it was reported that the two largest Baptist Sunday schools in the state in 1868 were at Waco (190 pupils and 19 teachers) and Brenham (185 pupils and 15 teachers).

In addition to promoting Sunday schools and their literature, the Union's constitution named another object to be the establishing of a system of colportage to provide religious literature. In pursuing this work, book depositories were established at Brenham and Bryan, and regular gifts to the book fund were solicited. At the close of this period in 1874, W. E. Penn, soon to be recognized as Texas' outstanding evangelist, was serving as president, J. T. Zealy as secretary, and J. B. Link, treasurer. The minutes of the meeting are deficient as to work accomplished, but the post-war depression curtailed activities radically. The name of the body was changed to the Texas Baptist Sunday School and Colportage Convention.

The exciting political events that led to the end of reconstruction and the return of the state government to the people were a harbinger of the brighter days ahead. The important place of Texas Baptists was emphasized in 1874 when the Southern Baptist Convention held its annual meeting at Jefferson, Texas, then a thriving commercial and transportation center of northeast Texas. Texas Baptists meeting there could compare their leadership with the outstanding Baptist preachers and laymen of the Southland. Doubtless many echoed the words of R. E. B. Baylor, who had died just a few months before this meeting, when he said, "I do not believe there is any portion of the United States that has a greater amount of talent, education, and piety than the Baptist ministers of Texas, . . ."

8

Closing Ranks

(1874–86)

☆☆☆

A new fabric of denominational leadership begins to appear in this period. The older stalwarts mingle with the new, strong leaders for a relatively brief time, then they start dropping out one by one. A priceless item has been preserved. Texas leaders urged R. E. B. Baylor on several occasions to write down reminiscences of his early comrades, and he finally did so. Most of his sketches seem to date between May and December, 1873, a year before his death in his eightieth year.

Some examples of his comments are given. He was complimentary to the Old Guard, yet distressingly honest at times. Huckins, he said, should not have read his sermons. Tryon he had heard preach in Alabama before he had become a Christian and had been greatly impressed by him. He loved Tryon and was close to him. Even his language reflected that devotion as he described Tryon's dark, flaxen hair, "His eyes were grey with a calm and soft expression," and he possessed a "pleasant smile which made you feel intensely the love he had for the brethren. . . ." He spoke of General Sam Houston "with his majestic form and noble bearing," and told of escorting the second Mrs. Houston to an entertainment in Selma, Alabama, while she was a young woman and of having saved her from drowning in the Alabama River. Of J. W. D. Creath he remarked, "No man has been in Texas whose benevolence and disinterested piety has surpassed him. . . ." He related how Anderson Buffington and "four others in Nashville when Campbellism had nigh destroyed the Baptist Church, stood firm by the old landmarks of our people, until Brother Howell came to the rescue and saved the church from ruin. . . ."

Baylor wrote only briefly about the imbroglio between Burleson and Clark who, said he, ". . . differed in the manner of conducting our literary institutions," and noted sadly that their conflict worked "most disastrously" for the school. Noah Hill, Baylor said, "in exhortation . . . had the power to shake the human soul." Patience B. Chandler was "perhaps too rigidly grave and silent." He spoke highly of D. B. Morrill whose "sun went down at mid-day." He greatly admired "Zet" Morrell (Z. N. Morrell), "double-soldier"—for Christ and for Texas. Eloquently he described how Morrell was a true fisherman for Christ—"Fish on, venerable brother, may God still continue to bless you until life's poor play is over." Of John Woodruff he said, "I believe he preached the first sermon ever delivered in Texas." (He dated this some time after Bays). He praised Hosea Garrett highly, then in a rare word of criticism remarked, "He was neither brilliant nor eloquent but then he was always zealous and deeply in earnest. This together with his known piety and honesty as a man gave his sermons great force and weight with his audience. . . ." Of Jesse Witt, a missionary from Virginia, he judged that he was "a man of spotless integrity . . . and a high order of intellect and as a preacher few excelled him. . . . He emigrated too late in life; old trees rarely do well if transplanted out of their native soil." A. W. Elledge he characterized as a "bold, outspoken man"; of B. B. Baxter, "He never seemed to be hitched fairly in the harness," probably because Baxter had difficulty providing for the physical needs of his family; Frank Kiefer "now stands among our ablest and best preachers"; Richard Burleson "is what the world would call a dry preacher," but his great merit was found in his educational work. These and scores of other candid comments by Baylor concerning the pioneer leaders make them appear to be real people instead of simply names. But all, he reiterated, were faithful and zealous.

This list of Baylor's contemporaries who were faithful could be extended to include many others like Noah Byars, William Carey Crane, J. W. D. Creath, R. H. Taliaferro, Jonas Johnston, C. C. Chaplin, and the four great laymen immortalized by J. M. Carroll —A. C. Horton, Aaron Shannon, T. J. Jackson, and A. G. Haynes. Most of them had laid down their burden before the end of this period, and new names become familiar as they are repeated in the historical documents of Texas Baptist life: names like F. M. Law, J. H. Stribling, B. H. Carroll, R. C. Buckner, Frank Kiefer, J. B. Link, A. J. Holt, O. C. Pope, J. B. Cranfill, J. M. Carroll, S. A. Hayden, and, of course, the dedicated lawyer W. E. Penn, who became a flaming evangelist after 1875.

A Great Forward Thrust

During the first half of this period (1874–81) it appeared that the new leadership would not be able to continue the rate of progress begun by their fathers. The State Convention supported only a few missionaries on the field during the time, and focused most of their attention on the San Antonio mission where J. W. D. Creath served his last days. The General Association did no better. In fact, several of their meetings were characterized as "inharmonious" and displaying "bitter feelings." Baylor University at Independence, under the leadership of William Carey Crane, made some progress, but the main building on the campus, Tryon Hall, which had stood unfinished year by year, was not completed despite a campaign to do so. Work was ordered stopped on it in 1881 because of lack of funds. A tornado swept through the community on February 27, 1882, seriously damaging many buildings on the campus. Repairs were rapidly made, but Tryon Hall remained half built. Baylor Female College at Independence fared better, but had three presidents before 1881—Col. W. W. Fontaine (1872–75), William Royall of North Carolina (1875–78), and J. H. Luther. Waco University, under Rufus C. Burleson, was the most prosperous of all Texas Baptist schools. Its enrollment reached almost 300 in 1873 and it graduated 85 students between 1874 and 1881. In 1881 the school was transferred from the sponsorship of Waco

Association to the General Association, who accepted it after a brief delay.

Not only was the work of Texas Baptists in general not impressive, but during this period a number of rival organizations sprang up and brought dissension in the ranks, as will be described shortly.

The situation changed radically after 1881. In that year the State Convention appealed to the Home Mission Society of New York for missionary assistance. The Society agreed that they would match dollar for dollar each $3,000.00 raised by the State Convention for work within the state. Not only so, but in the following year both the state Convention and the General Association accepted a similar offer from the Home Mission Board of the Southern Baptist Convention. Results followed promptly. The State Convention showed twenty missionaries on the field in 1882, thirty-seven in 1883, thirty-five in 1884, and forty-six in 1885. The same mushrooming effect was seen in the work of the General Association. In 1883 they reported sixteen missionaries on the field and in 1884, a total of fifty-nine. It will be noted that other rival general bodies also were assisted and put missionaries on the field. The educational situation after 1881 will be described in the story of unification.

Curiously enough, all of these factors—early hardships, the organization of rival bodies, bitterness and recrimination, and the affluence brought by sectional affiliation with northern and southern missionary bodies—led directly to unification of Texas Baptists in 1886. That story will now be told briefly.

"Wheels Within Wheels"

The increasing stability of the secular state government after 1874 encouraged Baptists in the various sections of the state to dream again of making Texas a great Baptist empire. There followed a frenzy of organizational efforts that coincided almost precisely with the end of the reconstruction period. J. M. Carroll sketched this development as follows:

> Things began to grow mightily. So rapid was the growth that our people became restless and hurried. They wanted to grow faster.

They became impatient with the tardiness and the seeming ineffi-
ciency of all the old general organizations, and it seemed to them that
the quickest remedy was to have new and more numerous organizations. In their enthusiasm and hurry they acted without due delibera-
tion. They created organizations within organizations—wheels
within wheels—until one wheel could not turn without interfering
with another. Different sections felt that they must have general
organizations rightly to care for their peculiar territory.[1]

As a result of this Baptist boom in general organizations, within a
decade the following bodies larger in scope than the district associations were active: five territorial conventions; two Sunday school
conventions; probably two ministerial conferences; two general organizations for women; a deacons' convention; and an education
society. There was overlapping, rivalry, and confusion.

> In some large sections one association would cooperate with one of
> the general bodies, and another association in the same section would
> cooperate with another. Very many associations were sadly divided in
> their sympathies and cooperation—some of the churches in an asso-
> ciation giving their sympathy and support to one, and other churches
> in the same association giving theirs to another. Sometimes individual
> preachers and laymen followed the same course.[2]

Furthermore, Texas Baptists also inaugurated twenty-nine district associations, whose territory extended as far to the northwest as
Sweetwater. The number of preachers grew rapidly. In the 1872
minutes of the General Association were the names of 508 Baptist
preachers in Texas, and it was noted that there were many more
that should have been included. A. J. Holt estimated that at the
close of this period (1886) there were over 100,000 white Baptists
in the state, 1500 white Baptist churches, and over 60 associations.

Five Territorial Conventions. At the opening of this period in
1874 there were two general bodies—the Baptist State Convention and the Baptist General Association. Three more general
bodies were soon formed. On December 12, 1877, at Overton, the
East Texas Baptist Convention was organized because, its founders
said, the two older conventions were not meeting the needs of east
Texas. On July 3, 1879, a small group withdrew from the General
Association to organize the North Texas Baptist Missionary Con-

vention. They claimed that a general body should not carry on educational enterprises and other benevolences, but should conduct only missionary work. However, after four years this body, whose constituency lived in the geographical area affiliating with the General Association, merged with the Baptist State Convention (who engaged in educational and other benevolences), which suggests that there were reasons for withdrawal other than those advanced. On November 12, 1880, the Central Texas Baptist Convention was formed to meet the needs of the territory between the Brazos River on the east, Belton and Lampasas on the south, the frontier on the west, and the Clear Fork of the Brazos River on the north, an area not being reached, it was alleged, by the existing general organizations.

Two Sunday School Conventions. The Baptist Sunday School and Colportage Convention, organized in 1865 at Independence, had been viewed as a state-wide body during the following decade, but on November 5, 1875, a Baptist Sunday School Convention was organized under the aegis of the Baptist General Association and was intended to foster the Sunday school movement in the territory of this Association.

Two Ministerial Conferences. A ministerial conference was formed by the State Convention in connection with its annual session on October 5, 1877, at Bryan, Texas, and J. M. Carroll indicated a similar body was developed by the General Association.

Two General Organizations for Women. The organizational structure involving two principal territorial bodies (the State Convention and the General Association) brought also the forming of two women's missionary societies. The earlier one developed in the territory of the State Convention. It was born in the midst of glory. Miss Ann Luther, daughter of President J. H. Luther of Baylor Female College, was stirred by the zealous preaching of General A. T. Hawthorne, who had become a voluntary exile to Brazil after the Civil War. His description of the needs in Brazil brought her to a conviction that God wanted her to go to that nation as a missionary. The gifted W. B. Bagby also felt a call to Brazil, and providentially these two met, were married, and together went to their mission field in 1881.

The spirit of foreign missions swept Texas. Z. C. Taylor and his wife, C. D. Daniel and his wife, E. A. Puthuff and his wife, and Miss Mina Everett surrendered for Brazilian service. Two other Texans, W. D. Powell, who had been active in the Sunday school movement, and Miss Addie Barton volunteered for Mexico.

In this atmosphere of dedication, when the Baptist State Convention convened at Austin in 1880 the women met separately. Their first local missionary society had been organized at Independence two years earlier, with Mrs. F. B. Davis, president, Mary Johnson (later became Mrs. C. H. Wedemeyer), recording secretary, Miss Ann Luther (later Mrs. W. B. Bagby), corresponding secretary, and Miss Roselle Davis (later Mrs. C. S. Robinson), treasurer, as their first officers. At the Austin meeting in 1880 representatives from twelve local societies attended, and the first state body was formed. Mrs. F. B. Davis also became the first president of the state organization, with Miss Addie Breedlove, recording secretary, Mrs. O. C. Pope, corresponding secretary, and Mrs. F. M. Law, treasurer. By 1886 this general body had raised more than $20,000.00 for their missionary activity.

Four years later (July, 1884), the women related to the Baptist General Association organized a similar body at Paris, Texas.

The Deacons' Convention was organized in 1877 principally for the purpose of supporting Buckner Orphans Home. The renewal of the Texas Baptist Education Society in 1869 has already been described.

Rival Newspapers. Adding to the developing rivalry between many of these organizations was the opportunity of influencing Baptist opinion through Baptist newspapers. It will be recalled that the Civil War scuttled the first Baptist paper, the *Texas Baptist,* and that at the close of the war the *Texas Baptist Herald* was begun by J. B. Link at Houston. In 1877 Jonas Johnston bought a half-interest in the *Herald;* at his death in 1881 Link again became sold proprietor. It was moved to Austin in 1883.

On January 3, 1874, the *Religious Messenger* was begun at Paris, Texas, with R. C. Buckner as editor and proprietor. It moved to Dallas in the following year and took the name the *Texas Baptist,* and it was used to promote Buckner Orphans Home. On

June 1, 1883, this was sold to S. A. Hayden. S. J. Anderson bought one-half interest, and became joint editor for two years, but then sold his interest to Hayden in 1885.

There were other papers of various sorts published by Baptists, but the principal controversy in the area of Baptist newspapers occurred between the *Herald* published at Austin by J. B. Link and the *Texas Baptist* at Dallas published by S. A. Hayden. As early as 1870 the *Herald* had been attacked by President Burleson of Waco University for espousing the development of a central university in Texas. For a decade, Burleson opposed the *Herald* and Link. When S. A. Hayden purchased the *Texas Baptist* in 1883, a controversy soon erupted between the *Herald* and the *Baptist*. A great deal of bitterness was reflected in the publications during the next several years.

Additional Sectional Tension

When the Southern Baptist Convention was formed in 1845, the northern benevolent bodies did not immediately withdraw their missionaries from the South. These bodies were the Home Mission Society of New York and the American Baptist Publication Society of Philadelphia. At the close of the Civil War, the Home Mission Society began to increase its missionary force in the South quite rapidly. In 1868, for example, the Society urged all Baptist state bodies to enter into cooperation with them. The Society offered to spend $75,000.00 in fifteen Southern states if those states would raise $43,500.00 for domestic missions. With reference to Texas, the Society offered to spend $3,000.00 on mission work in Texas if Texas Baptists would raise $1,000.00 for the Society.[3]

At the meeting of the Texas Baptist State Convention at Galveston in 1881 the question of state missions had become critical. The Home Mission Board of the Southern Baptist Convention had been unable to assist in the Texas work for about six years. That Board was still almost prostrate in the post-war depression. Evidently the initiative to get assistance from the Home Mission Society of New York, who had not had missionaries in Texas for over thirty years, came from O. C. Pope. Pope visited the Society in

New York on this matter. At the Galveston meeting of the Baptist State Convention, a committee consisting of O. C. Pope, W. C. Crane, F. M. Law, C. R. Breedlove, W. D. Johnson, G. W. Pickett, and J. H. Luther was appointed to take into consideration a plan of co-operation with the American Baptist Home Mission Society in its work in Texas. This "especially strong committee" recommended that the Convention enter into auxiliary relations with the Society.

The Convention adopted an agreement with the Home Mission Society by which the latter "shall appropriate to missionary work in the field of the Texas State Baptist Convention at the rate of one dollar in addition to every dollar raised on the field for the missionary work aforesaid, provided however, that the liability of the A.B.H.M. Society shall not exceed $3,000.00 for the year beginning October 1, 1881, . . ." It was agreed further that all missionaries should be appointed jointly by the Society and the State Convention and make duplicate reports to both bodies. It was also recommended that all contributions for missionary purposes "in the field of the Convention be made to these bodies direct in order that the Convention may have the means for determining on what scale missionary operations can be conducted as well as to avoid irregularities and inequality in the use of such funds."

Following the recommendation of the Society, O. C. Pope was elected corresponding secretary "whose duties shall include the general supervision of the missionary work, the raising of funds for the same, the education of churches in systematic benevolence and the dissemination of information about the work of the Society and of the Convention." J. M. Carroll noted in his history that one of the brethren seemed to feel such action might be construed as disloyalty to the Southern Baptist Convention's Home Mission Board, and offered a resolution commending that Board to the prayers and contributions of the brethren "in view of the benefits conferred upon Texas in the past. . . ."

At this same time the Society also entered into formal cooperation with the East Texas Baptist Convention whereby the Society provided two-fifths of the salaries of missionaries appointed, not to exceed $1,000.00 during the year. In 1882, the Society entered into cooperation with the North Texas Baptist Convention. The Texas Baptist General Association did not request cooperative relationship with the Society.

In 1883, the Home Mission Board of the Southern Baptist Convention proposed to both the State Convention and the General Association that they cooperate on the basis of the southwide Convention matching dollar for dollar to the amount of $3,000.00 per year for mission work. Both bodies promptly accepted this proposition. In addition, during this year the Home Mission Board proposed to the Texas Baptist General Association that they cooperate in employing a general missionary among the colored people on the basis of each paying half of the salary of a man to hold Ministers' Institutes and otherwise helping in the work. W. H. Parks was chosen and put into the field. Already the Texas Baptist State Convention had appointed A. R. Griggs as general missionary to the colored people in cooperation with the Home Mission Society and the State Convention of the colored Baptists.

As a result of the relatively large amount of missionary funds available, the State Convention, which had been struggling arduously to keep a few missionaries on the field, now appointed them in large numbers. At the end of 1885 Pope resigned as corresponding secretary to take a position with the Home Mission Society of New York.

A similar rapid advance took place in the work of the General Association. In 1881 and 1882 the body struggled to keep a few missionaries on the field. However, in 1883, with assistance from the Southern Baptist Convention, and under the leadership of A. J. Holt, the field was flooded with missionaries.

The correspondence of O. C. Pope of the State Convention reflected how much bitterness was involved in this sectional cooperation. After the State Convention had entered into the agreement with the Home Mission Society of New York, E. T. Winkler, president of the Home Mission Board, wrote an article protesting the "intrusion" of the Society into the South. During the next several years Baptist editors North and South entered into a vigorous editorial controversy. The South claimed that the Society should do its work in the North and Northwest (the Mississippi

Valley) and not try to "invade" the South. The Society, on the other hand, said that it did not recognize a line dividing North and South and that it was in the South to stay.

In January, 1885, O. C. Pope wrote a long letter for publication in the journal of the Society. He described how he had visited New York and laid the needs of Texas before the Society. Through his work, the State Convention had entered into cooperation with the Society. He denied that he was disloyal to the Southern Baptist Convention. If by loyalty, he said, you mean that

> . . . one must sit idle and see his State pass into the hands of other denominations, because the Southern Convention cannot supply the destitution; that one must despise and abuse every other organization but the Convention, and refuse to be helped when in distress, except by a Southerner—then I am not loyal, and I pity the narrow, contracted man who is. I see no reason why I should love a Baptist better because he lives in Maryland instead of Pennsylvania, in Kentucky, rather than in Indiana, or in Missouri instead of in Kansas.
>
> I do not think I am disloyal to Texas, or to the South, or to Jesus Christ when I wish, as I sincerely do, that we were less divided into Southern Baptists and Northern Baptist with sectional prejudice and sectional hate, but that American Baptists might be all one in Christ. If this be treason, make the most of it.[4]

In the opening years of the 1880's, therefore, Texas Baptists were in a shattered condition organizationally, and were developing increasing tensions in missionary activity, educational work, and among denominational newspapers. The only explanation for the rapid closing of ranks in 1886 must be found in the Christian maturity and stability of the leaders during that era.

"We Are Brethren"

In 1883, many Texas leaders declared that the existing organizational tension among the Baptist brethren was simply unthinkable. At Cleburne in 1883 B. H. Carroll made a very strong report to the General Association concerning the evils of the present situation. It is true, he said, that

. . . district associations have been divided in council; some rent asunder; churches have been torn by faction, brethren alienated and strife engendered. More than this, the saddest and most lamentable antagonism has been developed on the mission fields. By every consideration of our holy religion this ought not to be.

We venture to express the conviction that with the overwhelming majority of the churches and brethren in all the five general bodies, there is love for each other and no desire for any such conflict. On the contrary, they deplore this evil, and are impatient of its continuance.

Now, therefore, we recommend that this General Association send fraternal greetings to all general bodies in this State in correspondence with us, and respectfully request of each the appointment of a committee of five to meet with a similar committee from our bodies to confer in the spirit of Christ about this matter. And furthermore that these committees, if agreeable to other bodies sending them, confer together on the subject of State unification. . . .

In the following year at Paris, Corresponding Secretary A. J. Holt said to the General Association:

I speak my heart to the brotherhood in these words. I do not enter the field as a champion for the General Association. I shall not allow myself to become a sectionalist. My first work as a minister of Jesus in Texas was done in the State Convention. For seven years I lived and laboured in her bounds. No man can excel me in admiration and love for her choice spirits. When I left the Indian Territory I stopped at the first place I came to in Texas, just because I was not able to go any further. Thus I came to be a member of the General Association. My heart is state-wide, world-wide in its love for the brethren. But I do feel especially called upon to labor for the upbuilding of the Master's cause in that particular field where my lot is cast. I should feel the same way were I in Rio de Janeiro.[5]

The Achievement of Unification

The remarkable element in the unification of 1886 was the rapidity with which so many diverse movements were brought together. The story of unifying the general bodies and the educational institutions provides some overlapping, but for clarity they will be considered one at a time.

Consolidation of the Conventions. The General Association moved first toward unification of Texas Baptists. It will be recalled that B. H. Carroll in 1883 presented a resolution to that body urging that the several conventions appoint committees to discuss the question of state unification. Evidently there had been some spadework. Carroll, as a matter of fact, had preached before the State Convention at its 1882 session in Belton. It was unfortunate that at the 1883 meeting of the State Convention at San Antonio, the North Texas Convention, ". . . which, because of some feeling, had gone right out of the heart of the General Association territory," applied for affiliation with the State Convention and was admitted. A committee from the General Association had appeared at San Antonio with a proposition for unification from the Association, but instead the State Convention voted to recognize the North Texas Convention, which had broken with the General Association just four years before. This undoubtedly delayed statewide unification for several years. To make matters worse, the State Convention then adopted a resolution welcoming to its membership "all general Baptist organizations, district associations, churches or individuals in any part of the State of Texas who may desire it on the basis of membership prescribed by the constitution of the Convention."

However, at the July, 1885, meeting of the General Association that body again took the initiative for consolidation. A resolution was adopted which said that "the interest of our denomination in the State would be best subserved by the existence of one general body, and that this Association is willing to cooperate with other general bodies for the accomplishment of this end, on terms honorable and equal to all." When the State Convention met three months later, a resolution was passed noting that a desire had been widely expressed for the consolidation of the missionary bodies in the State and authorizing the appointment of a committee of five "to confer with any like committee that may have been, or may hereafter be appointed by the other bodies. . . ." This committee of the State Convention consisted of G. W. Smith, J. B. Link, A. S. Broaddus, Abram Weaver, and R. T. Hanks.

At a called session on November 25, 1885, the General Association appointed a similar committee composed of R. C. Burleson, W.

J. Brown, R. C. Buckner, H. B. Pender, and J. T. S. Park. At the same time the Association appointed a committee of fifteen in connection with consolidation of the schools and gave these twenty men "plenary powers to act for this body in all matters pertaining to consolidation of general bodies, provided the State Convention shall appoint a like committee with plenary powers."

The State Convention appointed a similar committee with plenary powers, and on December 9, the combined group met at Temple. Representing the General Association were J. W. Speight, J. M. Anderson, R. S. Taylor, M. D. Herring, R. C. Burleson, J. S. Allen, E. A. Sturgis, J. W. Gooch, John T. Flint, M. H. Standifer, J. C. McCreary, J. E. Elgin, A. M. Harris, Richard Coke, F. L. Carroll, W. B. Denson, R. C. Buckner, W. H. Trolinger, S. J. Anderson, J. B. Baker, J. W. Moffatt, J. W. Bryce, L. L. Foster, B. H. Carroll, S. L. Morris, S. A. Hayden, Kit Williams, A. J. Holt, D. I. Smyth, E. R. Freeman, and J. L. Whittle. Representing the State Convention were F. M. Law, A. W. Dunn, H. W. Waters, C. R. Breedlove, G. W. Capps, J. B. Link, R. J. Sledge, R. Andrews, O. H. P. Garrett, M. V. Smith, Harry Haynes, G. W. Breedlove, L. R. Bryan, Hosea Garrett, A. W. McIver, A. T. Spalding, William Howard, J. H. Stribling, Isaac Sellers, S. A. Beauchamp, A. Weaver, J. A. Hackett, W. R. Maxwell, C. C. Garrett, and S. F. Styles. These names are listed partly to show how few of the veterans of the older body were still in service and partly to enroll the new leaders in the pages of history. This group met for two purposes: to discuss the possible consolidation of Baylor and Waco universities, and to look to the possible unification of the general bodies. The former purpose will be considered shortly. The two five-man committees on unification of the general bodies met and presented the following recommendation to the joint session, which had been clothed with plenary powers to consummate the union:

We, your committee, believing that the consolidation of general bodies is desirable, recommend:

1. That the Baptist General Association of Texas be consolidated with the Baptist State Convention of Texas.

2. That the name of the consolidated body shall be "The Baptist General Convention of Texas."

3. That the basis of representation in the first meeting of the consolidated body shall be the same as heretofore. . . .

4. That the mission work be continued until the first meeting as heretofore under the direction of the two general bodies respectively, and be supported until that meeting.

5. That the first meeting of the consolidated body be held at Waco, beginning on Tuesday after the first Sunday in July, 1886.

This was adopted and the State Convention and General Association were thereby dissolved as separate bodies. J. M. Carroll, who attended the meeting, remarked that this, as well as the educational unification, represented a Christian compromise, with no party really securing just what it wanted.

It will be recalled that the East Texas Baptist Convention was formed in 1877. It had eight annual sessions and did a creditable work in east Texas from 1877 to 1885. In the latter year this Convention voted to disband and unite with the consolidated body.

The Central Texas Baptist Convention, which had been a separate body from 1880, also voted in 1885 to unite with the consolidated body. Total unification of all general bodies was thereby effectively secured.

Consolidation of Baylor at Independence and Waco University. After the Civil War a movement began to develop one central Baptist university in Texas. The reasons given for this were many: the principal existing schools at Independence and Waco were bitter rivals; the Independence location had been by-passed by the railroads and was almost inaccessible in bad weather; Texas Baptists could only support one first class university; supporters of schools at Independence and Waco and elsewhere in the state would never agree to relinquish their school in favor of any of those now existing; national educational circles were encouraging unification into an orderly system.

Considerable agitation pro and con continued until 1875 when the Central Baptist Educational Commission of Texas was formed for the purpose of raising $250,000.00 to found a central university which would be other than one of the existing schools. F. M. Law became the agent to raise these funds, and in two years he had led in securing over $80,000.00 in notes and lands. However, the movement began to wane and in 1884 the Commission dissolved, the assets reverting to the contributors or being disposed of according to their wishes.

Despite the uncertainty involved in these proceedings, both Baylor at Independence and Waco University made some progress, as described earlier. However, on February 27, 1885, there came a blow that for all practical purposes marked the end of Baylor at Independence. This was the death of President William Carey Crane, a noble and competent scholar. J. M. Carroll judged that "for more than twenty years the school had lived, and lived to a great purpose, largely through the transfusion of his own rich blood and the investment of his great life."[6] For a year Reddin Andrews, Jr. served as president at Independence, but the death knell of the school had been sounded. It was probably this situation more than anything else that caused the Baptist State Convention to look favorably toward unification of the several Baptist general bodies in the state as a means of solving the problem of the school. When the Baylor University trustees met on June 3, 1885, and subsequently on June 16 jointly with trustees of Baylor College, the whole question of the removal and consolidation of Baylor University with Waco University was referred to the State Convention for a decision. Reluctantly, that body voted removal from Independence, which prepared the way for the negotiations with the Baptist General Association, who operated Waco University. Baylor Female College was making relatively good progress at Independence when the State Convention decided upon removal. As suggested previously, Waco University was also prospering at this time under the leadership of President R. C. Burleson.

The matter of consolidating Baylor University with Waco University was closly related to unifying the two missionary conventions. The joint meeting on December 9, 1885, at Temple, resulted in an agreement that Baylor and Waco universities be consolidated under the name Baylor University to be located at Waco. The female department of Waco University was to be continued as it existed, with the suggestion that Baylor Female College be located elsewhere than at Independence. The consolidation of the two universities was thus consummated. Baylor Female College moved to Belton, opening there in September, 1886. The property at Independence was proffered to Union Association, who endeavored to operate a new school there, William Carey Crane College, but the school soon failed. The historic and valuable property at Independence was lost to Texas Baptists at that time through a questionable legal decision relative to its ownership.

Consolidation of the Two Baptist Newspapers. After the large steps of unifying the general bodies and the two universities were taken, there still remained the touchy question of the existence of two rival newspapers—the *Texas Baptist Herald* edited by J. B. Link and the *Texas Baptist* edited by S. A. Hayden. In contrast with the other unifying efforts, the denomination really had little jurisdiction in this matter because the papers were privately owned.

During the year following consolidation of the general bodies, the two editors and denominational committees many times met and discussed and disagreed on many points. Finally, a joint committee representing both papers agreed upon all but one thing; namely, where a consolidated paper should be located. Link preferred Waco, while Hayden wanted Dallas. It was finally agreed to ask the messengers attending the Convention at Waco in 1886 for a sort of straw vote on the matter. On July 1, 1886, not in an official sense but simply as an opinion, the messengers at Waco chose Dallas by a majority of one vote out of several hundred cast. A few hours after this vote, Hayden agreed to pay Link $10,000.00 for his paper, and Link was employed as co-editor for a few months. The new joint paper was called the *Texas Baptist and Herald*.

Unification of the Women's Work. The Texas Baptist Woman's Missionary Union (related to the State Convention) and the Ladies' General Aid Society (related to the General Association) were dissolved in 1886 and the two groups were united under the name Baptist Women Mission Workers. This name was retained until 1919 when it was changed to Woman's Missionary Union to parallel the name used by Baptist women in their organizations in other states. Mrs. Fannie Breedlove Davis was elected president and Mrs. S. J. Anderson became corresponding secretary.

Consolidation of the Sunday School Conventions. Although the move to bring consolidation of these two bodies (one affiliating with the State Convention and one with the General Association) was initiated later than similar movements to unify the general bodies, the schools, and the newspapers, the effort was successful earlier. After a meeting of committees from the two Sunday school bodies in 1884, the union was consummated in July, 1885. It is likely that the quick agreement in this area had an influence upon the successful consolidation of the general bodies and the schools that took place later on in the year.

Pure Religion and Undefiled. . . .

One of the great influences in keeping the hearts of Texas Baptists tender and responsive through the years has been the Buckner Orphans Home. Generally, the first evening session of the Baptist General Convention during its early years provided the opportunity for presenting the needs of the orphans.

> High tides of tenderest sentiment and religious fervor have often arisen during these evenings and swept on through the succeeding sessions, to the sweetening and inspiriting of all. The appeal of the Home to the hearts and purses of the laymen has helped pastors everywhere to win a way to their hearts for every other cause fostered by our Baptist brotherhood.[7]

Robert Cooke Buckner, in whose heart and noble character the orphans' home was conceived and nurtured, was born January 3, 1833, at Madisonville, Tennessee. He was educated at Georgetown College and by personal study completed the equivalent of a seminary course. He served as pastor and denominational worker in Kentucky, moving to Texas in 1859 in an effort to improve his health. Here he became successful pastor of the Paris church, then turned to the editorship of the *Religious Messenger* and the *Texas Baptist*. In the latter paper on December 7, 1877, he began a series of letters addressed to the deacons of Texas stating his intention of founding an orphanage which should be under the control of Baptist deacons.

Buckner himself described the story in the 1893 minutes of the General Convention: how on July 17, 1878, a deacons' convention met in Paris and named Buckner General Superintendent of an orphans' home yet to be established; how on December 2, 1879, in a rented cottage in Dallas, the Home officially opened with three children; how on September 25, 1880, Buckner selected a tract of forty-four acres on which the Home was to be built; how two days later five deacons, representing a quorum of the Board of Directors, led by Buckner, purchased the land and dedicated it and a small cedar log house as the new Home; and how on April 5, 1881, in a new frame house large enough for twenty-five children, the Home was opened on its own property with $59.45 balance after paying $841.19 for the erection of the house. On July 15, 1883, the Home Baptist Church was constituted with Buckner as pastor.

It should be mentioned that R. C. Buckner's relation to the Home was unique. The Directors voted him unconditional authority as General Manager. He purchased land, borrowed from the bank for improvements, and carried the financial obligations personally from the beginning. Yet all deeds were made to the Home, and the selfless Superintendent and founder mortgaged his own property to provide unencumbered titles for the Home.

The founding of such a blessed institution should rank with the great unification of 1886 in the important events of this period.

9

Finding Direction
(1886–1914)

☆ ☆ ☆

The journey of Texas Baptists from 1886 to 1914 was a turbulent one. The American nation was undergoing profound changes, by the turn of the century assuming the stature of a world power. Texas, too, was being transformed. Her population doubled; black gold was discovered all across the state; industry began to develop. The vast areas of west Texas were opened to relatively safe living. The Indian threat vanished, partly through the efforts of the United States army, more from courageous service by the Texas Rangers, perhaps mainly because buffalo hunters exterminated the meat supply of the Plains Indians.

In the midst of this turbulence, Texas Baptists made considerable progress, outdistancing population statistics in their growth and devising improved structures for benevolent activities. To provide a glimpse of the principal events of this period, this chapter will successively discuss organizational beginnings under the new consolidated structure, six painful confrontations through internal controversies, enlargement of the missionary thrust, a rash of Baptist schools, the development of many peripheral ministries, and some portents of the future.

The Shape of the New Convention

At the initial meeting of the Baptist General Convention of Texas in 1886, a constitutional committee was appointed consisting

153

of B. H. Carroll, F. M. Law, R. T. Hanks, W. H. Dodson, and
E. Z. F. Golden, representing both the old State Convention and
the General Association. A word should be said concerning the
nature of the constitution that was adopted.

The first four articles of the new constitution of the united body
followed almost precisely the old constitution of the General Association. Article II on Membership declared that the body was
composed of messengers from regular Baptist churches, and associations of Baptist churches, and Baptist missionary societies. Each
church was entitled to two messengers plus one additional messenger for each $25.00 contributed to the funds of the Convention,
but no church was allowed more than eight messengers. Each
association was allowed two messengers plus one additional messenger for each $100.00 expended in missionary work within its own
bounds, and one additional messenger for every $100.00 contrib-
uted to the funds of the Convention. Any Baptist missionary society was allowed one messenger for every $25.00 contributed to
the funds of the body, but no society could have more than four
messengers. Article III specifically said that all donations would be
designated and strictly applied according to the expressed will of
the donor. Article IV described the officers of the Convention. As
suggested, these first four Articles are taken almost word for word
from the old constitution of the General Association.

However, Article V completely departed from the philosophy of
the General Association, which annually had appointed a number
of boards to take care of the several benevolences fostered by the
General Association. This was the pattern of the Southern Baptist
Convention, which annually elected portions of Boards to carry on
the benevolent work of the Convention between sessions of the
body. The Baptist General Convention of Texas, however, in the
new constitution of 1886 adopted a feature which the State Convention had included in its constitution from the very beginning in
1848; namely, the annual election of a Board of Directors which
was authorized to handle convention business during the recess of
the annual body. This Board of Directors anticipated the formation
of an Executive Board subsequently structured by the Baptist
General Convention of Texas, as well as the Executive Committee
begun by the Southern Baptist Convention in 1917.

In addition to this Board of Directors, the constitution of 1886 provided for four other Boards: a Board of Trustees for Baylor University; a Board of Trustees for Baylor Female College; a Board of Trustees for the Baptist General Convention to hold properties and invested funds; and a Minister's Relief Board. Thus, in a sense, Article V of the constitution of 1886 united the best features of the State Convention and the General Association with respect to administration.

No change was made in the plan for financing the work of the new body. Usually cash offerings and pledges were taken at the annual meeting. The pledges, plus additional offerings and gifts, were collected by the Corresponding Secretary during the year. These gifts were generally listed in complete detail in the annual minutes of the body, both to inspire others to give and to provide accurate records that could be publicly checked. Corresponding to the major emphasis of one source of their income, Texas Baptists generally held a "fall round-up" and a "spring round-up" by which the benevolent work of the convention could be sustained. The united body wavered at first in setting forth the financial extent of its program, then began to suggest plans based upon a specified amount of money which it was thought could be raised during the year. Missionaries were appointed and institutions were assisted on the basis of estimated receipts. The funds expended were generally borrowed from banks in anticipation of the fall and spring offerings.

Fierce Controversies

Texas Baptists were divided over six controversies which raged during the last decade of the century. These will be considered briefly in the chronological order of their appearance, although some were considerably more significant than others. Three of them (Martinism, Haydenism, and Fortunism) were distinctly Texas quarrels, while the other three were southwide controversies that had their reflection in Texas Baptist life.

Martinism. This controversy sprang from the views of M. T. Martin, who as a member of the First Baptist Church of Waco expressed opinions as a young preacher in 1888 and 1889 that suggested unscriptural views on the subject of faith and assurance. In March, 1889, B. H. Carroll and the deacons of the church had a formal conference with the young minister, who not only declined to change his views but also applied for a letter of dismission so that he might join another church.

Whereupon, the deacons brought charges against him for teaching "doctrines contrary to our acknowledged standard of faith and polity, thereby causing division and trouble in our denomination." He was charged with the violation of six doctrines which were specifically identified as being a part of the New Hampshire and Philadelphia Confessions of Faith. With the concurrence of other Waco pastors, Martin was tried and convicted, and his credentials as a minister were withdrawn. He was then granted a dismission as a layman.

He departed soon thereafter to Georgia, where he was licensed to preach by a church there. He returned to Texas and joined the Marlin church, which was also in fellowship with the Waco Association. In a church council by the Marlin church on November 28, 1889, it was voted that Martin should be restored to his former ministerial functions. At a church conference on December 1, 1889, the Marlin Baptist Church asked the Waco church to restore the credentials of Martin. If this could not be done, they inquired, would it be a bar to fellowship between the Waco church and the Marlin church if the latter should invest him with credentials? Before the Waco church made official reply, the Marlin church restored the credentials of Martin in February, 1890.

At the meeting of the Waco Association, the Waco church preferred charges against the Marlin church because it had "violated Gospel order, the sanctity of discipline, the comity acknowledged by the Baptist churches, Christ's law of love and fellowship binding the churches, and has brought our form of church government into reproach in the presence of its enemies." As a result, fellowship was withdrawn from the Marlin church.

In the following year, after personal conferences, the Marlin church was restored to fellowship. As late as 1895 the Waco Association took notice of the extensive confusion caused by the preaching of Martin, and urged that all Baptist bodies declare non-fellowship for the doctrines and followers of Martin. In that year the state convention adopted a resolution to the effect that anyone presenting himself as a messenger who believed or taught Martinism should be rejected.

Gospel Missionism. Another controversy affecting Texas Baptists involved T. P. Crawford, a veteran missionary of China, and the Foreign Mission Board of the Southern Baptist Convention. Early in his missionary career in China, Crawford had witnessed abuses in the use of mission funds. As early as June, 1884, Crawford insisted upon a conference with the Foreign Mission Board relative to the best method of carrying on foreign mission work. On October 27, 1884, a special committee of the Board along with missionaries from Africa and Italy, heard the statements of Crawford, who at this time advocated confining appropriations strictly to work done by missionaries, and eliminating native workers. The Committee felt that such a change in policy would be unwise. After several years of agitation, Crawford published a book entitled, *Churches, To the Front!,* in which he openly attacked in very strong language the use of Boards and Conventions in missionary work. The local church, he said, not a Board, should be the agency by which missionary work should be done. All missionaries should be self-supporting, and native helpers, subsidy money, and Board control of the missionaries should be eliminated.

This movement had important repercussions in China and in some of the States along the seaboard, but in Texas the principal result was the withholding of funds from the Foreign Mission Board. Many were indoctrinated with the idea that Boards should be eliminated to save expenses, and mission money should go from the churches on a direct route to the missionaries. These arguments greatly impressed some Texans, for they reflected the local church emphasis of J. R. Graves, who had been very influential in Texas for an entire generation. The movement was also important in that it emphasized the cleavage between churches and Boards, quite similar to the disagreement in the Hayden controversy.

Haydenism. This controversy was probably the most virulent of all the quarrels Texas Baptists have ever known. It had roots that were quite complex, involving partly a clash between personalities, a popular appeal to democratic and church authority as over against centralization, and a renewal of other tensions in church and denominational life in Texas. Its importance may be measured by the fact that it brought J. B. Gambrell to Texas to lead the fight against it, and it provided the determinative answer in the ecclesiological issue that had been raised both in Martinism and Gospel Missionism. These controversies had agitated the question of whether sovereign churches made up the state bodies, or whether the Convention was composed of individual messengers who neither brought authority from the churches nor carried authority back from the Convention.

The agitation began when S. A. Hayden, a member of the Executive Board and the editor of the *Baptist Standard*, wrote a letter on April 2, 1894, to all members of the Executive Board with a complaint that the expenses of the Board, particularly the salaries paid to some of the leadership, were excessive. He said that some of the missionaries were in great financial need, the debt of the state body was increasing year by year, and the work being done was decreasing annually. The Board met one week later and appointed a committee to investigate the charges set out in this letter. The committee report sustained the operation as it was being conducted and denied the allegations of imbalance. B. H. Carroll offered a conciliatory resolution designed to placate Hayden and at the same time to defend the administration of the work.

However, Hayden began publishing his allegations in his newspaper and became increasingly critical. A called meeting of the Board was held on June 26–27, 1894, and in the resolutions adopted at this time, there was evidence of a hardening of the position against Hayden. When the Baptist General Convention met at Marshall in the fall of 1894, there came additional friction between the followers of the two groups. Unfortunately, distinguished names were counted on each side of the controversy. Rufus C. Burleson, who had been president of the General Convention, had publicly taken the side of Hayden, and evidently as a direct result was not reelected to his office with the Convention. The Corresponding Secretary, J. M. Carroll, was unanimously reelected, and it was reported that all of the debts of the body had been paid as a result of a brief campaign. However, J. M. Carroll later lamented, the new Convention year in 1895 began "with an empty treasury and with a field that had recently been closely gleaned and also with an unsilenced and unweakened opposition."[1] Carroll announced that the illness of his wife demanded that he resign the office of Corresponding Secretary, and in January, 1895, he was replaced by M. D. Early.

The Hayden attacks on the leadership of the Convention subsided somewhat during the year 1895, primarily because of the agitation over the Martinite and Fortunite quarrels. However, in 1896 the explosion took place. The Board gave an extensive report of the work done during the previous year and called attention to the harsh attacks by Hayden. "Very crushing have been his burdens and responsibilities and sorely has his administration been shot at by the archers," remarked B. H. Carroll concerning the stewardship of Early during the year. In the report, signed by W. H. Jenkins, president of the Board, and George W. Truett, secretary of the Board, it was noted that in cooperation among Baptists, the leadership becomes contemptible if it is not protected from the contempt of the constituency. In dramatic sentences, the report came to its climax:

> For several years past an agent has been at work in our state Capitol undermining the mission work, drying up the mission spirit, and sowing down our once fertile fields with salt. That agent has persistently, ruthlessly, and openly in public print attacked this board, its methods and work, charging it directly and indirectly, and by various methods of innuendo and insinuation, with misappropriation, wanton extravagance, and reckless waste of public funds. Through an unwitting instrument, unconscious of what he was led by him to sign, he has published virtual charges of embezzlement against the secretary, and by fair implication, the board itself. With this agent nothing pertaining to this work is sacred or ever settled. He evinces open disrespect of the decisions of this body, going back each year behind its approved and finished work to dig up and galvanize such issues or events as by his unrighteous use of them may best contribute to add to the general distrust, discord and divisions he himself has gendered. . . .
>
> . . . Is there no end of patience? Shall sickly sentimentality about peace forever usurp the throne of justice? Shall we wait until the

mission cause, now bleeding, is stamped out of existence? Who, then, is this agent? His name is S. A. Hayden, of Dallas.[2]

This report recommended that Hayden not be allowed a seat in the body. However, six of the forty-eight members of the Board entered a protest against the recommendation against Hayden on the ground that the Board of Directors did not have the right to arraign a person for trial before the Convention. Finally, after much wrangling, a motion was passed expressing by the Convention "their strong disapproval and condemnation of the course of said Hayden, as editor and publisher of a Baptist paper, in persistently attacking through the columns of said paper, editorially and otherwise, the board of directors of this Convention, both as individuals, and as the servants of this Convention, in reference to the matters entrusted to them by this Convention." A protest containing thirty-three signatures was made to this action. Rufus C. Burleson, president of Baylor University, was one of the principal signers. Among the four items of protest, the second raised the ecclesiological issue that finally became central. It asserted "that the arraignment of an individual, apart from the church from which he was an accredited messenger, is in direct conflict with the constitution of this body, and the usages of Baptists the world over."

In the midst of this controversy, M. D. Early was unanimously reelected corresponding secretary over his protest; he promptly resigned the office. The Board chose James Bruton Gambrell of Georgia as Early's successor. He began his work in December of 1896, and his first activity was an attempt to bring reconciliation with Hayden. His efforts were unsuccessful.

When the state convention was held on November 5–9, 1897, in San Antonio, Hayden was refused a seat at the Convention after almost four days of controversy. This action seemed to loosen the restraint of Hayden altogether. He charged that the whole issue was a struggle between the Board of the Convention and the churches of Texas; he condemned the "Roman Catholic" policy of withholding information from the people; he caricatured the work by suggesting that the Board would pay $5.00 each for baptizing adults, $2.50 each for children under fifteen, $100.00 each for bankers, etc. Also, he said, the Board would give $200.00 for organizing a board party church of twenty or more members; would pay $125.00 for splitting an independent Baptist church; for abusing Hayden, $5.00; and $2.50 for telling that Hayden was dead. He addressed Gambrell as "my dear pontiff," and said that he himself would be true to the interests of the pontiff if he were given a paying position. Hayden also distributed a special edition of his paper at the meeting of the Southern Baptist Convention in Norfolk, Virginia, airing his charges and sullying the name of Texas Baptists. The Convention refused to seat Hayden again in 1898.

The issue finally reached a climax in 1899 when the Convention met in Dallas, the center of Hayden strength. His party nominated candidates for all of the offices of the Convention. The amount of support for the Hayden movement can be glimpsed in the fact that the opposition got about half as many votes as the incumbents. For example, R. C. Buckner received 1,424 votes for president, while Hayden's candidate, H. B. Pender, received 760 votes. Total messengers numbered 2,494. However, after the defeat of the Hayden party in the election, there came a deterioration in the strength of the movement. An amendment was offered (the first amendment to the constitution since it was adopted in 1886) which stated that if any church, association, or society shall by a majority vote of the Convention be declared to be in an attitude of general or continued hostility or unfriendliness to the work or purposes of the Convention, or when any person is declared to be in such attitude, then such church or association or society shall by majority vote be denied the privilege of sending messengers to the Convention, and such person shall be denied a seat as a messenger from any other body. This, remarked J. M. Carroll, completely stopped the long wrangles at the sessions of the Convention. It was repealed in 1913, partly because loyal members of the Convention feared it might be used to coerce legitimate dissent.

On April 28, 1898, Hayden filed a suit for $100,000.00 damages against thirty-three leaders of the Convention for denying him a seat. Subsequently, three additional suits were filed. Seven years later, on April 28, 1905, J. B. Cranfill, without the knowledge of any of the other defendents, paid $100.00 and court costs in each of the cases to end the litigation. Cranfill felt that Hayden was thriving on the continued litigation and that the Convention was compromising its dignity in continuing in this way.

Meanwhile, a new Baptist body emerged from this schism. After several unofficial meetings of the followers of Hayden, the East Texas Baptist Convention (whose name was changed in a few months to the Baptist Missionary Association) was organized at Troup, Texas, on July 6, 1900. Although Hayden had objected to organizing a separate body, he aligned himself with this body until his death in 1918. Several efforts to reunite this body with the Texas General Convention in the twentieth century have failed.

This controversy articulated the basic ecclesiology that has been held by Texas Baptists since that time. Hayden contended that the Convention consisted of the sovereign churches which sent their delegates and that the Convention could not refuse to seat the accredited delegates without overwhelming the authority of the church. The ruling by President R. C. Buckner was that the Convention consisted of messengers who had no delegated power from the churches. As a matter of fact, this question had arisen at the Belton convention in 1895 in connection with the Martinite controversy. At that time, after considerable discussion and the appointment of a committee, the Convention voted that "the Convention is composed of persons chosen by churches, associations, and missionary societies as their messengers, and that when said persons are convened they, and not the churches are the Convention.[3] Three years later, at the Waco convention, Burleson confirmed the ruling that the Convention was composed of messengers, not of churches.

Fortunism. George M. Fortune, who became pastor of the First Baptist Church of Paris, Texas, in the fall of 1891, created an exciting controversy in 1894 when he published two sermons on the atonement which were widely circulated in the state. At the 1895 Convention his views were condemned, and on February 11, 1896, an *ex-parte* council met at Paris and condemned a dozen of his beliefs, including his doctrine of inspiration, of the substitutionary death of Christ, and many other views he had championed.

Fortune continued to preach to the church until the summer of 1897, when he abandoned the church and the ministry and opened a law office in Indian Territory. Suit was entered to recover the church property by the minority, who constituted the Baptists still holding to the doctrines and practices that had characterized the church before the controversy. However, on January 15, 1900, the Supreme Court of Texas awarded the property to the majority, even though that group had departed from the original doctrines and practices of the church.[4]

The Whitsitt Controversy. During the Hayden controversy in 1896, Texas Baptists entered into another southwide controversy over the views of President W. H. Whitsitt of the Southern Baptist Theological Seminary in Louisville, Kentucky. A resolution was passed condemning Whitsitt's interpretation of Baptist history, and earnestly requesting the trustees of the Seminary to bring a report on the matter to the Southern Baptist Convention which would meet at Wilmington, North Carolina, in the following spring. In the following year, after a great deal of discussion about Whitsitt's views on Baptist history, a committee was appointed by the Texas body, which said that the seminary and the work of the Boards of the Southern Baptist Convention were being affected by all of this agitation. It was urged that Whitsitt should retire from his position as president of the Southern Baptist Theological Seminary, or, if he were unwilling to do so, he should be retired by the trustees. B. H. Carroll reflected this attitude at the Southern Baptist Convention in the following year when he announced that he would propose a constitutional amendment cutting off the Seminary from the support of the Convention. However, Whitsitt resigned in 1898, and the controversy died away.

The Sunday School Literature Controversy. The last of the six controversies in Texas during this period involved the competition between the Southern Baptist Sunday School Board, which had been organized in 1891, and the older American Baptist Publication Society of Philadelphia. J. B. Gambrell had been a member of a committee at Birmingham in 1890 that had established the Southern Board, and had been outspoken in favor of allowing each individual or church in the South to purchase literature from either the Publication Society of the North or the Sunday School Board of the South. The Publication Society had assisted Texas in many ways in its work, including providing colportage wagons for the distribution of tracts.

On March 18, 1896, the Publication Society made a proposition to the Sunday School Board that the Society should publish all the literature for the South, in return for which it would pay the Board one-half of the profits on the series. This began several years of agitation in Southern Baptist life. At the meeting of the Convention in Wilmington, North Carolina, in May, 1897, J. M. Robertson, one of the Texas Baptist leaders and also district Bible Secretary for the Society, made an open attack on the program of the Sunday School Board from the platform of the Southern Convention. The backlash from this attack, however, undermined the Publication Society in its place among Southern Baptists, and many who had not favored the Sunday School Board now became its champions.

The Missionary Thrust

How much benevolent work can be accomplished, one asks, with the frequent changes in leadership, the bitter controversies, the financial depression, and the years of excessive drouth that occurred in the 1890's? A glance at the records shows that between 1886 and 1900 a surprising amount of state, home, and foreign missionary activity occurred. After 1900, the accelerated progress made in these areas marked this as a distinct period in missionary growth.

A. J. Holt's Administration (1886–89). As indicated in discussing the controversies, there were five corresponding secretaries between 1886 and 1914. None served more than three years and there can be little doubt that the harsh attacks of S. A. Hayden were influential in driving four of them out of office. A. J. Holt served from 1886 to 1889, but due to an unfortunate disagreement in his church at Dallas, he declined to accept reelection. During his term of service, the amount raised for state missions increased each year, the total in 1889 being $19,237.78. The number of missionaries among the Anglo-Americans fluctuated, with an average of about 115 employed annually. The first mission church among the Mexicans was begun at Laredo in 1887. In the same year, in cooperation with the Negro convention, twenty-six missionaries were employed to work with them. In 1888 and 1889, two missionaries worked among the Mexicans, while in those two years the Negro missionaries increased to twenty-seven and thirty, respectively. In addition, in 1888 two missionaries were employed to work among the Germans, while in the following year five missionaries worked among the Germans and one among the Scandinavians, the first worker to be employed for this latter group. In the three years covered by his service, Holt reported that about eight thousand people were converted through the work of the missionaries and about three hundred and seventy-two churches were organized.

J. B. Cranfill's Administration (1899–92). When A. J. Holt declined reelection in 1889, J. B. Cranfill was chosen to succeed him. In both of the years for which Cranfill reported, an excellent showing was made. In 1890 there were 121 missionaries among the Anglos, plus five with the Mexicans, three with the Germans, thirty in cooperation with the Negroes, and 103 churches organized. In 1891 he reported the largest number of missionaries ever employed by Texas Baptists, a total of 143, with $35,510.00 (including cooperative work) raised. Four active mission churches were serving the Mexicans, four missionaries were at work among the Germans, and thirty-five missionaries were employed cooperatively with the Negroes. A total of 107 new churches were organized during the year. Cranfill evidenced continuing interest in the frontier, which now was the Panhandle area and the western high plains. In his last report, Cranfill mentioned that three new associations had been formed in the Panhandle, while farther south one new association had been organized involving thirteen new churches. At San Angelo a new association was organized and the outlook was bright.

In 1889 J. M. Carroll was named Statistical Secretary of the Convention, and in 1890 he made his first report. Carroll felt that his figures were below the actual numbers because of poor reporting, but "they are the best that could be secured." His report showed 87 associations composed of 2,221 churches, who had baptized 10,598 in that year. The net gain in membership was shown as 8,987. Church buildings were reported as numbering 406, valued at over $647,000.00. There were about sixteen pastor's homes reported with a value of almost $43,000.00. Of the 2,221 churches, 376 were without pastors; 1,318 contributed nothing to associational missions, 1,410 contributed nothing to foreign missions, 2,033 contributed nothing to home missions, and nearly one-half of the churches failed to contribute to any kind of missions. Carroll estimated that there were 1,971 Baptist preachers in the state, of whom 889 were pastors, 169 were state and associational missionaries, and 78 of these missionaries were also pastors.

During 1890, Corresponding Secretary Cranfill began a monthly paper devoted exclusively to the mission work of the Convention, taking the title *State Mission Journal*. Under various names and with occasional lapses, this paper continued for over twenty years. Cranfill resigned on March 31, 1892, to assist in beginning a new Baptist paper, the *Baptist Standard*. J. M. Carroll was named as his successor and took office on April 1, 1892.

J. M. Carroll's Administration (1892–94). J. M. Carroll served during the period from April 1, 1892, to December 31, 1894. In each of the three years of his service, Carroll reported that approximately $18,000.00 (including the assistance from the Home Mission Board) was raised each year for state missions. As will be pointed out, Carroll was entrusted with raising funds for home missions, foreign missions, and old minister's relief, in addition to state missions. As a typical year, in 1893 he reported that the state work was still in debt, as it had been in the previous year, but named a number of items that contributed to the difficulty in raising money, including the campaign for Baylor University, the resignation of several key figures in the organization, the widespread drouth that had brought great suffering, and the financial depression. Carroll's report was vivid in describing each of these deterrents, and particularly the last named:

> Then came the financial depression. We do not remember anything like it. It seemed at times as if the bottom would drop out of everything. The whole country seemed on the verge of bankruptcy. Banks and mercantile houses were failing. Manufactories, mines, and

mills were suspending work. Thousands of people were being thrown out of employment. Money could not be had at any interest. Those few who had money became frightened and hid it away.[5]

Early that year, despite these handicaps Carroll said that over $11,000.00 had been collected on the field, while three missionaries had been sustained among the Germans, three among the Swedes, five among the Mexicans, sixteen among the Negroes, and seventy-eight among the Anglos. Carroll estimated the strength of Baptists in Texas as being 130,000 members, with 2,300 preachers, 2,400 churches, and 92 district associations among the whites. The Negroes had 90,000 members, 1,343 churches, 900 preachers, and 32 district associations.[6]

M. D. Early's Administration (1894–96). J. M. Carroll resigned on December 31, 1894, and immediately M. D. Early was elected to fill the remainder of the year and served, in addition, one more year. Under the circumstances, with the increasing agitation by Hayden, Early gave excellent leadership. A total of $17,739.19 (including $4,000.00 from the Home Mission Board) was available for state missions, in which 93 missionaries were employed, who organized 77 new churches, and reported 1,516 baptisms in 1895. During this year the American Baptist Publication Society donated a chapel car, which was quite useful in railroad centers in the distribution of tracts and the preaching of the gospel. A. S. Stuckey and his wife were in charge of the car, which was maintained by Texas Baptists for several years. In 1896, only a little more than $11,000.00 was raised in cash for state missions, which reported only sixty-six missionaries. All of the work was suffering from the controversy initiated by Hayden during this time.

J. B. Gambrell's Administration (1896–1910). Early abruptly resigned as Corresponding Secretary after his election in the 1896 election, and J. B. Gambrell of Georgia was chosen as his successor. Gambrell began his work in December, 1896. A debt on the state mission fund of $1,700.00 was paid, and over $18,000.00 was raised for state missions, by which 66 missionaries were supported. In the years 1898–1900, the leadership of Gambrell, the loosening of the depression, and relatively good crops in Texas reflected increases in the receipts and the reports of the work done. In 1898, 122 missionaries were employed; in 1899, 149; and in 1900, 164. Baptisms into the mission churches were 997, 1,641, and 1,983, respectively. Cash collections for state missions were $21,706.56, $24,094.07, and $35,091.62.

With the cessation of the Hayden agitation and the good spirit engendered by Gambrell, the state missionary work showed great advance. In 1901, for example, there were 198 missionaries employed and $52,462.00 was raised for state missions; while in 1910, when Gambrell resigned, the number of missionaries had increased to 447, who had baptized 8,035 members into the mission churches, had organized 159 new churches, and had raised $133,945.00 for state missions. There was no slowing of the pace after Gambrell resigned on February 10, 1910, to become editor of the *Baptist Standard*.

F. M. McConnell's Administration (1910–14). McConnell, a successful pastor and evangelist, took up the task and continued the excellent progress. At the close of this period in 1914, for example, the number of missionaries had grown from 447 in 1910 to 482 in 1914, and gifts for state missions had increased from $133,945.00 in 1910 to $147,370.00 in 1914.

During this period, Texas Baptists began to develop a consciousness of the large role they would one day play in movements beyond their own borders. Home and foreign mission receipts increased rapidly. In 1914 the former amounted to over $63,000.00 and the latter, $72,793.38. Statistician J. M. Carroll displayed this consciousness in his statistics for 1901. He noted that Baptists had more than 2,700 churches, 2,200 preachers, and probably 1,200–1,500 Sunday schools in Texas. Southern Baptists, he continued, had a total of 760 district associations; of these, one hundred, or more than one-eighth, were in Texas. In the South, there were 19,653 white Baptist churches affiliating with the Convention; one-seventh of these, or 2,745, were in Texas. In these churches were 1,638,039 white Baptists; Texas had 198,367, or nearly one-eighth of them. In all the United States, including the colored churches, there were 4,249,615 Baptists; more than one-thirteenth, or 340,012 were in Texas. In the world there were

5,044,302 Baptists, more than one-fifteenth of whom were in Texas. Of the 62,812 net increase in the white Baptists of the South in the previous year, more than twenty-two percent, or 14,218 were in Texas. There were 1,158 state missionaries in the Southern Baptist Convention territory; of these, 204 were in Texas. During 1901, Southern Baptists contributed to state missions a total of $192,259.46; Texas contributed $42,773.92, or nearly one-fourth of the whole amount. During the same year Texas contributed to state, home, and foreign missions a total of twenty-five percent more than any other Southern state. While Texas contained not quite one-eighth of the church membership of the Southern Baptist Convention, she contributed in 1901 more than one-sixth of the gifts to state and foreign missions.

Advance in Texas Baptist Education

It is rather paradoxical that in the consolidation of Baylor and Waco Universities in 1886, Texas Baptists felt that they had shown wisdom in unifying all of the people in getting behind one great university which could be adequately supported. The founding of William Carey Crane College at Independence after the departure of Baylor and the removal of the Female College to Belton in 1886 were simply a foretaste of the large increase in the number of Baptist schools of every sort during the period from 1886 to 1914. These included at least thirteen schools, along with others whose records cannot be found.

Multiplication of Baptist Schools. Through the efforts of J. D. Robnett, pastor of the First Baptist Church of Brownwood, Howard Payne College was founded by the Pecan Valley Association on June 29, 1889. It was named after Robnett's brother-in-law, Edward Howard Payne of Missouri, who made a substantial gift for that time toward the founding of the school. It opened September 16, 1890.

Simmons College was fostered by the Sweetwater Association, first under the name of Abilene Baptist College and then, when James B. Simmons, a Baptist minister of New York City, made a generous donation to the college, it honored him by using his name.

Although preparations were made to open in 1891, the school had its first session in September, 1892, at Abilene, Texas.

In June, 1891, the North Texas Baptist College was chartered under the tutelage of Jacksboro, Macedonia, Palo Pinto, Stephens County, and Lake Creek Baptist associations. It was opened at Jacksboro in 1891, but lived for only a few years.

Several cooperating Baptist associations founded the Northwest Texas Baptist College at Decatur, which was chartered on December 21, 1891. It opened two years later.

The Cherokee Baptist Association chartered the East Texas Baptist Institute on July 18, 1895, and it opened at Rusk on September 2, 1895.

Burleson College was chartered in February, 1895. In September of that year it opened at Greenville, Texas, and soon was adopted by Hunt County Baptist Association.

In 1898, the South Texas Baptist College opened at Waller, Texas, but closed in two years for lack of patronage.

In 1905 the Baptist General Convention of Texas accepted a coeducational school known as Canadian Academy, located at Canadian, Texas, but it closed in 1913 through lack of patronage.

In 1905 another coeducational school was transferred to the Convention, known as Goodnight Academy. It became a Junior College in 1913, but was closed a few years later because of the lack of patronage.

On July 20, 1907, a charter was secured by Baptists of southwest Texas for San Marcos Baptist Academy, which was accepted in 1910 by the Baptist General Convention of Texas.

In August, 1908, through a gift from James Henry Wayland, Wayland Literary and Technical Institution at Plainview was chartered. The name was changed two years later to Wayland Baptist College.

In 1910, a coeducational school at Bryan, Texas, known as Bryan Baptist Academy, was transferred to the state convention, but before many years it was closed because of dwindling attendance.

On October 23, 1912, a charter was granted for the College of Marshall (now East Texas Baptist College). On August 25, 1913, Thurman C. Gardner became the first president, and at the close of the first period in 1914 the school had been accepted by the Baptist General Convention of Texas as a junior college.

After the consolidation of Baylor at Independence and Waco University, under the name of Baylor, located at Waco, the school opened in 1886 with 337 students, the majority of whom were young men. In the first report of the Board of Trustees at the 1887 Convention, President B. H. Carroll of the Board described the procuring of a charter on August 7, 1886, and the considerable disorder of getting started.

> Caesar in the battle of Nervai was not in greater straits than has been this board for the whole year. We had everything to do at one time. Chaos, doubtful complications, past irregularities, continued drouth, and invincible impecuniosity were among the formidable adversaries with which we had to cope.[7]

In the following year the trustees said that S. L. Morris had been continued as the Financial Secretary and was doing good work, but in 1889, Carroll reported that J. B. Cranfill had undertaken that post. At the 1889 meeting of the Texas General Convention, Cranfill was elected Corresponding Secretary to replace A. J. Holt, and was forced to discontinue his work with Baylor.

The report of B. H. Carroll in 1890 spoke of the need of Baylor for a Financial Secretary who could effectively meet the needs of the school. In 1891 Carroll said that they had found such a person in George W. Truett, a young man who had been teaching school at Whitewright but had agreed to serve as Financial Secretary before completing his education at Baylor. In 1892, Carroll reported that he and Truett had raised $33,000.00 in cash to pay on the debts of the institution. In 1893, in the absence of Carroll, Truett read the report for the Board of Trustees and said that the debt had been lifted from Baylor at Waco. In addition to announcing a matriculation of 470, including forty-one ministerial students, the report said that a Bible Department had been formed. The entire sum collected by Carroll and Truett was reported as about $83,000.00.

In the internal administration of Baylor at Waco, President Rufus C. Burleson was made President emeritus for life on June

11, 1897. Two giants succeeded him in the active presidency. Oscar H. Cooper, called by Professor Frederick Eby "unquestionably the greatest educator Texas has produced as a native son," was named president in 1899. In his four years of service the school made tremendous strides. In 1902 the immortal Samuel Palmer Brooks succeeded Cooper and was serving valiantly at the close of the period in 1914.

B. H. Carroll suggested in 1893 that since the Waco school had been relieved of its debt, the whole state now "unite, earnestly, faithfully, and prayerfully in the work of redeeming from all encumbrance, our Baylor Female College at Belton." Year by year President J. H. Luther and Board of Trustees President F. M. Law appealed to the Convention to meet some of the financial needs of this school. By 1890, the debt had reached $100,000.00. For that school year, there was an enrollment of 300 students who were taught by twenty teachers. Professor P. H. Eager of Mississippi was elected to succeed Luther, but served only two years. Professor E. H. Wells of the Belton faculty succeeded him, but resigned after two years. In September, 1896, W. A. Wilson of Missouri was elected president and realistically faced the needs of the College. J. M. Carroll had been elected general agent and financial manager of the College in 1895 and he reported the debts of the institution were over $140,000.00. Carroll struggled with the question of how to appeal to the whole constituency of Texas when the large number of local schools, each with its own financial problems, seemed to cut out appeals for Baylor College.

The plan of correlation for Texas Baptist schools probably owed more to J. M. Carroll than any other person. The direction he took was influenced by the work of the American Baptist Education Society, which had been organized in 1888 and had received generous gifts from the philanthropy of John D. Rockefeller. The Society "would not assist any state in its educational program unless the leaders agreed to pay off all debts on their schools, limit the number of schools so as to diminish competition and build a permanent system."[8]

The Plan of Correlation. In this context, J. M. Carroll worked out a program by which the debts on the schools might be retired.

The plan embraced the idea of paying the debts on all our schools which had debts, and to such as had no debts—Baylor University and Simmons College—to give them some bonus, with all the schools to enter a "Federation" and to be under the control and direction of the Baptist General Convention, both as to appointing trustees and fixing curriculum, Baylor University to be the head of the Baptist school system.

This was in substance the plan Carroll formulated. It required the raising of about $200,000.00.[9]

To carry out this plan, J. M. Carroll turned to Colonel C. C. Slaughter of Dallas, who had made a donation of $5,000.00 to Baylor College in the previous year. Carroll consulted with Slaughter, who promised $25,000.00 to begin with, and a similar amount to be given later on as a stimulant to the campaign. Carroll called a meeting for September 15, 1897, at Fort Worth, involving one representative from each of the Baptist schools. As a result of this meeting, a recommendation was made and approved at the Convention in San Antonio in 1897 whereby a committee of five brethren not officially connected with any existing Baptist school, along with one representative of each school, making a total of thirteen, would meet to consider the federation of the schools and their relationship to each other. A Convention resolution agreed that if as many as five of the schools, including the two Baylors, agreed to unite in the confederation, that this committee of thirteen should become the Education Commission for Texas Baptists with power to raise funds to promote the financial interest of schools so agreeing.

Pursuant to this authorization, a committee consisting of J. B. Gambrell, J. P. Crouch, George W. Baines, J. B. Carter, and W. M. Harris, none of whom were related to any of the schools, and B. H. Carroll for Baylor at Waco, C. C. Slaughter for Baylor at Belton, R. T. Hanks for Simmons College at Abilene, S. J. Anderson for Burleson College at Greenville, J. H. Grove for Howard Payne College at Brownwood, J. L. Ward for Decatur College at Decatur, J. H. Thorne for East Texas Baptist Institute at Rusk, and J. C. Lindsey for North Texas Baptist College at Jacksboro met for conference on November 30, 1897, at Dallas. As a result, the two Baylors, Howard Payne, Decatur, and East Texas Baptist Institute agreed to enter the program. It provided that Baylor University at Waco would be the head of the system, with the power of granting degrees. Baylor College at Belton would be recognized as a four year college for young women. All other schools agreeing to this program would confine their work to the academy and two years of college work. Their graduates would be received into their junior year by Baylor University and Baylor College. Burleson College at Greenville and Simmons College at Abilene were not willing to enter into this confederation.

The Education Commission promised, in view of this affiliation, to raise a sum of $212,000.00 to liquidate existing debts. Since Baylor University at Waco had no debts, J. M. Carroll recommended that the Waco school should receive a pro-rata share of what was raised to become a part of Baylor's endowment. On January 1, 1899, B. H. Carroll accepted the leadership of the Education Commission, while his brother (J. M. Carroll) served as his assistant. Despite the handicap of the Hayden controversy and other factors, the final report showed that $211,251.51 had been raised by November 7, 1901.

Other Activities

Texas Baptist were busy on many fronts.

Buckner Orphans Home. At the organization of the Baptist General Convention of Texas in 1886, a resolution was offered by R. T. Hanks commending Buckner Orphans Home to the support of the churches and brethren in the state, particularly in view of the Home's need for buildings and endowment. No mention was made of the Home in the 1887 convention. In 1888 a resolution was passed commending the Home and recommending that thereafter the convention receive a report from the Home.

At the 1889 convention, for the first time R. C. Buckner submitted a report on the Home, consisting of nine short sentences about the operation of it. During the previous year there were 127 children in the Home, and its expenses amounted to over $7,000.00. Under construction was a brick central building "which should be finished at once, not only for the extra room it will give, but to increase the comforts of the inmates and as safety from fire in wooden buildings." The committee on the Home recommended that the Baptists of Texas cooperate in the work of the Home and allow Buckner to take pledges to the building fund and receive other offerings. In 1890, Buckner gave a detailed report on the operation of the Home. The property consisted of four two-story buildings, a combination school and chapel, and several farmhouses and barns.

Buckner's industry was phenomenal. In 1890 he traveled about 3,000 miles, preached about 160 sermons, delivered 100 public addresses, answered 2,500 letters, printed and distributed 20,000 circulars, had written numerous newspaper articles on the work, approved applications of all children entered into the institution, etc. In addition to this, he operated almost single-handedly the dairy and poultry activities of the Home and other details of operation for the 130 children. Mr. and Mrs. A. F. Beddoe had been added to the staff as principal of the school and matron of the Home, respectively.

From 1890 until 1914, when the Home was officially presented to the Convention, the institution grew in favor with the people. It was not included in the regular budget of the Convention, but each year Buckner, usually surrounded by a large crowd of orphans, would present the report to the Convention and receive a very liberal offering. In 1904, for example, it amounted to more than $33,000.00, while in 1911, $40,000.00 in pledges and cash were received.

One of the great tragedies in the history of Texas Baptists came on the night of January 15, 1897, when the frame building housing the boys caught fire and burned to death twenty of the children. Growing out of this tragedy, a new large brick hall for the boys was completed in that year, and other brick structures were built for the nursery in 1906, the Chapel in 1908, the power house in 1910, Manna Hall in 1911, and school rooms for the children. In addition, until the founding of Baylor Hospital, a children's hospital was provided for the campus; and in 1905 the first buildings for the housing of aged people was constructed. These several ministries laid the foundation for the extensive program which will be discussed in a later chapter.

In 1914, at the end of this period, R. C. Buckner, then 81 years of age, requested that the Home be sponsored by the Convention through a committee of twenty-seven men, named by the Convention, from whom could be chosen the Board of Directors of the Home. In this year Buckner reported that the organization at the Home consisted of ten men and twelve women and a budget of $108,756.20. A debt of $7,582.50 remained for the year.

Aged Ministers. Another activity of the Convention concerned the care for aged ministers. Since the majority of ministers during the early years in Texas carried on secular labor to support themselves and their families in addition to preaching, they were looked upon as any other member of the community, who, upon getting old, would live with a relative or otherwise spend his last years.

The year before the unification, the Pastors' Conference held their two-day session preceding the meeting at Lampasas, and they discussed the need for a plan to aid aged and disabled ministers. A committee was named to prepare a plan, which was later submitted to the Convention, who approved it. This plan recommended that a Board of Relief for Disabled Ministers be appointed by the Convention to consist of eleven members, one-third of whom should be appointed annually by the Convention. Ministers applying for aid must furnish a certificate of good standing from the association to which they belonged. No appropriation should exceed $400.00 per annum. It was urged that each Baptist in Texas become a regular contributor to this fund.

The Convention named a Board consisting of J. M. Carroll, H. M. Burroughs, E. W. Holman, W. Wedemeyer, A. P. Anderson, Harry Haynes, J. M. Brown, H. J. Chamberlain, N. Moses, A. W. McIver, and J. R. Miller. H. M. Burroughs was chosen as agent of the Board, and later in the year 1885, W. A. Mason assisted him. From 1887 to 1892 this Board annually reported approximately thirty annuitants and income of approximately $1,500.00 to $2,000.00. In 1892 a new method was developed. H. M. Burroughs, using his private funds, built a home at Lampasas, which had fifteen rooms and was quite comfortable. This was used as a home for the aged ministers and their wives. However, the three old couples who stayed in the home during the following year suffered from loneliness away from the community in which they were reared, and finally asked to be returned there. In 1893 the Convention appointed a committee to look into this work. Their report urged that the entire control and management of the Relief Fund be put into the hands of the Executive Board of the Convention. The home at Lampasas was discontinued so far as the Convention was concerned.

Between 1895 and 1914 the number of beneficiaries slowly increased, while the receipts fluctuated between a low of $1,101.39 in 1901 and a high of $5,663.23 in 1907. In 1914, the closing year of this period, the Executive Board reported that 81 beneficiaries were on the roll, each receiving $10.00 per month, and that the fund for this work had been overdrawn by $4,000.00.

Hospitals. Another very significant activity of Texas Baptists was the development of hospitals. Early in 1903, J. B. Cranfill and R. C. Buckner discussed in the *Baptist Standard* the need for a hospital operated by Baptists. A corporation was organized, of which Buckner was president, George W. Truett was secretary, and C. C. Slaughter was treasurer. The charter was dated October 16, 1903. On October 30, a committee from the Board of Directors purchased hospital property in Dallas for $23,400.00. When the Convention met in Dallas in November of that year, Truett presented a resolution which approved the establishment of the Texas Baptist Memorial Sanatorium in Dallas and pledging sympathy and support. This Sanatorium was opened on March 11, 1904, in the old building, and a new building was occupied on October 14, 1909.

A building for the training of nurses, another for Baylor Medical College, and other essential structures were gradually provided. Year by year the Convention elected trustees for this institution. Truett became its spokesman. By 1914, at the close of this period, the hospital reported free service amounting to almost $130,000.00, plus receipts of $153,682.68. The Convention was challenged by an offer from C. C. Slaughter to give $200,000.00 on the condition that $300,000.00 should be secured from other sources besides the fees of patients.

Shortly after the founding of the hospital in Dallas, Baptists in Houston, led by L. T. Mays and D. R. Pevoto, began writing about the need for a hospital in Houston and making plans for it. Mrs. Rachel Stuart, a member of the First Baptist Church in Houston, gave the first $1,000.00. In the late summer of 1907 Pevoto purchased a seventeen-bed hospital, and on September 1, 1907, this was named the Baptist Sanatorium. Pevoto gave up his plan to enter Baylor University as a student and remained as financial agent of the new hospital. Mrs. Ida J. Rudisill, from whom Pevoto had purchased the hospital, was retained as superintendent; a training school for nurses was promptly opened. Pevoto soon became superintendent of the Sanatorium. At a special meeting of the Board of Directors of the Baptist Sanatorium on November 9, 1910, at Houston, the Sanatorium was offered to Texas Baptists. It was accepted by the Convention, and the name was changed to the Baptist Sanatorium and Hospital. In 1911 a four-story reinforced concrete building was added, and this was increased to seven stories in 1914. In that year the superintendent reported total receipts of $59,918.00. Charity amounted to $6,702.25, while total service rendered was listed as $42,906.50.

Sunday School and Colportage Convention. Still another of the activities of Texas Baptists during this period was the Sunday School and Colportage Convention, which has been referred to in the previous period. This body, made up of the same people who were leaders in the state convention, continued from 1886 to 1900 as a separate activity. It served as an agency to distribute Bibles (sometimes sold and sometimes donated), as well as other religious books. Donations were made by both the American Baptist Publication Society and the Home Mission Board of the Southern Baptist Convention, and, after 1891, by the Sunday School Board of the Southern Baptist Convention. In 1894 this Convention began utilizing Sunday School Institutes, which were effective in reaching all races in Texas. In 1898, for example, the body reported holding 182 institutes and conventions for the purpose of assisting the Sunday school. In 1900, the last year of its existence, it reported

165 institutes. It published a paper briefly for the purpose of promotion.

Doubtless, however, its principal work was the organization of Sunday schools. It is estimated that between 2,000 and 3,000 Sunday schools were organized by this body between 1886 and 1900. During the last eight years, for example, it reported the following figures on Sunday schools organized: in 1893, 106; in 1894, 207; in 1895, 217; in 1896, 123; in 1897, 409; in 1898, 384; in 1899, 291; and in 1900, 331.

Its leadership was effective during this period, although Corresponding Secretaries changed rather rapidly. Jeff D. Ray served from 1886 to 1888; B. F. Clayton, 1889–90; J. C. Wingo, 1890; L. E. Peters, 1890–91; R. A. Lee, 1891–92; D. H. LeSueur, 1892–93; W. C. Luther, 1893–96; and E. C. Everett, 1896–1900. In 1900 the organization was consolidated with the Baptist General Convention of Texas.

Newspapers. Another activity of Texas Baptists involved the publication of newspapers. Until 1914, these were primarily individual enterprises closely related to the denomination. From 1886 to December, 1888, after the consolidation of the two newspapers in the former year, the *Texas Baptist and Herald,* edited by S. A. Hayden, was the only newspaper in the field. The recognition that the sharp attacks by Hayden on the denomination required another denominational organ brought several prominent Texas Baptists to the decision to publish other newspapers. A small paper known as the *Baptist News* was begun in Honey Grove, Texas, in December, 1888. It was swallowed up by the *Western Baptist,* published at Dallas by R. T. Hanks. In February, 1892, M. V. Smith and J. B. Cranfill purchased this paper and changed the name to the *Texas Baptist Standard.* After the death of Smith in 1893, Cranfill was aided by H. J. Chamberlain, C. C. Slaughter, George W. Carroll, and others, in financing and publishing this paper. Cranfill remained editor until 1904, when J. H. Gambrell succeeded him and continued until 1907. J. M. Dawson replaced J. H. Gambrell in 1907 and served as editor until April, 1908, when J. Frank Norris assumed the post. On February 10, 1910, J. B. Gambrell resigned as Corresponding Secretary and accepted the editorship of the

Standard. In January, 1914, the paper was sold to the Baptist General Convention of Texas, and E. C. Routh became its editor.

There were numerous other papers published in various parts of the state, such as the *West Texas Baptist,* the *Western Evangel,* the *Missionary Visitor,* the *East Texas Baptist,* and the *State Mission Journal,* but the emerging denominational state paper was the *Standard,* purchased by the Convention in 1914.

Continuance of Conferences for Deacons and Pastors. Brief reference should be made to the continuation during this period of the Deacon's Conference, developed by R. C. Buckner in connection with the organization and support of the Orphan's Home, as well as the Minister's Conference, which was regularly held immediately preceding the meeting of the General Convention and exercised a great deal of influence over the thinking of the Convention. The general format for the latter Conference consisted of simply a series of questions on various items of immediate interest, with a panel of two or three speakers to discuss each one briefly.

Training Union. During this period, also, began the movement in Texas now known as the Baptist Training Union. Not long after the Civil War, active efforts to enlist young people in training and Christian fellowship were made in many denominations. In 1867, for example, the First Baptist Church in Brooklyn, New York, formed a young people's association, and by 1876, with eight other local associations, developed a city organization known as the Young People's Baptist Union of Brooklyn. The Congregationalists began their Christian Endeavor movement on February 2, 1881. Other denominations followed quickly in the organization of their young people, ofttimes in a fellowship extending beyond the local churches.

In this context, the Broadway Baptist Church of Fort Worth in 1888 formed what is generally called the first young people's organization in Texas. In 1891 a state convention of messengers from twenty-six such organizations in Texas was held in Fort Worth. The Baptist Young People's Union of Texas was organized with T. S. Potts as president and A. E. Baten as corresponding secretary. In 1901, this body appointed a committee to arrange an encampment, which met regularly thereafter at La Porte from 1902 to

1905, and then after 1906 at Palacios. A state B.Y.P.U. secretary in the person of E. E. Lee was secured in 1907, but he served for only one year. Joe English led the work for a part of the year, then he was succeeded by W. T. Curtis, whose ill health kept him from serving for more than a few months. J. R. McGill began his work in this post in 1912 and at the close of the period in 1914 he could report approximately 400 unions in Texas. A significant movement occurred in July of 1900, when the first Junior union was organized in Waco with forty members. This anticipated the enlarging of the scope of the training union from simply involving the young people until in later days it would include every age. The enrollment in 1914 was approximately 15,000.

Southwestern Baptist Theological Seminary. Another activity, which J. M. Carroll called the most significant achievement of Texas Baptists, was the organization of a theological seminary in Texas. In 1872, after one year as pastor in Waco, B. H. Carroll became assistant to the president as teacher in the Theological Department at Waco University. In 1893, in Baylor at Waco, the trustees established a Department of Bible with Carroll in charge. In 1901 a Department of Theology was created under Carroll as Dean. A curriculum leading to the Bachelor of Theology degree was offered.

Early in 1905 Carroll came to a conviction that God wanted him to establish a theological seminary in Texas. By a private canvass of individuals, Carroll secured pledges amounting to $32,000.00 to support the seminary for three years. He then submitted to the trustees of Baylor a proposal to establish a theological seminary as a school of the University, and this proposal was unanimously adopted. In 1907 the Baptist General Convention approved resolutions from the trustees of Baylor authorizing the chartering of the seminary and its removal to a new location. On March 14, 1908, the charter was secured, creating Southwestern Baptist Theological Seminary. In the summer of 1910 the seminary moved to Fort Worth.

Carroll remained president of the school until his death in November, 1914, when he was succeeded by L. R. Scarborough. The first faculty of the new seminary, in addition to Carroll who taught English Bible, consisted of A. H. Newman in church history, Calvin Goodspeed in systematic theology, C. B. Williams in New Testament and Greek, J. J. Reeves in Hebrew, Jeff D. Ray in Homiletics, Lee R. Scarborough in evangelism, and Fred W. Freeman as financial secretary. During the first year in Fort Worth, there were 190 ministerial students and a number of men and women studying for special Christian service, representing four foreign countries and eleven states and territories. The report to the Convention in 1914 showed 208 students matriculated, of whom 128 were ministers and 5 were laymen; and 75 young women were in the training school.

Baptist Women Mission Workers

After unification in 1886, it will be recalled, the Woman's Missionary Union of the State Convention and the Ladies' General Aid Society of the General Association were consolidated into a new body which took the name Baptist Women Mission Workers.

Three presidents served the body in the period from 1886 to 1914: Mrs. Fanny Breedlove Davis (1886–1895); Mrs. W. L. Williams (1895–1906); and Mrs. F. S. Davis (1906-end of period).

Three corresponding secretaries served under Mrs. Fanny B. Davis: Mrs. S. J. Anderson (1886–87); Miss Minnie Slaughter (1887–89); and Miss Mina Everett (1889-to the end of Mrs. Davis' presidency).

The record of receipts is an indication of the progress made. In the first year of the united body, slightly more than $3,000.00 was raised for mission purposes. Despite the severe depression that raged in the 1890's, the receipts from 1890 to 1895 showed gains. In the last-named year they totaled $23,193.55. Translated into life, these funds built schools and orphanages in Mexico and assisted in mission work in South America; established missions among the Mexicans in Corpus Christi, San Antonio, and Laredo; and paid the salary of a teacher in a girls' school in Mexico. A forward thrust in receipts was shown in 1890 because the women appointed Miss Mina Everett as general agent for organization and inspiration. Her own background was impressive. She came from an unbelieving home. She gave herself as a missionary to Mexico, but went on to Brazil instead, and only returned to Texas because the tropical diseases there threatened her life. Another forward step was the publication in Houston in 1889 of the *Texas Baptist Worker,* with Mrs. F. B. Davis as editor. Mrs. Davis represented Texas in the organization on May 11, 1888, of the Southwide Woman's Missionary Union.

Mrs. F. B. Davis was succeeded by Mrs. W. L. Williams in 1895 as president of the body. She immediately faced several difficulties. The state Boards which had paid the expenses of Miss Mina Everett, the corresponding secretary, discontinued this support. A rent-free office was tendered by the American Baptist Publication Society at Dallas, and this was accepted. The women undertook the support of Miss Everett, and this crisis became a victory, resulting in more money raised and more societies organized than in any previous year. Another element of crisis was the opposition of several of the brethren, including the giant B. H. Carroll. The grit of Miss Everett carried the day, as she stood her ground.

With sly humor, Mrs. F. S. Davis described how, fourteen years later, B. H. Carroll came before the Executive Board making plans to build a Woman's Training School at Southwestern Seminary, and on this occasion, Carroll thoroughly supported, with illustrations from history and Scripture, the work of the women. Still another critical moment came in 1897 with the resignation of Miss Everett, whose seventeen years of fruitful service in Texas had brought outstanding results. For a part of 1896–97 Mrs. W. C. Luther and Miss Ella Yelvington each served for a time as corresponding secretary. Mrs. J. B. Gambrell was elected to this post at San Antonio in 1897 and held the office at the end of the presidency of Mrs. Williams.

Extraordinary progress was made in every direction under the leadership of Mrs. Williams and the corresponding secretaries who served with her. The receipts by 1906, when Mrs. Williams retired, reached $57,816.96, by far the largest amount in the history of this organization. A specific emphasis of Mrs. Gambrell was work with the foreign populations, the Mexicans in particular. The inspiration of the Mexican Preachers' Institutes, which she helped promote, led to the organization of a Mexican Baptist Convention of Texas.

The successor to Mrs. Williams in 1906 was Mrs. F. S. Davis (Mary Hill Davis) who served for the next twenty-five years as president of the body. She was greatly assisted by the dedicated work of Mrs. J. B. Gambrell, who, however was removed by death on January 15, 1911. Her successor was Mrs. Addie Buckner Beddoe, the daughter of R. C. Buckner and the wife of Dr. A. F. Beddoe, an ordained Baptist minister and medical doctor; and mother of Dr. Robert Beddoe and Albert Beddoe, the first of whom was a medical missionary in China and the second an ordained Baptist preacher. She had served two years as assistant to Mrs. J. B. Gambrell and in March, 1911, was made corresponding secretary.

The achievements under the presidency of Mrs. Davis and her co-workers were remarkable. For ministries as diverse as the building of a girls' school in Kaifeng, China, and the raising of $50,000.00 for a dormitory at Southwestern Baptist Theological Seminary, the sensitive hearts of the women of Texas responded. In October, 1911, the Womans' Training School was organized as a part of the seminary at Fort Worth. The burgeoning receipts between 1906 and 1914, the close of the period, speak of the extent of the service rendered. In 1906 the receipts were almost $58,000.00; in 1907 about $49,000.00; in 1908 about $44,000.00; in 1909 almost $71,000.00; in 1910 almost $47,000.00; in 1911 over $112,000.00; in 1912 over $153,000.00; in 1913 over $195,000.00; and in 1914 over $206,000.00.

Straws in the Wind

Several events in this period pointed to future directions in Texas Baptist life.

Indications of Additional Centralization. During this period foundations were being laid for the unification of many areas of work within the Convention, which would finally be accomplished in 1914. In 1892, after the resignation of J. B. Cranfill as the Corresponding Secretary and General Superintendent of Missions, the Board of Directors reported that J. M. Carroll had been elected to succeed Cranfill, but that before Carroll had accepted, the Foreign Mission Board had been contacted to see if it were possible to consolidate the work that had formerly been done by two agents. After fair and impartial discussion "the Board very nearly unanimously decided that it was its deliberate conviction that the time had come for such consolidation." By 1896, the collections and disbursements for Home Missions, Foreign Missions, and Ministerial Relief were added to the task of the corresponding secretary who supervised state missions. "What before had been done by four salaried agents was now committed to one."

By 1905 Corresponding Secretary J. B. Gambrell could report that the Convention had assigned to the Board of Directors every type of mission.

> The Board, in spirit and intent, is just as much a Home Mission Board as it is a State Mission Board, and just as much a Foreign Mission Board as it is a State Mission Board. This includes the upbuilding, strengthening and training of the churches, the fostering of Sunday schools, the building of church buildings, the co-operation with associational organizations, and the unifying agency between the associations and the Southern Baptist Convention.

In 1908 Gambrell reported that "This Convention is rapidly becoming the center of unity for the aggressive missionary forces of Texas. . . . There is a constant and growing movement for State-wide and State-through unification." In 1910, the Convention adopted a statement by A. J. Barton which looked toward developing plans to allow the great number of causes fostered by the Convention to be considered in an orderly and wise way.[10]

Promise of Future Progress. The move toward increased organizational efficiency also spoke eloquently of the bright days ahead for Texas Baptists. The need for an improved structure testified to the rapid enlargement of the ministry of the general body. In the 1913 meeting of the Convention, for example, in addition to the lengthy report of Secretary F. M. McConnell involving all of the work of the Southern Baptist Convention and the state body, a total of thirty-one special committees reported, and dozens of appeals were made for various aspects of the work. Four days were crammed with business, and on Monday evening, when time for adjournment came, a considerable amount of unfinished business was referred to the Board of Directors. This kind of agenda year after year guaranteed that growth would be measured in geometrical rather than arithmetical terms.

Not only so, but meeting the need for an improved structure revealed the kind of able leadership that guaranteed future progress. B. H. Carroll, the preeminent leader during this period, died in 1914, bringing a close to an era in a sense, but other mature leaders like J. M. Carroll, R. C. Buckner, and J. B. Gambrell continued their service. In addition, a remarkably gifted group of younger men was taking up the mantle. Some of them were brought into public focus by the several controversies of the period; others, through magnificent leadership in some sphere of Convention ministry; and yet others, by the display of stability and faithfulness during difficult hours. Names such as George W. Truett (who became the acknowledged leader of Texas Baptists in the next period), F. M. McConnell, A. J. Barton, W. B. McGarity, W. T. Tardy, J. R. Jester, L. R. Millican, S. J. Porter, and the layman M. H. Wolfe are found in almost every annual meeting at the forefront of denominational ministries. Other important laymen were Colonel C. C. Slaughter, F. L. Carroll, and William Reeves, who made generous gifts to the Baptist cause; A. H. Newman, the eminent church historian; and John C. Townes, the dedicated teacher. An army of noble women was laying strong foundations for the next generation. Simply to name some of those preaching the annual sermon discloses the wealth of manpower in Texas Baptist life: R. T. Hanks, A. J. Fawcett, R. B. Garrett, B. H. Carroll, S. M. Harris, J. S. Tanner, K. I. Smythe, O. L. Hailey, Jeff D. Ray, G. W. McCall, Forrest Smith, W. A. Hamlett, George W. Baines, and B. A. Copass.

It was during this period that the man called "our first Texas Baptist evangelist" came to his mature ministry. This was W. E. Penn, titled Major Penn because of his service in the Confederate army. He was a successful lawyer and outstanding Sunday school leader before 1875. In that year at the age of forty-three, under the influence of J. H. Stribling, pastor of the First Baptist Church, Tyler, Penn turned from a lucrative law practice to serve as an evangelist during the remaining twenty years of his life. He was a lay preacher until December 4, 1880, when he was ordained at Galveston and continued in an impressive ministry. He died in 1895 after winning thousands to Christ. He prefigured a mighty host of evangelists that would carry the gospel to every border of Texas during the coming years.

Relation to Ecumenical Movements. It will be recalled that one of the Baptist newspapers that circulated most freely in Texas during her formative years was the *Tennessee Baptist,* edited by J. R. Graves, the founder of Landmarkism. Graves himself was a frequent and popular speaker in Texas. Landmarkism, of course, stressed the authority of the local Baptist body as the only scriptural institution and turned away from the growing ecumenical trend. It is not surprising, then, that in 1913 a distinct pronouncement of Texas Baptists on the ecumenical movement, while acknowledging the spiritual union of all believers and proffering cooperation "with all our fellow Christians and our fellow citizens, whether Protestant or Catholic, whether Jew or Gentile, in every worthy effort for the moral and social uplift of all men in all lands," pointedly said:

> Our message to our brethren of other communions is, that since the present divided condition of Christendom is unquestionably the result of departures from the simple teachings of the Scriptures, the only possible road to organic union is back to the Scriptures, fairly interpreted. If it be said that this is, in our present state, impracticable and impossible, we reply, that if that be so, then organic union is impossible with Baptists, for we are unalterably bound to the Scriptures as our law and guide.[11]

10

A New Era
(1914–29)

In his first report to the Convention in 1915 under the new consolidated structure, Corresponding Secretary J. B. Gambrell rhapsodized:

> The growth of Texas Baptists is almost alarming. Their numbers run into the hundreds of thousands. They hold a large part of the wealth of this rapidly growing state. They have already well laid foundations upon which to build indefinitely. Texas Baptists can and do send abroad annually an army of missionaries to work on all lines of kingdom building. We have attained a good degree of unity and denominational discipline. We are growing in every direction. Our preachers are growing in numbers, in preaching power and in leadership. The churches are growing, many of them into giant strength. Every department of the work is growing. Enlargement is the key word to the whole situation.
>
> . . . . No people on earth ever had a greater incentive to do their best than Texas Baptists have today, for a convert now may mean one hundred further on.
>
> Are we sufficient for our day and generation? . . . . Our thinking must be broad, our spirit generous, our leadership masterful, our giving far beyond what it is today. We must merge our individualism into an army without losing it. The plans of the Convention must be made for world conquest. Mere localisms and personal ambitions and individual plans must perish or become harmonious parts of an onward movement. This Convention never saw a greater hour than this. Are we ready to match our plans and our daring with the

188

situation we are in? If we are, a new era in Texas Baptist history will open with this Convention![1]

It was indeed a new era. It opened with the founding of Executive Board through a constitutional revision in 1913–14. It closed with a number of important events, the chief of which was the world-wide financial collapse on October 24, 1929. In this period the world conflagration known as World War I took place, alternately bringing war depression and war inflation, followed by a severe post-war recession in the 1920's. Drouths, floods, and hurricanes were interspersed in Texas to keep the economy completely off balance.

The Executive Board Formed

A constitutional revision in 1913–14 completed the movement toward inner consolidation that had begun in the 1890's under J. M. Carroll. Two significant changes were made in the constitutional revision: (1) no president may serve more than three consecutive years; and, more important, (2) an Executive Board was structured which "shall have charge and control, except when otherwise directed by the Convention, of all the work of the Convention, including missions, education and beneficence, in the interim between its sessions." This Executive Board elected its Corresponding Secretary annually and "shall fix salaries, make financial arrangements, and have such other powers and authority as may be necessary to carry on the work of the Convention."[2]

Under this revised constitution, the new Executive Board met in December and elected M. H. Wolfe as president, J. B. Gambrell as corresponding secretary, and F. M. McConnell and B. A. Copass as assistant secretaries. Despite the fact that he was seventy-three years old, Uncle Gideon (as Gambrell was known) responded to the call of his denomination.

J. B. Gambrell's Second Administration (1914–18)

Gambrell's first report to the Convention at Austin in November, 1915, was filled with his well-known pungent wisdom and down-to-earth language. He grouped the convention's work under the three heads set out in the constitution: benevolence, education, and missions. Under the first head were included Buckner Orphans Home, the hospitals, and the old ministers' relief program. The correlated system of schools constituted the area of education. Under missions, Gambrell listed not only state, home, and foreign missions, but also the Baptist Women Mission Workers, the B.Y.P.U., and the Sunday school.

Benevolence. Gambrell's plan was to assign a particular time of the year to campaign for each of the interests. The emphasis was first on benevolence in the spring of 1915. However, said Gambrell,

> . . . the churches were unused to it, and they were busy cleaning up church debts which had accumulated during the depressing months preceding, when religious activities were at a standstill. The campaign was not very encouraging. Do what we could, it was like trying to strike a wet match.

The several interests making up the benevolence section made progress in spite of this poor beginning. In 1914 R. C. Buckner requested that the Convention assume trusteeship for the Home, and this was done. In the four years between 1915 and 1918 the reports were optimistic. Approximately 600 orphans lived at the Home during this time. In 1915 the receipts of the Home were almost $82,000.00. In the following year they reached $167,432.50, which disposed of a deficit at the beginning of the year amounting to $28,700.00. In 1917 the receipts exceeded $165,000.00, and in 1918 they were approximately $113,000.00. On April 9, 1919, Sir Great Heart, as R. C. Buckner was called, went to his reward.

The two hospitals prospered during these years. In 1915 the Dallas hospital had 5,485 patients. Receipts totaled over $192,000.00. The Houston hospital reported 2,155 patients. Receipts totaled about $45,000.00. In the following year the receipts of the Dallas hospital were over $182,000.00, with 7,096 patients, while Houston reported receipts of over $65,500.00, with 2,761 patients. In this year R. E. Burt, one of the Houston trustees, offered to match dollar for dollar any gift made to the Houston hospital up to $300,000.00. In 1917 the Dallas Hospital reported receipts of almost $300,000.00, with 7,832 in-patients, while Houston reported receipts of $123,649.22, with 3,132 in-patients. In the last year of Gambrell's administration, the Dallas hospital reported $324,924.87 in receipts and 7,079 in-patients. Colonel C. C. Slaughter, in this last year of his life, made a gift of $150,000.00 to the hospital. The Houston hospital in 1918 showed receipts of $114,520.68, with 3,036 in-patients.

Secretary Gambrell also gave attention to aged ministers' relief. Receipts for this cause varied from about $5,000.00 to $11,000.00 annually during these years. In 1918 the new Relief and Annuity Board of the Southern Baptist Convention was formed, partly because of urging from Texas Baptists. It was located at Dallas, Texas, with William Lunsford as Secretary, and began a period of increased benefits for aged ministers and their wives under the ministry of the Southern Baptist Convention.

Education. As he began his work in 1914, J. B. Gambrell remarked, "We are in an educational jam." When the Executive Board assumed control of educational interests from the Education Board in 1914, it found that regular deficits, augmented by the outbreak of World War I, had brought a most serious situation. The deficit in 1915 was shown as $95,897.70. Part of the difficulty was the mushroom-type growth of the schools. Gambrell remarked in his first report in 1915 that eighteen years before, Texas Baptists had six schools; now, he noted, we have nineteen. In attempting to interpret this crisis, Gambrell said that all denominational education was faced with the competition of state schools where taxes provide all of the resources. The state university at Austin was even recognizing Bible teaching as a part of its curriculum. The farther a student goes in education, Gambrell said, the relative cost per student is greater, which meant that academies may live on the tuition charged but universities will die without endowment. For the present he urged that either individual campaigns in limited territories for each school be instituted or, as was done in 1898, have a state-wide campaign to clean up everything. He favored the former because large subscriptions had already been made to some of the schools.

Despite heroic efforts in intensive campaigns, the "jam" still remained. The deficit in 1917 was shown as $215,896.24, and as $223,083.82 in the following year. Baylor University at Waco was straining every nerve to match endowment funds conditionally promised by the General Education Board. Baylor Female College at Belton had huge debts and was expending large sums each year for interest.

A concentrated effort was begun in December, 1915, to raise in four years the sum of $1,000,000.00 in money, not pledges, to ease the pressure. George W. Truett gave three months of his time and raised $265,905.74 in 1916; L. R. Scarborough of Southwestern Seminary led in a sixty-day campaign in 1917 and raised $281,784.81; the campaign in 1918 was hurt by bad weather in January and February and only $154,893.85 was secured.

In March, 1918, the Executive Board appointed a special committee headed by T. V. Neal, along with H. L. Kokernot, J. C. Hardy, J. L. Smith, R. E. Burt, and Cullen F. Thomas. This committee thoroughly studied the eleven Baptist schools (including Southwestern Seminary) and among other findings reported that the total indebtedness of the schools was about $1,000,000.00 and that they were showing a deficit in operating expenses of almost $25,000.00 a year. The committee recommended a state-wide campaign to raise $300,000.00 in cash each year, and urged that meanwhile a bond issue should be floated in the amount of $1,000,000.00 to fund the debts immediately. The resignation of Gambrell in 1918 delayed briefly any action on the recommendation.

Missions. The mission work was impressive in view of the financial stringency of this period. Gifts for home missions hovered around $63,000.00 per year until 1918, when the war inflation enabled the raising of $94,645.42. The foreign mission offering rose from $73,893.85 in 1914 to $131,710.86 in 1918. State missions, which Gambrell called "the heart of all our denominational, constructive, co-operative effort," also showed impressive statistics. The receipts during these years averaged around $100,000.00 per year. Missionaries employed generally numbered about 350, never exceeding the high of 482 in 1914. Baptisms reported by the missionaries were usually between 5,000 and 6,000; churches organized averaged around sixty; members added to the church each year numbered around 12,000; the number of Sunday schools organized by these missionaries generally averaged around 275. The year 1916 probably would be a typical year. The number of missionaries was 339, of whom five were to the Germans, one to the Bohemians, two to the Italians, and twenty-two to the Mexicans. The Board also cooperated in the support of seventy-one associational missionaries. As well, a great deal of religious work was done among the many soldiers stationed in the various army camps of Texas.

The auxiliaries to the mission task (Sunday schools, B.Y.P.U.'s, and the Baptist Women Mission Workers) developed dramatically during this period. The field secretary for Sunday school work, W. E. Foster, retired in 1915 after three years of laying foundations. By that time the Sunday school enrollment in Texas had reached 214,687. In the following year William P. Phillips became General Secretary of the Sunday School Department, and served at this post for the next ten years.

The B.Y.P.U. movement made phenomenal progress. J. R. McGill was acting as field secretary when the Executive Board was formed in 1914, but resigned in that year. In the December meeting of 1915, T. C. Gardner, then president of the College of Marshall, was named State B.Y.P.U. Secretary. His leadership in structuring effective forms and promoting enthusiasm among the leadership made him one of the principal architects of this movement among Baptists. The numerical measure of his success during this brief period may be seen in the fact that the number of unions grew from 552 in 1916 to 1,575 in 1918, and from 16,554 members in 1916 to 34,194 members in 1918. The number of associational organizations grew from two in 1916 to twenty in 1918.

The inspiring record of the Baptist Women Mission Workers in the period of Gambrell's secretaryship can only be sketched briefly. Mrs. F. S. Davis was president during these years, and Mrs. A. F. Beddoe was corresponding secretary-treasurer. The Woman's Missionary Training School building at Ft. Worth, to which this body had subscribed $50,000.00, was completed and dedicated in 1915.

Statistically, Mrs. Beddoe reported 1,378 societies, 598 Sunbeam bands, 200 Y.W.A. and G.A. chapters, and 41 Royal Ambassador organizations. Receipts in 1915 totaled $12,127.87. Both receipts and organizations increased regularly in 1916, 1917, and 1918. In the last named year, receipts totaled $20,902.76, and 2,004 organizations were reported, in addition to 111 associational unions and 12 district bodies.

Corresponding Secretary Gambrell vigorously advanced every interest in Texas Baptist life until his resignation on June 11, 1918. He served as president of the Southern Baptist Convention from 1917 to 1921, and upon leaving the secretaryship of Texas Baptists, fulfilled a lifelong ambition to teach at Southwestern Seminary, where he remained until his death in 1921. During his four years as Secretary, Gambrell struggled constantly with financial needs. In 1915, for example, there was a deficit of $131,704.51 in operating funds, and the Board's indebtedness on October 31, 1915, was $228,213.03. This debt was made up of $128,198.56 deficit from state missions and $95,987.70 from the schools. By 1918 this indebtedness had reached $374,091.19, the principal items being a deficit of $328,083.19, in education and about $45,000.00 in missions.

New Leadership

After the resignation of Gambrell, the Convention turned to Frank S. Groner, pastor of Columbus Avenue Baptist Church, Waco, a tested and effective leader; after his resignation in 1928, T. Luther Holcomb left the First Baptist Church, Sherman, to succeed him at the close of this period.

It is not easy to list outstanding names among the hundreds of leaders in this period, for each annual report of the convention included new ones. The matchless figure was George W. Truett, pastor of First Baptist Church, Dallas. J. M. Carroll served until his death in 1931; A. J. Holt, J. M. P. Morrow, W. T. Tardy, and Jeff D. Ray were some of the veterans still active. Other active ministers were L. R. Scarborough, I. E. Gates, J. B. Cranfill, Marshall Craig, J. H. Pace, W. W. Melton, J. L. Ward, S. E. Tull, S. J. Porter,

J. L. Gross, O. L. Hailey, G. W. Parks, Forrest Smith, and M. M. Wolf. Faithful women leaders included Mrs. F. S. Davis, Mrs. A. F. Beddoe, Mrs. J. M. Dawson, and Mrs. W. B. McGarity, among many. Stalwart laymen served faithfully—men like O. S. Lattimore, Col. C. C. Slaughter, George W. Carroll, John G. Hardin, George Cowden, Giles H. Connell, H. L. Kokernot, John Z. Means, F. W. Johnson, M. H. Wolfe, R. E. Burt, W. H. Fuqua, J. K. Wadley, A. D. Foreman, Sr., T. G. Hendrick, Earl B. Smyth, Carr P. Collins, Pat M. Neff, T. C. Yantis, S. P. Brooks, Cullen F. Thomas, J. C. Hardy, J. D. Sandefer, Robert H. Coleman, and H. Z. Duke.

The situation between 1918 and 1929 continued in many respects quite similar to the one prevailing during Gambrell's administration. The financial scene showed little improvement. It will be recalled that just before the retirement of Gambrell, a committee recommended the issuance of $1,000,000.00 in bonds as a means of meeting the needs of the schools. Under the leadership of Educational Secretary T. V. Neal the plan was approved by the Board in December, 1918, and during February, 1919, the bonds were issued and oversubscribed by thirty percent. For a brief period the schools were emancipated from the back-breaking debts, but operating deficits soon clouded the picture again.

The Seventy-Five Million Campaign. When the Southern Baptist Convention met at Atlanta in May, 1919, it voted unanimously to enter into a campaign to raise $75,000,000.00 in the following five years for the causes of the Convention. President L. R. Scarborough of Southwestern Baptist Seminary was named General Director of the Campaign, while in Texas, Secretary Groner became the Campaign Director along with T. V. Neal as State Organizer, J. M. Dawson as Publicity Director, and Mrs. A. F. Beddoe, corresponding secretary of the Baptist Women Mission Workers, as Organizer for Texas women. Texas Baptists were asked to raise the sum of $15,000,000.00 as their quota. However, the Texas leadership voted to include $1,000,000.00 additional in order to care for the Loyalty Bonds which had been sold during the previous months. The following allocations were made to the various causes in Texas:

Foreign Missions	$3,726,000.00
Home Missions	2,275,000.00
State Missions	1,750,000.00
South-wide Education	640,000.00
Ministerial Relief and Annuity	730,000.00
Texas Baptist Memorial Sanitarium	500,000.00
Houston Baptist Sanitarium and Hospital	475,000.00
Central Texas Baptist Sanitarium, Waco	250,000.00
Abilene Sanitarium	100,000.00
San Antonio Sanitarium	150,000.00
Brownsville Sanitarium	25,000.00
Orphanage (For Buildings Only)	300,000.00
Baylor University at Waco	1,000,000.00
Baylor University at Dallas	500,000.00
Baylor College	750,000.00
Southwestern Baptist Theological Seminary	500,000.00
Simmons	500,000.00
Howard Payne	300,000.00
Burleson	100,000.00
Wayland	100,000.00
Decatur	100,000.00
Marshall	100,000.00
Rusk	100,000.00
San Marcos	100,000.00

The state was thoroughly organized during the remainder of the year, and the subscription period was planned for the week of November 30–December 7, 1919, designated as Victory Week. In 1920, it was reported that subscriptions had finally reached $16,560,000.00. In 1921, the Board organized a Redemption Campaign to call upon the people to redeem the pledges which were now due. Secretary Groner recited some of the problems which were faced:

Our local campaigns have been beset by difficulties the most numerous, varied and menacing with which we have ever been confronted. The general economic depression has been the most serious in the memory of man; the cotton crop was very short except in one small section of the state, and the cotton price not at all satisfactory; the decline in the price of cattle and oil; the failure of a number of banks and other business concerns, together with the general low morale incident to the unsettled business condition of the country; all has conspired to slow up and hinder the collection of pledges, or the securing of new subscriptions.

At the Board meeting in December, 1921, B. W. Vining was elected as Conservation Secretary. At the suggestion of the Southern Baptist Convention's Conservation Commission, a Reenforcement Month was set for November and early December in an attempt to secure new pledges from members who had joined since the Seventy-five Million Campaign was originally begun and from others who did not at that time make pledges. In addition, at the Board meeting in Dallas on July 20, 1922, it was agreed to institute a Catch-up Campaign in the fall to urge all who had pledged to pay up to date. An extensive campaign was waged for three months, including an All-State Motor Tour which reached nearly two thousand churches in September. It was noted that for the first three years of the campaign, despite unusual financial depression, Texas Baptists had raised over $4,000,000.00 compared to the three "unusually prosperous years" preceding the campaign when less than $2,000,000.00 was raised.

In 1924 Secretary Groner reported that a complete tabulation of the subscription list showed that only about $12,000,000.00 had been subscribed instead of the $16,500,000.00 that had been reported. A little over $1,000,000.00 was received in 1924. The Seventy-five Million Campaign officially concluded December 31, 1924.

Our receipts did not reach our expectations, but they were far in excess of anything ever realized before. Our regular receipts through the channel of the Dallas office to the Seventy-five Million Campaign account were $7,034,411.50. The Conservation Commission of Nashville requested all the states to secure information about special gifts and to make a report of same. This we have done, and including these special gifts together with our orphan's home receipts and our associational missions, both of which items were counted in the regular 75 Million Campaign budget in all the other states, the total financed results of the 75 Million Campaign in Texas was $8,720,060.65. This is about $2 million more than was raised by any other Southern state during this period for the same objects.

The Attacks by Norris

J. Frank Norris, who accepted the pastorate of the First Baptist Church in Fort Worth in 1909, indicated opposition as early as 1914 to the program of Texas Baptists. The Seventy-Five Million Campaign completed the rupture. At first he announced generous support of the program through his newspaper, then repudiated it and began to oppose the movement. During 1921 he vigorously attacked a teacher in Baylor University, alleging that evolution was espoused, and created dissension at the Convention meeting. In 1922 a large committee of Texas leaders condemned these attacks as embodying "misrepresentations, insinuations, and reflections upon the proper conduct in office of the appointed and trusted leaders of this Convention; . . ."[3]

Secretary Groner, in discussing the Seventy-five Million Campaign in 1922, said that one of the most serious hindrances was "the relentless, persistent and cruel opposition waged by a certain opponent of our work, both through the columns of his local church paper, which was sent free to thousands of our Baptist people throughout the state, and also through the columns of the secular press, both in the form of contributed articles and paid advertisements." In the following year Groner reported that "we have had waged upon our work the most violent, incessant and heartless attacks that the opposers to constructive Christianity and the world-wide missionary program could contrive." In that year the messengers of the First Baptist Church, Fort Worth, were not seated by the state body. Norris was permanently excluded in 1924. In 1927, due to continued attacks by Norris, a long history of the agitation and the condemnation of Norris were made a part of the Convention records.[4] Norris formed his own fellowship outside of Convention life, but continued to harrass both the state body and the southwide body for the next twenty years.

This Will We Do!

It is inspiring to observe the leadership and the people, while struggling to regain financial stability, resolutely go about the work which was theirs to do. During the Seventy-Five Million Campaign, for example, the whole program of Texas Baptists was accelerated. In 1924 Secretary Groner compared the achievements during the 75 Million Campaign with those of the previous five years. During the Campaign, gifts for home missions went beyond $716,000.00, almost $290,000.00 above the gifts of the five years previous. Gifts to foreign missions doubled, reaching over a million dollars. Gifts to state missions also doubled, reaching almost one and one-half million dollars. Gifts to Christian education far more than doubled, reaching $2,167,000.00, compared with $862,528.00 in the five years previous to the Campaign. Relief and Annuity gifts were almost six times as much; gifts to the hospitals, ten times as much; and gifts to Buckner Orphans Home, almost four times as much. The number of baptisms from 1915 to 1919 was 112,445, while from 1920 to 1924, they totalled 146,729. The number of Texas Baptists increased between 1915 and 1919 to 395,547, while between 1920 and 1924, the number increased to 471,140. The assets of Texas Baptist schools more than doubled between 1919 and 1924, being valued at over nine million dollars; houses of worship of Texas Baptist churches increased in value from $9,434,071 in 1919 to $18,600,000 in 1924.

Similar impressive statistics show growth in every aspect of Texas Baptist life for the period from 1925 to 1929. Church membership soared to the half-million mark in the latter year, about 400,000 were enrolled in Sunday school, almost 10,000 were enrolled in Vacation Bible School during the summer, and the Training Union reported 4,431 unions with 121,083 members, 92 associational organizations, and 17 District Conventions. In 1925 Sunday School Secretary William P. Phillips resigned and was succeeded by Granville S. Hopkins. Sunday school enrollment in that year was 368,171.

New departments of work were developed between 1919 and 1929. In 1920 J. P. Boone became the first Baptist Student Secretary to promote the religious interests of students both in denominational schools and in the state schools. In that same year a Publicity Department was structured at the January meeting of the Board, and Coleman Craig acted as part-time leader at first.

Throughout all of this period the cooperation of the *Baptist Stand-ard* and its editor, E. C. Routh, was highly praised. Its reports year by year showed an increasing influence in the work. In May, 1925, a Department of Evangelism was approved and W. Y. Pond be-came its head. As usual, the women, now known as the Woman's Missionary Union of Texas, faithfully carried on an increasingly active program of missions, missionary education, and the collection of funds for missionary objects.

In 1925 the ownership and operation of Southwestern Baptist Theological Seminary, Ft. Worth, was transferred to the Southern Baptist Convention.

Beyond the regular work being carried on by Texas Baptists, the financial crisis of the 1920's brought some very significant changes in the basic organization and method of work of Texas Baptists. In the first place, for the first time the Convention faced squarely the problems involved in guessing how much work to carry on in state missions by borrowing funds, without having an inkling of whether or not the program was too large or too small for the resources to be made available to them later on. Before the Seventy-Five Million Campaign, the normal method of raising funds for the work of Texas Baptists and state missions in particular was to have two great roundups each year—one in the fall and one in the spring. Gener-ally, at the meeting of the Convention in the fall, offerings and pledges were made to the many interests reported on at the Conven-tion. In addition, most of the institutions had field men whose prin-cipal task was to secure pledges for the institution represented. Oc-casionally, the institutions had special campaigns for the purpose of raising sums of money for their needs.

This method made it impossible to know even approximately how much money would be available for state missions, for exam-ple. Should the fall roundup be impeded by unusual weather, whether rain or drought, an epidemic of some sort of illness, or some other factor that diverted the finances or interests of the constituency, the amount available for state missions would fluc-tuate considerably. The same thing was true with the spring round-up. Since the money generally came in two large lump sums during the year, it was necessary for the Executive Board to borrow

large sums of money from the banks in order to pay expenses
during the remainder of the year until the offerings were received.

As a result of their experience in the Seventy-Five Million Campaign, Texas Baptists began to look closely at the deficiencies involved in this system. At the 1920 meeting of the Convention in El
Paso, the Board made several recommendations. One urged that a
campaign be instituted to promote systematic giving, both in paying
the pledges for the Seventy-five Million Fund and for the regular
work of the churches. The Board suggested that from January 15 to
March 15, 1921, an active state-wide effort be made to assist the
churches in developing budgets for local support and for the denominational work. As a result, it was felt, the churches would
remit the denominational funds to the Dallas office every month.

Secretary Groner felt that three "happy" results would be accomplished by this: First, this would eliminate the peril of rainy
weather right at the close of the Campaign, which often threatened
to defeat a large ingathering of funds, and thus impair the credit
and demoralize the work of Texas Baptists. Second, thousands of
dollars in interest would be saved the denomination by providing
funds regularly through the year. Third, other thousands of dollars
would be saved to the cause by the systematic collecting of subscriptions that might otherwise be lost by a lack of interest in
pledges that were not regularly looked after.

However, the Board felt that the semi-annual campaigns in the
fall and spring should also be continued in order to collect unpaid
subscriptions and secure new subscriptions and contributions from
those who had not subscribed to the work. It was suggested that the
month of November not be utilized by either the state convention
or the associations, so that this time would be clear for taking the
cash roundup.

In connection with the organization of the Cash Roundup Campaign planned for 1920, Groner remarked that "we have among the
Baptists of Texas no ecclesiastical hierarch or oligarchs; no big
denominational boss who wields the denominational whip. . . ."
But, he continued, "to all who run and discern the signs of the
times, it must be apparent that there has developed among our
Baptist constituency in Texas an *espirit de corps*, that expects of

every church whole-hearted loyalty—one hundred percent loyalty —to a great cause, and to all our great programs."

In 1921 it was reported that some worthwhile progress had been made in the budget movement, but "we have a long road yet to travel." Superintendent O. E. Bryan of the Home Mission Board, it was noted, would be in Texas during December to assist churches in installing the budget system. In December, 1921, B. W. Vining was named Conservation Secretary in an effort to secure tithers and encourage regular giving both to the local work and to the denominational program. In 1924 Secretary Groner reported the death of Vining and announced the appointment of T. V. Herndon as Budget Director for the Board. In this year it was reported that of approximately 650 churches, there were now 143 churches operating on the budget plan in whole or in part and remitting to the Dallas office monthly. The Board in December, 1923, voted that no appropriations would be made to churches until such churches had adopted the budget plan both for local support and denominational work. In an effort to magnify the budget system, the Board voted in June, 1925, that all special campaigns in behalf of any cause or institution would cease with the calendar year of 1925 because these campaigns hurt the general budget. In 1926 the Board recommended that every church in the state put on a simultaneous, thorough, every-member canvass during December, 1926, emphasizing the budget plan.

"We have gone a long way toward finding ourselves," wrote Secretary Groner in the opening portion of his report to the Convention in 1927. In ringing words, the Board reaffirmed their confidence in the budget plan and urged Every-Member Canvass Campaigns during December, 1927. The Board felt it necessary to institute a special Conquest Campaign for funds to apply on the indebtedness against the institutions and causes. A Budget Promotion Committee elected by the Executive Board urged in 1928 that all churches adopt the budget plan of financing and report to the Dallas headquarters "how much money may be expected from them each month for the work of a co-operative program." In 1929 it was reported that 916 churches had adopted the budget plan of church finance and promised to remit monthly for denominational causes.

Thus, although the budget movement was slow in developing, Texas Baptists were on the way to eliminating the guessing-borrowing-deficit syndrome that had plagued them for all of their history.

A second significant movement of this period was the development of a structure to control the burgeoning expenditures that year by year was bringing large operating deficits to the Board. In 1925, in addition to emphasizing the importance of the budget method of supporting local and denominational work, a special committee reported that at the July, 1924, Executive Board meeting several principles were adopted with respect to denominational activity in Texas. Some of these referred to the Seventy-five Million Campaign and others to recommendations from the Southern Baptist Convention.

The principles adopted that brought expenditures under control were interspersed in this long report. The more important of these were: (1) The Board will no longer advance funds to institutions, but will remit monthly to them the available money. (2) All institutions receiving money from the Board shall make full financial report to the Convention; the Board of Trustees of all such institutions shall be appointed or approved by the Convention; and unaffiliated institutions receiving funds from the Convention shall be approached to work out a method of affiliation. (3) All institutions affiliated with the Convention or receiving money from the Executive Board shall make monthly reports of all contributions received, whether part of a campaign or otherwise. (4) All institutions and causes will be permitted to seek large gifts outside of the denominational program, provided this does not interfere with the denominational program and that no collections or a general canvass among the membership of the churches be made. No institution may have a solicitor in the field except by approval of the Executive Board. (5) Soliciting of scholarships for any schools outside of the denominational campaign budget will be discontinued. (6) No general campaign for endowment may be conducted by any institution except with the approval of the Executive Board.[5]

In 1926 a Budget Control Committee was named "to keep in touch with all the institutions of this Convention and so assist them in the financial affairs as to keep their operating budget within the limits of their income." This Committee, made up principally of financially successful laymen, examined the schools and hospitals of the Convention and reported that in general most of them were in excellent condition and needed no suggestions. In a few instances, there was some lack of business efficiency, and suggestions of the Committee were promptly followed.

In 1927 this Committee recommended that a Finance Committee of the Executive Board be appointed to make a careful study of the expenses of the Executive Board for the purpose of effecting substantial reductions in the expenses. Such a Finance Committee was appointed, submitted a carefully prepared budget at the December, 1927, meeting of the Board, and kept constant oversight of all expenditures during the year. The Committee continued this type of careful scrutiny of the financial aspect of the work during the remainder of this period.

The Budget Control Committee found itself embroiled in a very noisy controversy as the result of another recommendation to the Convention in 1927 at Wichita Falls. They suggested that an Education Commission be appointed to make "a careful study of our correlated school system to determine if there should be any steps taken looking to the possible consolidation and relocation of some of our schools." A Commission of sixteen, of which H. L. Kokernot was chairman and some of Texas' strongest leaders were members, met on April 28, 1928, after months of careful study, and passed a resolution to the effect that the city of Dallas had pledged $1,500,000.00 in cash, plus a large amount of land, which would be available for Baylor University if it would move its campus from Waco to Dallas, and recommended that the offers be accepted and the school be removed to Dallas.

The response perhaps was surprising to some, for the entire denomination reacted with intense agitation. On May 10, 1928, the Commission met again with a committee of Waco citizens, who proposed that the city of Waco would expend $1,000,000.00 on a building program for Baylor at Waco with the understanding that Texas Baptists would raise a like sum, the total amount to be paid on the indebtedness of the school and/or added to the permanent endowment of the university. The first unit of such building program would be a chapel to cost approximately $350,000.00.

The citizens of Waco also declared their desire to assist Baylor in its future enlargement if it remained in Waco. This proposal was considered at length, following which the Commission rescinded its former action and voted to accept Waco's new proposal. This was reported to the Executive Board on May 11, 1928, and on June 5, 1928, in Waco, a called session of the Convention ratified the proposal that Baylor should remain at Waco, and agreed that the denomination enlarge its program by adding another million dollar item for Baylor at Dallas.

Growing out of this a Baylor Campaign Commission composed of one hundred Baptist men and women was named to assist in carrying out the action just voted to raise one million dollars in Waco and one million dollars for Baylor in Dallas. In 1929, when the Budget Control Committee made its report, they approved this campaign in preparing the budget for the new year. The cheering report was made that by reason of the Conquest Campaign, begun in 1926 at the San Antonio Convention, the debts of the institutions had been reduced by $691,258.78. During the year 1928–1929, because of the work of the Budget Control Committee, the debts of the agencies included in the report were reduced by $244,-529.88. The net indebtedness of these agencies (including the Executive Board) on August 31, 1929, amounted to $4,850,587.65.[6]

A third significant financial step was taken during this period. This was a definite, aggressive effort to stop the deficits that were occurring year by year in operating expenses and to begin payment on the debts at once. As indicated above, the deficits were in part slowed by assuming control over the expenditures of the various agencies under the supervision of the Convention. The debts, so very large at first, were slowly cut down by payment of principal and interest as shown above. The Conquest Campaign, kicked off at San Antonio in 1926, was an all-out effort by one hundred leaders among Texas Baptists to encourage the churches to have a part in retiring the indebtedness against the Executive Board representing the Convention. The results of this Campaign by 1929 are shown above.

Finally, during this important period, Texas Baptists learned to integrate their state program with that of the Southern Baptist Convention. Notice has been taken that in 1918 the Texas body sold a one million dollar issue of bonds to pay the debts on their educational institutions, and that in the following year, another heavy financial demand was made (somewhat overlapping) in the beginning of the Southwide program of the Seventy-five Million Campaign. There was some misunderstanding among the constituency about the two efforts to raise money, but the friction subsided in the practical outworking of the two programs together.

Influenced by the program of the Southern Baptist Convention and in turn influencing that body, Texas Baptists helped in the development of what is known as the Southern Baptist Convention's Cooperative Program in 1925. The Seventy-five Million Campaign from 1919 to 1924 showed the desirability of enlisting all of the membership in the churches in all of the work of the Convention. The budget program encouraged monthly support of denominational interests, but the next step was the building of support for all denominational activities. After considerable committee work, the Southern Baptist Convention adopted what was known as the Cooperative Program in 1925, which urged that the constituency no longer designate how their gifts would be used. Designation, of course, was not eliminated, but encouragement was given for all Baptists to give undesignated funds, which would be divided among the agencies to the extent of their needs as far as possible. In the relationship between the Southern Baptist Convention and the state bodies, it was agreed that the states should collect the funds and remit an agreed percentage of undesignated gifts to the southwide body.

Despite the heroic efforts of Texas leaders to extricate themselves from the financial problems besetting them, the closing years of this period showed a deterioration of their financial condition. After the Seventy-five Million Campaign the situation was serious. The report to the 1925 Convention showed an operating deficit of over $256,-000.00. In the following year Secretary Groner said that the total denominational indebtedness of Texas Baptists amounted to $6,-144,624.00. In 1927, Secretary Groner reported that the books showed an operating deficit of $214,348.74. In 1928 the excess of liabilities over assets was shown as almost $830,000.00, and in 1929, as over $732,000.00. Each of the last two years brought an increasing amount of operating loss, and the tide had not yet turned. On October 24, 1929, just before the messengers assembled for the meeting of the Convention at Beaumont, the bottom fell out of the stock market, and the nation was in the grip of financial panic.

11

Depression and War

(1929–45)

☆ ☆ ☆

Every historian uses superlatives in speaking of the depression of the 1930's and the war of the 1940's. In fact, the clinging, suffocating depression, although attacked with every weapon national planners could devise, was lifted only with the bustling activity of World War II.

Both of these events shaped the history of Texas Baptists. Of the first, Secretary J. Howard Williams said in 1932 at the very depth of the financial trauma:

> The work of the past year has been carried on under what is likely the most trying conditions the world has faced in the past two generations. It has been a time of widespread unemployment, unparalleled overproduction, five-cent cotton, the cheapest wheat in decades, continued decline in commodity prices, and the nervous discontents which accompany such conditions. Our National Government has loaned and spent billions of dollars to stabilize affairs, England has deserted the Gold Standard, the world at large has been staggering in abject economic helplessness. It has been a time of political upheaval, bewilderment, and cataclysmic changes.

The war needs no description for those who lived through it. Secretary W. W. Melton commented on it in his report to the Convention in 1943:

The story of 1943 will probably be the blackest page in the history of our civilization. The tragic savagery which has laid its cruel hands on the peoples of the earth since we last met is a story that beggers description. No historian can record it; no artist can paint it; no orator can portray it. . . .

Twenty million men lie dead, and many millions have been maimed for life. . . .

Four hundred billion dollars have been spent in slaughter and destruction. . . .

In the midst of this kind of depression and this war of fearful proportions, Texas Baptists, along with other citizens of the United States, were forced to face severe restrictions in their religious activity. The war, in particular, caused the cancellation of many important denominational meetings (including the annual gathering of the Southern Baptist Convention). Yet all along the road between the collapse of the stock market in 1929 and the ending of the war in 1945 the reports of Texas Baptist leadership speak with gratitude of God's presence. In 1935 Secretary Williams said that

. . . genuine progress is being reported all along the battlefront, and we feel that in times that have taxed the strengths and the resources of every kind of organization and institution, it has been nothing short of the grace of God that has enabled us to emerge from the great depression without the loss of a single institution, with more than $7,000,000 of added assets and debt reduction, and with 100,000 members being added to our churches by baptism during the past three years.

Near the close of the period Secretary Melton described the world war going on and the interruption of the entire economic order, then remarked, "yet the hand of God has been about us as a strong wall. . . . The spirit of God can work and none can forbid Him."

This period is characterized by some positive achievements on the part of Texas Baptists in the areas of leadership, integrity, organization, and an enlarged program.

New Vigorous Leadership

Four secretaries served during these sixteen years. Each was an experienced denominational statesman, and each possessed peculiar gifts that matched the immediate needs of the occasion.

The first was W. R. White, a native Texan. He agonized long before leaving his church at Lubbock to accept the post in 1930, and remained in the office for one year only. As a matter of fact, through holding revival meetings, he raised a substantial part of his salary during this year. Even after his resignation as Executive Secretary, he continued to display his leadership in Baptist state affairs as chairman of the important Finance Committee, which played such a large part in saving the Texas convention from possible bankruptcy. His leadership in establishing the Baptist Foundation was a monument to his business insight and denominational sagacity.

From 1931 to 1936 the Secretary was J. Howard Williams, another native son of Texas, who came to the secretaryship from First Baptist Church, Corsicana. His administration was noted for its aggressive advance for Christ, thorough organization, and the indoctrination of the people. When he resigned to accept the pastorate of the First Baptist Church, Amarillo, his successor lauded this "beloved, honored, and highly successful Secretary" as the one inaugurating the district missionary plan and developing its effective use.

In 1936 R. C. Campbell came from the pastorate of the First Baptist Church, Lubbock, where he had been very successful in the teaching and promotion of stewardship. His secretaryship, continuing until 1941, was characterized by an emphasis on stewardship and evangelism, and great progress was made in these areas.

The fourth Secretary during this period was W. W. Melton, who was called in 1941 from his service of a generation at the Seventh and James Baptist Church, Waco, to lead Texas Baptists. This eloquent and stable pastor possessed the maturity and wisdom for the days when the depression was transformed by a world war into a time of affluence and prosperity.

It is impossible to name the wealth of denominational leaders serving among Texas Baptists during this period. The presidents of the Convention were men of great stature: L. R. Scarborough, J. C. Hardy, J. B. Tidwell, J. Howard Williams, A. D. Foreman, W. R. White, and E. D. Head. The faithful recording secretaries were J. L. Truett and D. B. South until 1942, when Roy L. Johnson succeeded J. L. Truett.

Those who preached the convention sermons were strong leaders. They were Marshall Craig, M. A. Jenkins, M. M. Wolf, Harlan J. Matthews, W. W. Chancellor, E. T. Miller, G. L. Yates, W. H. McKenzie, E. D. Head, J. Howard Williams, J. Ralph Grant, A. J. Holt, E. S. James, George W. Truett, J. M. Dawson, E. F. Cole, and Porter M. Bailes. More than a dozen Texas Baptist churches had over 4,000 members, led by Truett's successor at the First Baptist Church, Dallas, W. A. Criswell; followed by Perry F. Webb, First Baptist Church, San Antonio; Wallace Bassett, Cliff Temple Baptist Church, Dallas; and W. Marshall Craig, Gaston Avenue Baptist Church, Dallas. Some of the outstanding laymen of this period were G. S. Hopkins, R. A. Springer, T. C. Gardner, Robert Jolly, Robert H. Coleman, Pat M. Neff, J. K. Wadley, M. H. Wolfe, R. E. Burt, H. L. Kokernot, A. D. Foreman, Sr., Earl B. Smyth, Carr P. Collins, William Fleming, O. S. Lattimore, and "the largest benefactor to Baptist causes in Texas," John G. Hardin. A few of the scores of able women leaders were Mrs. B. A. Copass, Mrs. W. D. Howell, Mrs. Carlton Winn, Mrs. Olivia Davis, Mrs. R. L. Mathis, Mrs. E. G. Townsend, Mrs. T. C. Jester, Mrs. George W. Truett, Mrs. E. N. Henley, Miss Della Carroll, Mrs. J. H. Gambrell, Mrs. J. M. Dawson, and Mrs. F. S. Robertson.

Baptist Honor and Integrity

Most of this period was characterized by a continuing financial stringency that brought bankruptcy to many commercial businesses. The financial depression came at a particularly bad time for Southern Baptists, for practically every state convention and the southwide institutions were heavily in debt before the midnight of the depression arrived. The temptation came to all state bodies, as well as the Southern Baptist Convention, to negotiate a settlement of debts on a reduced basis. Many of the creditors were willing to accept payment of debts at ten cents on the dollar in order to recoup at least a part of their investments.

This, however, Southern Baptists did not do; and no other state faced a greater struggle with debts than did Texas Baptists. The state's debts were enormous in 1929 and had been increasing annually because of deficits in operation. The Loyalty Bonds issued in 1918 still lacked $200,000.00 of being retired; the expenditures in the 75 Million Campaign of 1919–24 had brought indebtedness to almost every institution of Texas Baptists, amounting to over six million dollars; and several unfortunate tragedies involving the accidental burning of some of the buildings of Texas Baptist institutions, added to the operating deficit, brought despondency and discouragement. When W. R. White made his first report as Secretary in 1930, he soberly took note of the terrific financial adjustments that had taken place, including the stock market crash in October, the lack of a Secretary in November, and the continuing failing crises and increasing unemployment. The liabilities of the Board itself in that year were $1,127,565.84.

Under the capable leadership of White, Williams, Campbell, and Melton, the Convention utilized the tools they already had and produced new ones to attack the overwhelming debt situation. The Budget Control Committee, appointed at the convention in 1926 and combined with the Finance Committee in 1931, was specifically instructed "to assist the executive secretary and the Executive Board in keeping the expenditures of the board within its income," and was doing its work well. The Board paid cash for current necessities in 1931, and a reduction of debts every month was shown. In addition to the work being carried on, for example, the Board paid on indebtedness in the following year a total of $128,731.01. Expenditures at headquarters were cut to the very bone. Salaries were slashed, expenses were eliminated, and economy prevailed on every side.

An interesting story during the secretaryship of J. Howard Williams gives a typical picture of the determination of Texas Baptists to pay their debts. It was necessary for Secretary Williams and Treasurer George Mason to make trips across the state on the train, and in order to save money, they simply purchased one Pullman bed, where one of them slept a part of the night and then arose and let the other one sleep the remainder of the night in the same bed.

The Conquest Campaign, begun in 1926 at San Antonio, continued to bring receipts into the Dallas office. The Budget Control Committee and the Budget Promotion Committee, as well as the Finance Committee, operated within the structure of the Executive Board. Year by year an increasing emphasis was given to the Every-Member Canvass in an effort to secure subscriptions to a budget that included both the local work and denominational activity. Great stress was laid upon the Cooperative Program every year in an effort to magnify undesignated giving through the budget for denominational purposes. In May, 1932, the Southern Baptist Convention adopted a plan known as the Hundred Thousand Club, which was an effort to secure 100,000 Baptists in the South to give one dollar per month over and above their regular gifts to pay on the debts. This movement was vigorously promoted among Texas Baptists.

In addition, appeals were made to generous donors, and names like Mr. and Mrs. John G. Hardin, Mr. and Mrs. George Bottoms, and others were immortalized by memorials from their generous gifts. Another instrument that helped lift the financial burden of this decade was the close cooperation between Texas Baptists and the Southern Baptist Convention. The southwide body provided tracts, leadership, information on achievements in other states, and an aggressive program to help eliminate the staggering debts.

Many stories of this period deserve a place in the heroic annals of Texas Baptists. The Executive Board, constantly harried by a debt of over one million dollars, was forced to make many arbitrary decisions that brought sleepless nights to the leadership. For example, when John G. Hardin made a magnificent gift to Howard Payne College, he structured it in a conditional way so that the remainder of the debts of the College had to be paid to get his gift. This involved an additional outlay of money that threatened the very life of the Executive Board, but without hesitation the Board assumed this additional obligation as a means of securing a long-range benefit in the financial situation.

The burden of indebtedness began to decrease rapidly toward the close of this period. By 1945 the Executive Board was budgeting substantial sums for post-war missions, and the debt had been lifted.

Even the statistics that illustrate the trials and victory of this period of financial stress are inspiring. In 1930, for example, mission gifts amounted to $1,157,753.00 and total gifts of every kind to $6,708,643.00. Both of these figures dropped year by year until 1933, when the sum of $578,392.00 was given for missions, and total gifts of $3,860,515.00 were shown, a 50% drop from 1930. The figures slowly increased during the remainder of the 1930's, and in 1939, mission gifts went over the one million dollar mark for the first time in seven years. In 1945, the end of this period, mission gifts had risen to $3,688,383.00, while total gifts reached a new high of $18,619,999.00.

New Organizational Forms

The District Plan. A far-reaching organizational form was developed during this period by J. Howard Williams, at the time a member of the Executive Board and pastor at Corsicana. At the 1930 Convention he read a report on "Plans for Better Enlistment of Associations and Churches," which was approved. It called for a new organizational structure, known as the "District," to be inserted between the associations and the state body. Associations were grouped geographically into seventeen Districts with a missionary for each District. R. A. Springer remarked that Williams probably introduced this because the Woman's Missionary Union had been successfully using this kind of organization, and, as a matter of fact, so had the Sunday School and Training Union Departments. Williams had first approached the Executive Board with his program, and it had met with immediate enthusiastic response, although there was some opposition. This structure provided a vehicle for improved communication and promotion between the Executive Secretary and over one hundred associations and three thousand churches. The promotion of stewardship and evangelism and the new laymen's movement that developed early in the 1940's, as well as the regular mission and benevolent work carried on by the Convention, were greatly enhanced by this structure. A typical year was reported in 1942, when Secretary Melton listed the missionaries for each district, as follows:

District 1:	Morris A. Roberts	Longview
District 2:	C. M. Spaulding	Jacksonville
District 3:	O. E. Martin	Beaumont
District 4:	Lem Hodges	Houston
District 5:	C. J. Carter	Kingsville
District 6:	Willis J. Ray	San Antonio
District 7:	J. A. Kidd	Alpine
District 8:	W. C. Harrison	Odessa
District 9:	J. Lowell Ponder	Plainview
District 10:	J. C. McKenzie	Amarillo
District 11:	John M. Reddell	Wichita Falls
District 12:	J. D. Brannan	Seminary Hill
District 13:	E. W. Marshall	Dallas
District 14:	M. O. Cheek	Waco
District 15:	John Archie McIver	Austin
District 16:	J. R. Hickerson	Brownwood
District 17:	J. Henry Littleton	Abilene

Secretary Melton said of these men:

> They are to the district what the pastor is to the church and what the General Secretary is to the whole state. These men seek to promote every interest of the Kingdom of God. They seek to enlist all churches in their district in a full, well-rounded program. They are general directors of our work for their particular district. Their work is essential to the on-going of a full program.[1]

The Baptist Foundation of Texas. Another important agency founded during this period involved the investment of endowment funds. On November 13, 1930, the Convention meeting at Amarillo heard a report by the Budget Control Committee, which recommended the creation of a corporation to be known as the Baptist Foundation of Texas, whose sole interest would be the investment and handling of endowment assets. It was felt that Texas Baptists had men and women with unique gifts for this service, who were qualified to handle the investing of such assets better than committees from the trustees of the several institutions. Despite some opposition, Secretary W. R. White was able to secure the adoption of this new organizational structure, reminding the people that the administration of the funds would be under the constant observation of each institution being served and of the Convention itself, thus keeping the Directors of the Foundation alert to invest the funds "only in such securities as would involve a minimum of risk, consistent with a fair rate of return."

Following approval of the Foundation by the Convention, a charter was secured on February 28, 1931. On March 23 of that year the Foundation elected H. L. Kokernot as President, Carr P. Collins as Vice-President, and Paul Danna as Secretary-Treasurer. On May 3, 1931, George J. Mason was elected Executive Secretary of the Foundation, in addition to his duties as Treasurer of the Executive Board of the Convention. Despite the fact that the Foundation was organized at the very depth of the depression, the sagacity of its leadership gave it immediate stability. By 1945, the end of this period, the funds for investment from the institutions of Texas Baptists amounted to $9,968,457.40, and its net income reached a high of $345,587.55.

Men's Baptist Brotherhood. During these depression years, an unusual thrust came in the work of laymen. It will be recalled that as early as 1915 an organization for laymen on a statewide basis was set up and some progress was made. In 1933, however, the report of a Committee on Laymen's Work urged that Texas Baptists join with the Southern Baptist Convention in the movement known as the "Men's Baptist Brotherhood," and that a statewide organization be developed. It was suggested that a Christian layman be employed as the Brotherhood State Secretary. Growing out of this, on March 2–8, 1935, a statewide laymen's conference was held in Dallas, and a thorough organization was developed. Earl B. Smyth was elected president of the state organization, and a chairman for each of the seventeen districts was appointed to promote the work. In 1938, R. A. Springer was elected State Brotherhood Secretary

along with his duties as Treasurer of the Executive Board, beginning his long and distinguished service to Texas Baptists. Because
of the war and other factors, it was difficult in the early years to
secure specific information on the enrollment of men in the various
Brotherhoods, but in 1945 the report showed 15,805 men enlisted
in 703 organizations. L. H. Tapscott was named as Secretary of the
movement in that year.

Department of Church Music. In 1945 the Executive Secretary
reported that a new department, known as the Department of
Church Music, had been created in the previous year and was
under the direction of J. D. Riddle.

Endowment Department. At the 1938 Convention, Secretary
Campbell recommended to the Convention that an Endowment
Department be organized with a Secretary to inform the people
and promote the securing of endowment gifts for the institutions
and agencies of Texas Baptists. In December, 1939, J. W. Bruner
was recommended for this position and elected, but because of his
duties with Southwestern Seminary he was unable to assume the
post until May 1, 1940. He promptly began seeking prospects for
endowment gifts, conferred with prospective donors, and soon published a Guide Book on the Texas Baptist institutions.

Soldier Centers. The entrance of the United States into World
War II brought the need for supervision of the Soldier Centers in
the various cities where training camps were located, and A. C.
Miller was named to head this task. By the end of the period, he
had so organized his work that he was able to give part of his time
to the interracial ministry also.

The Continuing Task

Even while Texas Baptists were valiantly striving to eliminate
the huge debt and weather the severe depression of these sixteen
years from 1929 to 1945, they were able to enlarge their regular
program of missions, education, and benevolences in a remarkable
way. All four of the secretaries (White, Williams, Campbell, and
Melton) stressed the winning of people to Christ through every
type of missions and evangelism, and the enlistment of all Texas

Baptists in this task. Every report in each year emphasized making undesignated gifts to the Cooperative Program for the cause of missions, and, in addition, described the needs of the foreign fields, the home fields, and, in great detail, the call of the state mission fields. In 1936 Texas Baptists began an intensive promotion of evangelism, and heartily joined in the movement by the Southern Baptist Convention to inaugurate a Southwide movement for evangelism under the leadership of L. R. Scarbrough, Southern Baptist Convention president, and R. Q. Leavell, Superintendent of Evangelism of the Home Mission Board.

In each annual report the Executive Secretary called attention to the fact that Texas had a foreign mission field within its own borders. Beginning with 1929, John A. Held led in the ministry to Europeans, which included 750,000 European-speaking people. The Mexican population in Texas in 1938 was reported at over 800,000, while 845,000 Negroes were counted within the borders. Charles T. Alexander became head of the Negro work in 1937.

The extent of the ministry of Texas Baptists in the area of missions during this period may be glimpsed in the regular increase, during the most stringent years of the depression, in gifts to the Cooperative Program. The following chart will illustrate this advance.

1929	$ 548,694.25
1930	511,766.69
1931	431,255.88
1932	364,351.01
1933	310,072.85
1934	364,516.12
1935	454,855.46
1936	482,938.39
1937	601,588.20
1938	634,462.73
1939	710,272.45
1940	752,127.80
1941	871,613.56
1942	1,292,395.13
1943	1,576,806.63
1944	1,852,055.80
1945	2,944,370.62

The accelerated rate of recovery after 1938 is reflected in the reports on the debt retirement. In 1938 the Convention had an indebtedness of $907,805.66. In 1939 it had decreased to $776,642.34; in 1940, $618,800.00; in 1941, $487,300.00; in 1942, less than $100,000.00; and in 1943, Secretary Melton reported that the indebtedness of the Convention had been completely paid in the previous year.[2] Nearly $600,000.00 had been paid in interest in the retirement of these debts.

A very practical measurement of the ministry of Texas Baptists from 1929 to 1945 can be glimpsed in other statistics. During these sixteen years, 584,555 people were baptized into Texas Baptist churches, which was more than the entire church membership in 1933. Total church membership increased from 521,462 in 1930 to 920,952 in 1945. The number of churches increased from 2,973 in 1930 to 3,262 in 1945. Remarkable progress was made in all of the adjuncts to the missionary task: the Sunday school, Training Union, Brotherhood, and Woman's Missionary Union. Between 1930 and 1945, under the leadership of Granville S. Hopkins, Sunday school enrollment increased from 419,615 in 1930 to 573,522 in 1945. The work of the Training Union, under the direction of T. C. Gardner, showed similar unusual achievements. The enrollment increased from 122,774 in 1930 to 173,544 in 1945. The enrollment of the Woman's Missionary Union increased from 52,904 in 1930 to 97,143 in 1945. Figures for Brotherhood enrollment were not available before 1943, but by 1945 it was reported as 15,805. Enrollment in Vacation Bible School jumped from 10,098 in 1930 to 109,797 in 1945, an unbelievable increase.

Leadership for Woman's Missionary Union during this difficult period was given by two presidents, Mary Hill Davis (1906–31) and Mrs. B. A. Copass (1931–46). From 1929 until 1944 the Executive Secretary's post was separate from that of Treasurer. Mrs. J. E. Leigh held the former office from 1929 until 1937, when she was succeeded by Mrs. E. F. Lyon, who served until 1942. From 1942 to 1944 no Executive Secretary was elected, but in 1945, Mrs. R. L. Mathis was named both Executive Secretary and Treasurer. From 1929 to 1944 the faithful Treasurer was Mrs. Olivia Davis.

A very significant factor in the growth of Texas Baptists was the *Baptist Standard*. The editor in 1929 was F. M. McConnell. In the dedication of the 1943 *Texas Baptist Annual* to him, it was remarked that in the sixteen years he served as editor (1929–1944), the circulation had grown from 15,000 to over 100,000. In 1944 David M. Gardner was elected editor to succeed McConnell, and in 1945 the circulation was reported as being over 155,000.

The educational activity of Texas Baptists likewise increased considerably after the beginning of the period in 1929. In that year eight schools were reported: Baylor University at Waco; Baylor Female College at Belton; East Texas Baptist College at Marshall; San Marcos Academy at San Marcos; Wayland Baptist College at Plainview; Decatur Baptist College at Decatur; Burleson College at Greenville; and Howard Payne College at Brownwood. Simmons University at Abilene elected its own trustees and to that extent was not controlled by the Convention. In 1945, with the exception of Burleson College, which closed its doors in 1931, these schools were still operating, and Simmons, now Hardin-Simmons University in Abilene, was controlled by the Convention through the election of its trustees.

These eight schools faced trying problems in the early 1930's due to financial stringency and during World War II when many young people became involved in the military struggle. However, a glimpse of the remarkable financial progress of these eight schools may be seen in the fact that in 1931, when the Baptist Foundation took over the endowment resources of the educational institutions of Texas Baptists, the assets totaled $1,531,414.44, while in 1945 the endowment assets of the schools totaled almost $5,300,000.00 (not including over $1,785,000.00 held for Southwestern Baptist Theological Seminary) and a reserve of almost $280,000.00.

The medical school of Baylor University was moved from Dallas to Houston and opened there on July 12, 1943. This move was made in response to an offer of a $2,000,000.00 gift from H. L. Kokernot, and a $500,000.00 gift by the city of Houston if the school were moved there.

At the beginning of the period Texas Baptists owned and controlled two hospitals: Baylor at Dallas and the Memorial Hospital at Houston. In 1930 there were five additional hospitals operated under the auspices of the various associations: at Fort Worth, Harlingen, Abilene, Waco, and San Angelo. In 1945, Baylor at Dallas and the Memorial Hospital at Houston were thriving institutions, and in addition, three of the associational hospitals had come under the control of the Convention: the Valley Baptist Hospital at Harlingen, Hendricks Memorial Hospital at Abilene, and Hillcrest Memorial Hospital at Waco.

Buckner Orphans Home at Dallas rendered a remarkable service during all of this period. In addition, in 1944 the Convention assumed control of the Mexican Baptist Orphanage at San Antonio.

Many things suggest that 1945 marked the end of a period in Texas Baptist life. In that year World War II came to an end, turning the thoughts of Texas Baptists from the war to the challenge of post-war tasks. In addition, the burdensome debt under which Texas Baptists had been laboring for over a decade had been removed, and Texas Baptists were eager to move forward in challenging activity. Furthermore, during World War II there came a reversal of the sluggish economy which Texas Baptists had known for almost two decades. Secretary Melton in 1944 warned the Convention of the peril of affluence, equal in danger to the perils of indebtedness and depression. Not only so, but 1945 marked the resignation of W. W. Melton as Secretary of the Convention, and his successor, J. Howard Williams, began a new type of accelerated program. Finally, the death of George W. Truett in 1944, L. R. Scarborough in 1945, and others of the giants who had led Texas Baptists for a full victorious generation, turned the leadership to younger men who had been well trained during the depression years to carry vast burdens in the work of the Convention.

12

Flowers and Fruits

(1946–69)

☆ ☆ ☆

This last twenty-four year period in the story of Texas Baptists has been one of constantly increasing economic affluence. During this time their work has had a two-fold emphasis: (1) a rapidly expanding ministry; and (2) a radical restructuring of Board and Convention for more efficient service.

Three gifted men have held the chief executive office during these years: from January 1, 1946 to June 9, 1953, J. Howard Williams; from September 1, 1953, to December 31, 1960, Forrest Feezor; and from January 1, 1961, to the present, Thomas A. Patterson.

It is difficult even to summarize the most basic ministries and achievements of these twenty-four years. The reports to the Convention alone occupy a full shelf and total approximately eight or nine million words. Many important people, events, and statistics must be mentioned only briefly or left out entirely.

It would hardly be proper to list some contemporary leaders and omit others in describing the events of this modern period. In a brief summary like this, the only logical solution has been to mention those holding the highest offices of the Convention or those who have been specifically singled out in the *Annuals* for recognition. The convention presidents were E. D. Head (1945–46), Wallace Bassett (1947–48), William Fleming

(1949–50), Forrest C. Feezor (1951–52), James N. Morgan (1953–54), J. Ralph Grant (1955–56), E. H. Westmoreland (1957–58), M. B. Carroll (1959–60), James H. Landes (1961–62), K. Owen White (1963), Abner V. McCall (1964–65), J. Carroll Chadwick (1966–67), Gordon Clinard (1968–69), and Jimmy R. Allen (1970). Roy L. Johnson and D. B. South were the Recording Secretaries until 1959, when Cecil G. Goff replaced Johnson and served during the remainder of the period. R. A. Springer and J. Earl Mead continued as Treasurer and Secretary of the Corporation, respectively.

The convention sermons were preached by C. E. Hereford, A. D. Foreman, Jr., Forrest Feezor, J. H. Landes, R. H. Cagle, A. B. Rutledge, Perry F. Webb, Carl Bates, W. Herschel Ford, Grady W. Metcalf, Sterling Price, H. Guy Moore, James Leavell, Gordon Clinard, John Rasco, Vernon Elmore, W. M. Shamburger, Woodson Armes, Herbert Howard, James Coggin, W. Fred Swank, B. J. Martin, and Ralph Langley.

Indicative of their recognition of outstanding service, Texas Baptists dedicated their state convention *Annuals* to Mr. and Mrs. Robert Jolly, Walter H. McKenzie, J. Howard Williams, H. L. Kokernot, J. W. Bruner, George J. Mason, William Fleming, E. S. James, D. B. South, David M. Gardner, Thomas H. Taylor, T. C. Gardner, E. Hermond Westmoreland, R. A. Springer (with the first "Second Mile Award" for 20 years of distinguished denominational service), Carroll Jones, Forrest C. Feezor, C. B. Jackson, E. A. Reiff, W. F. Howard, John G. Dudley, Wallace Bassett, T. A. Patterson, O. D. Martin, E. N. Jones, and Earl M. Collier.

Special reference was made in the *Annuals* to financial gifts by Mr. and Mrs. William Fleming, Mr. and Mrs. A. L. Wasson, Mr. and Mrs. H. R. Cullen, Mr. and Mrs. R. W. Smith, T. G. Hendrick, and Carr P. Collins, Sr.

Presidents of Woman's Missionary Union during this period were Mrs. Earl B. Smyth (1946–49), Mrs. R. L. Mathis (1949–55), Mrs. Clem Hardy (1955–60), Mrs. Bert Black (1961–63), Mrs. C. J. Humphrey (1964–67), and Mrs. H. C. Hunt (1968). Executive Secretaries were Mrs. R. L. Mathis (1945–47), and Miss Eula Mae Henderson (1947–69).

J. Howard Williams (1946–53)

All Texas Baptists had great confidence in Williams. They felt that this man, who had led so dynamically in the depression-ridden 1930's, had the wisdom and gifts to direct them in a post-war period of affluence that could turn into a depression at any time. The situation, of course, was completely different from the one that Williams faced when he took this position at the depth of the depression in 1931. The depression had now vanished, funds were available to meet many challenges that financial stringency had earlier obscured, and the denomination was strong and united. The general confidence in the new Secretary was indicated quickly. In May, 1946, the Southern Baptist Convention adopted a plan to raise $3,500,000.00 to repair and replace property, particularly on the foreign mission fields, that was damaged or destroyed during the war. Texas was asked to raise about $450,000.00 as her quota. Although Williams had been in office for only a few months, he was able to lead in the raising of $711,011.92 by October.

Williams showed the same creative leadership he had exercised over a decade before. His secretaryship was characterized by the formation of new departments for benevolent work, by the promotion of a vigorous Five-Year Program, and by advances in all areas of the Board's activities.

New Departments. The staff on January 1, 1946, when Williams became secretary, had already made an impressive record. At the headquarters office in Dallas, the Treasurer was R. A. Springer; the Sunday School Department was headed by Granville S. Hopkins; the Training Union by T. C. Gardner; the Baptist Student Union Department by W. F. Howard; the Endowment Department by J. W. Bruner; the Music Department by J. D. Riddle; the Brotherhood Department by L. H. Tapscott; and the ministry to minorities by A. C. Miller. Closely related to this central organization was the Baptist Foundation with George J. Mason as Secretary; Woman's Missionary Union of Texas with Mrs. R. L. Mathis as Executive Secretary-Treasurer; and the *Baptist Standard* with David M. Gardner as editor. The five bookstores, operated jointly with the Sunday School Board, were under the supervision of George J. Mason.

In the field were seventeen district missionaries, supported in part through the state budget. These were S. H. Maples, V. G. Garrett, O. D. Martin, J. L. Ponder, R. R. Lloyd, Hal C. Wingo, R. L. Wittner, J. W. Arnett, B. N. Shepard, J. C. McKenzie, S. F. Martin, J. D. Brannon, J. I. Gregory, M. O. Cheek, Lemuel Hall, J. R. Hickerson, and J. H. Littleton.

In addition, over eighty pastors were being financially assisted in churches too weak to maintain their own work, along with specialized workers among the Mexicans, Negroes, the Europeans, workers in city missions, and prison evangelists. Among the institutions related to the Convention were Buckner Orphans Home, of which Hal F. Buckner was president, and the Texas Mexican Baptist Orphanage of which J. L. Moye was the head until his untimely death. Also functionally related to the state office were eight schools and five hospitals. Pat M. Neff was president of Baylor University; Gordon J. Singleton, of Mary Hardin-Baylor College; J. L. Ward, of Decatur Baptist College; Thomas H. Taylor, of Howard Payne College; Rupert N. Richardson, of Hardin-Simmons University; H. D. Bruce, of East Texas Baptist College at Marshall; J. W. McDonald, of Wayland Baptist College; and R. Wilbur Herring, who became president of San Marcos Academy on August 15, 1946.

In the five Baptist hospitals related to the Convention, Lawrence R. Payne was administrator of Baylor University Hospital, Dallas; E. M. Collier, of Hendrick Memorial Hospital, Abilene; J. H. Pace, of Hillcrest Memorial Hospital, Waco; Robert Jolly, of the Baptist Memorial Hospital, Houston; and K. P. Walker was Superintendent of the Valley Baptist Hospital, Harlingen.

Immediately, Secretary Williams noted that the Convention was striving to exert leadership in several important areas that were not represented in the organizational structure at Dallas. With the assistance of committees, Williams moved to assure proper leadership in some of these areas by restructuring the state organization.

Department of Evangelism. The first new expanded area of assigned responsibility in the state structure came in evangelism.

Texas Baptists through the years have emphasized evangelism in our churches. Under the leadership of our executive secretaries, it has had full time evangelists on the field serving our churches. In the beginning of this year, 1946, under the direction of the leadership of Secretary Dr. J. Howard Williams, the Board decided that there should be created a Department of Evangelism for the purpose of studying evangelism and acquiring methods that would meet present day conditions. The Department of Evangelism was actually created May 1, 1946, and Dr. C. E. Matthews, pastor of Travis Avenue Baptist Church, Fort Worth, was elected superintendent.[1]

The staff of evangelists to serve with Matthews were C. Y. Dossey, who resigned his pastorate in Port Arthur to accept the post; C. B. Jackson who resigned his pastorate at Greenville; J. Frank Weedon, who resigned his pastorate at Denton; and Jesse Yelvington, a returned chaplain. In a remarkably short time this department organized a program to emphasize the winning of souls. In 1948, when C. E. Matthews resigned to accept a similar position with the Southern Baptist Convention's Home Mission Board, C. Wade Freeman, an experienced and successful pastor, became Superintendent.

Department of Radio. The second organizational expansion came on May 1, 1947. A committee reported to the convention that year that "during the early part of this year a radio department was set up. Dr. R. Alton Reed, the brilliant and efficient pastor of the Park Cities Baptist Church in Dallas, was persuaded to take over this most important work on May 1st."

Department of Public Relations. In June, 1947, a third new department was established when Andrew Q. Allen was named head of the new Department of Public Relations. In 1949, when Allen was named to head the Sunday School Department, the Radio and Public Relations Departments were combined under R. Alton Reed.

Rural and City Missions. In 1949 Floyd Chaffin was named Assistant Executive Secretary, in which post he served until 1952, when he resigned to become Executive Secretary for Louisiana Baptists. Chaffin was placed in charge of Rural and City Missions. Secretary Williams explained that emphasis had been placed upon rural work throughout several departments of the Convention, but that from the study of the Committee on Survey, a new thrust in rural rehabilitation and an advance in city mission work within the state were being actively promoted.

Christian Life Commission. In his address at the Convention in 1949, Secretary Williams urged "that this convention should initiate some plan by which we can help our people to understand the grave issues of our day in terms of Christian faith and practice." A special committee was appointed to study this matter, and in 1950 the Convention authorized the Executive Board to elect a commission to foster this area of interest. This became known as the Christian Life Commission, and A. C. Miller, who was directing work with minorities, was asked to head it. He was succeeded in 1953 by Foy O. Valentine.

Christian Education Commission. In the report of the Committee on Christian Education at the Convention in 1950, the committee discussed several serious problems facing Baptist education in the future and made an important recommendation, which was approved by the Convention, that

> the Executive Board be instructed to examine very carefully the feasibility of giving the Executive Secretary a special assistant who shall be a professional school man, and shall give his time to studying educational problems in Texas and their effect upon Baptist schools. He shall advise the Executive Secretary and Board in all matters relating to education, and shall spend a generous portion of his time actually out on the field "selling" Christian education to our whole Baptist constituency.[2]

In 1952 a Christian Education Commission was created

> to determine the division of Christian education funds, to determine the bounds of the curriculum of the several institutions, and to study the needs and problems of the Christian education program of Texas Baptists with the object in mind to find means of supplying those needs and solving those problems without interfering with their internal administration or usurping the prerogatives of the Boards of Trustees of the individual institutions.[3]

Harold A. Haswell was named Executive Coordinator of this Commission.

Department of Church Loans. In connection with the program of rural rehabilitation and city missions, it was observed that many of the churches already existing were in drastic need of loans for buildings. A committee was appointed by the Executive Board to study the matter, and it recommended that a church loan agency be established with an initial capital of $250,000.00 "for the purpose of making available funds to be loaned to churches throughout our state." This program was approved by the Convention in 1951, and A. B. White was named as its Secretary. A corporation called the Church Loan Association was organized to serve the churches in Texas through this Department.

On July 17, 1952, the Executive Board authorized this Department to establish and operate a new corporation known as the Baptist Church Loan Corporation, which would make loans to Baptist churches in the pioneer states of the West and Northwest.

The Department reported in 1953 that seventy-eight loans and sixty-eight commitments totaling $3,194,787.20 had been made in Texas, while in the West, a total of twenty-six loans closed and twenty commitments for a total of $1,063,500.00 had been processed. Special offerings from the churches and a three million dollar bond issue during 1953 provided capital for assisting the western churches.

Other Expansion. In addition to these new departmental structures created during the secretaryship of J. Howard Williams, several other extensions in the ministry of the Convention were developed.

On June 30, 1952, the Baptist Memorial Hospital, San Antonio, was transferred to Texas Baptists from the Southern Baptist Convention. The administrator, A. Moede, was succeeded by F. R. Higgenbotham in the following year.

A new school, the University of Corpus Christi, was established on April 1, 1947, under the aegis of the Executive Board, and E. S. Hutcherson became its first president.

In 1948 the Survey Committee of the Executive Board recommended that Buckner Baptist Benevolences develop three additional institutions under their leadership: a home for the aged, a mission for unwed mothers, and a boys' ranch. These institutions were organized. Meanwhile, on June 1, 1952, Hal F. Buckner was succeeded by Ellis L. Carnett as president and general manager. In 1953 Carnett reported to the Convention that the Mary E. Trew Home for the Aged in Dallas would probably open in the following year, and plans had been made for a similar Home in Houston. Bethesda Welfare Home at San Antonio had cared for thirty-five unwed mothers. Buckner Boys Ranch at Burnet had thirty-six boys in that year. Perry F. Evans was named supervisor of the ranch, while Bill J. Baker was supervisor of Bethesda.

On March 6, 1950, the Executive Board voted to approve a recommendation brought by a committee appointed by Secretary Williams that the Convention accept the offer of Mr. and Mrs. Louis M. Hanna to build and equip a home for needy and homeless children at Round Rock. The institution was titled the Texas Baptist Children's Home. Herbert D. Dollahite was named Superintendent of the new Home, which was formally dedicated on September 5, 1950. In 1953 it was reported that the Home was housing one hundred and forty children.

In 1951 Mrs. Laura L. Boothe of Beeville donated a section of land about eighteen miles from Beeville to care for homeless children. In December, 1952, the Executive Board voted to accept this Home as an agency of the Convention. J. M. Lunsford was named Administrator, and in 1953, in its first complete year of operation, the South Texas Children's Home reported that they were caring for thirty-eight children.

Five-Year Program. In December, 1946, the Executive Board authorized the appointment of a Survey Committee to study the total work of the Convention as a means of noting immediate needs and of planning a long-range program. The committee was composed of Perry F. Webb, chairman, along with Wallace Bassett, E. H. Westmoreland, H. L. Kokernot, A. D. Foreman, Sr., W. A. Criswell, and George J. Mason. Their report presented a challenging five-year program of advance. Secretary Williams remarked in 1949:

> This is the first year of our new century of organized Convention life. We set for ourselves a monumental task in adopting the report of the Committee on Survey which was made to the Convention last

year. That report, which envisioned a general advance along all lines, called for a five-year plan which has indeed become the program of the Convention.[4]

In the next five years (after which Secretary Williams resigned to become president of Southwestern Baptist Theological Seminary), the strength of Texas Baptists increased greatly. The number of churches between 1948 and 1953 grew from 3,214 to 3,478; total gifts for all causes increased from $30,818,160.00 to $54,648,025.00; the Sunday school enrollment increased from 711,801, to 923,516; the average Sunday school attendance, from 342,858 to 459,704; the Training Union enrollment increased from 219,194 to 356,678; the average attendance in Training Union, from 111,948 to 190,698. Baptisms in 1948 were reported as 49,339, while in 1953 they were shown as 62,512. As a matter of comparison, in the five years prior to 1948 the total number of baptisms was 224,680, while in the five year period from 1948 to 1953, total baptisms numbered 294,475. The church membership increased from 1,044,258 in 1948 to 1,307,054 in 1953. Mission giving increased from $4,536,605.00 in 1948 to $10,401,921.00 in 1953. Total gifts of Texas Baptists increased from $31,225,465.00 in 1948 to $55,506,986 in 1953. The value of church property in Texas increased from $85,110,909.00 in 1948 to $200,253,276.00 in 1953.

In 1949 Granville S. Hopkins retired as Sunday School Secretary after serving faithfully and effectively for twenty-three years. He was succeeded by Andrew Q. Allen.

These remarkable gains in the financial and numerical aspects of Texas Baptist work developed partly from the burgeoning economy, but principally from the vision and leadership displayed by Secretary Williams, his staff, and the Executive Board.

The established agencies of the Convention without exception reported unusual progress. The Direct Missions Department reported that during the five year period closing with 1953, a total of 713 rural churches had been assisted in securing proper buildings, for which the outlay amounted to $322,627.12. For the same period, city churches totaling 354 had been aided with land purchases in the sum of $561,889.60. The salaries of 113 mission pastors were supplemented, as well as the salaries of the seventeen district missionaries and forty associational missionaries. L. D. Wood, Coordinator for the State Board and the Home Mission Board in Spanish work in Texas, reported that thirty-two Latin American missions and churches had been assisted through the Mary Hill Davis offering during the year in 1953. During the year 130 pastors and workers in Latin American missions and churches had received salary supplements from the State Board.

In July, 1951, George J. Mason retired as Secretary of the Texas Baptist Foundation after two decades of distinguished service. He was succeeded by A. B. Culbertson. The Foundation reported in 1953 that its total funds amounted to $20,276,888.37.

The *Baptist Standard,* edited by David M. Gardner, had a circulation of 267,441 in 1953.

During 1949, the Sunday School Board, with whom the Convention jointly owned the bookstores, made an offer of $125,502.87 for the state's half-interest in the five bookstores in Texas. This offer was accepted.

As one scans the *Annuals* of the Convention for the years of Williams' ministry, it becomes apparent that he desired many more things and dreamed much more than he was able to do. In 1951, for example, his closing word to the Convention was titled "More Beyond." He noted that the Convention had doubled its membership in twenty years in many departments and that giving was twenty times greater than twenty years before. This, he commented, should not bring bragging. "In comparison with our actual abilities, the achievements registered are unworthy," he said.

However, other things he did accomplish included a closer relationship between the district and associational missionaries and the moderators of associations, the encouragement of the youth revival movement, the development of a better schedule for pre-Convention and post-Convention meetings, and the continuance of the Survey Committee that would prepare new goals for the new Secretary after Williams resigned. He led in the erection of a new headquarters building, in cooperation with other Baptist bodies. The new five story building was formally opened in June, 1952.

Secretary Williams was greatly loved by the constituency.

Stricken by a non-fatal heart attack in 1948 and unable to attend the annual meeting, he wrote tender words to the Convention and received similar sentiments from them. He delighted to call the evening service to consider the state mission program the "Family Night." His resignation in 1953 was the occasion for many expressions of appreciation for him.

Forrest C. Feezor (1953–60)

On July 10, 1953, the Executive Board elected Forrest C. Feezor, then pastor of the First Baptist Church, Waco, Texas, as the new Executive Secretary. He had been a distinguished educator, pastor, and administrator. All of his talents were called into play in the challenging post to which he had been named. His administration included another Five-Year Plan, an impressive list of achievements in the many sided activities of Texas Baptists, and the development of the most important Survey Committee that Texas Baptists have ever known.

New Personnel. Not only did the Board lose the services of J. Howard Williams, but in addition J. W. Bruner, Secretary of the Endowment Department, had reached retirement age; A. C. Miller, Secretary of the Christian Life Commission, resigned to accept leadership of the Christian Life Commission of the Southern Baptist Convention; and R. Alton Reed resigned to join the Annuity Board of the Southern Baptist Convention. Other important leaders in the state program also resigned.

To replace these losses, J. Woodrow Fuller, who had been serving as Acting Secretary since the resignation of Williams, was named Assistant Executive Secretary in charge of the Department of Direct Missions and Promotion. L. T. Daniel was elected Endowment Secretary; L. L. Holloway, Director of Public Relations; R. H. Dilday, Associate Sunday School Secretary; Foy Valentine, the Christian Life Commission; L. B. Cobb, assistant in the Department of Direct Missions and Promotion; Ross Coggins, Associate in the Student Department; Robert B. Chapman, Royal Ambassador Secretary; and Miss Amelia Morton, Young People's Secretary of the Woman's Missionary Union.

Five-Year Program. Although Feezor had been in office for only about a month at the time his report was made to the Convention in 1953, he spoke of the excellent achievements of the previous year by each of the departments of work. A new Advance Committee headed by E. H. Westmoreland, appointed by the Executive Committee, named a number of goals to be accomplished during the following five years. Many of these goals were set with such a large annual increase over the statistics shown in 1953 that it appeared impossible even to approximate reaching them. Probably it was felt that it would be better to aim too high and not to achieve the total goal than to set a lesser challenge before Texas Baptists.

Each of the fifteen areas of work enthusiastically set itself to carrying out these goals during the following five years.

At the end of the first year the prospects for reaching many of these goals seemed good. The goal for baptisms in 1954 had been 65,000, and the total at the end of the year was 66,634. The goal for new churches was 100, and the 1954 report showed 91 more churches than were reported in 1953. The goal for church membership had been set at 1,400,000, while the actual figure was 1,363,685. The goal for Sunday school enrollment was 1,000,000, and the report for 1954 showed an achievement of 1,009,385. The Sunday school awards goal was 125,000, and the achievement numbered 139,105. The achievement for Vacation Bible Schools exceeded the goal of 3,100 by three schools. The goal for Training Union enrollment was 400,000, and the achievement was shown as 384,643. The number of Training Union awards in 1954 exceeded the goal of 175,000 by 2,628. The goal of a Brotherhood enrollment of 61,000 was exceeded by 3,690, while the goal of 135 new Brotherhoods was short by only 34. The goal of 160,000 Woman's Missionary Union members was exceeded by 12,745. The number of W. M. U. organizations had as its goal 8,400, while the report showed 10,147 in 1954. The goal for *Baptist Standard* circulation had been set at 280,000, while the report of 1954 showed the circulation as 281,000.

The goal for total gifts of $58,000,000.00 was exceeded by over $3,000,000.00. The goal of $5,500,000.00 in undesignated Cooperative Program receipts was exceeded by over $84,000.00. The goal of designated Cooperative Program receipts of $2,500,000.00 fell short by about $90,000.00.

The goal of $24,000,000.00 in assets for the Baptist Foundation was missed by almost two million dollars. The goal of assets for the Church Loan Fund was $4,000,000.00, while the report shows assets of $2,522,580.85.

During the remainder of this Five-Year Program, the reports revealed that good progress was made in every department of work. Many of the numerical goals were not reached at the end of the five years. It is interesting to note that the goal for total gifts for all causes was $74,000,000.00 for 1958, while the attainment showed $80,294,137.00; the Cooperative Program gifts goal of ten million dollars was exceeded by over one million dollars in 1958.

Beyond all of these numerical and financial goals, however, a glance at the reports of the various departments of work of the Convention during this five-year period reveals an extraordinary ministry in every way.

Educational Efforts. It has been mentioned that Harold A. Haswell was named Executive Coordinator of the Education Commission in 1953. He was also elected Secretary of the Texas Baptist School Administrators Association, a voluntary organization of college presidents developed in September, 1952. Immediately the Commission, working with the Administrators Association, developed a formula for Texas Baptist Christian education amounting to twenty-five percent of the distributable budget plus one-third of the over-plus.

In 1954 Arthur Tyson was named president of Mary Hardin-Baylor to replace A. C. Gettys. Plans were developed for meeting capital needs and endowment, as well as for seeking future students. In 1955 the Commission reported that the major emphasis of the year had been on the improvement of the instruction. A five-year master plan for development of Texas Baptist schools was adopted in December, 1954, looking to give maximum support to the improvement of existing institutions and to assist all schools to attain membership in the Southern Association by January, 1960. Guy D. Newman succeeded Thomas H. Taylor as president of

Howard Payne College in 1954. The 1956 Convention approved establishing junior colleges in Houston and Dallas, with San Antonio a possible site for a third such school in the future.

Benevolent Ministries. The six hospitals operated by Texas Baptists showed good progress year by year. Julian H. Pace was the Administrator of the Hillcrest Memorial Hospital at Waco; John G. Dudley, of the Memorial Hospital at Houston; T. H. Morrison, of the Valley Baptist Hospital at Harlingen; Boone Powell, of the Baylor University Hospital at Dallas; F. R. Higgenbotham, of the Baptist Memorial Hospital, San Antonio; and E. M. Collier, of the Hendrick Memorial Hospital at Abilene. In September, 1957, a new hospital was accepted by the Convention—the Baptist Hospital of Southeast Texas, at Beaumont, of which Guy H. Dalrymple was Administrator. Also in September, 1957, the Convention accepted the Baptist Memorial Geriatric Hospital at San Angelo, with Mrs. Louis Gayer as Administrator.

The ministry of Texas Baptists among the orphans and other needy groups was enlarged during this period. In 1953 E. L. Carnett reported that the Home in Dallas, the Ranch at Burnett, and the Home for unmarried mothers at San Antonio had ministered to about 775 persons during the year. The Mexican Baptist Children's Home at San Antonio had increased its enrollment of children to ninety-six, its capacity. There were 140 children at the Texas Baptist Children's Home. The South Texas Children's Home had cared for thirty-eight children.

The Buckner Home report for 1954 announced the retirement of Robert Cooke Buckner on June 19, 1954. The Mary E. Trew Home for the Aged opened at Dallas on September 19, 1954, and soon was taxed to its capacity of twenty-four persons. In 1955 Buckners opened a new home for elderly people in Houston under the supervision of James C. Wilson. Jarel I. Cartlidge was named Superintendent of the Texas Baptist Children's Home in October, 1954. On December 15, 1955, Buckner Girls Ranch, Breckenridge, was opened with facilities for six girls. Its Supervisor was J. C. Hood. In 1956 James S. McNabb became Administrator of Texas Baptist Children's Home, Round Rock. On January 1, 1957, Buckner Orphans Home secured property at Lubbock and on March 8,

1958, opened the Buckner-Milam Girls Home. In 1957 Buckners added a Social Service Department to foster home care, adoption service, and mother's aid. Effective January 1, 1960, all of the benevolent homes of Texas Baptists became participants in the Cooperative Program distribution of Texas Baptists.

Direct Missions and Promotion. This department under the leadership of J. Woodrow Fuller continued its emphasis in behalf of rural churches, city missions, and mission salary supplements for pastors. In addition, the Board continued to provide financial assistance on the salaries of the seventeen district missionaries and forty associational missionaries. In cooperation with the southwide stewardship emphasis, preparation was made to magnify stewardship in conferences in each association, to be climaxed in a week of stewardship study. Fifteen hundred schools of stewardship were doubtless responsible in large part for increasing budget gifts over a million dollars from the year before.

Good progress in the Spanish missions under L. D. Wood and the City and Rural Extension program under R. Elmer Dunham was reported. A vigorous beginning was made in a church-centered approach to Jewish work. In 1955 a World Missions Conference on the state level was held in mid-March in Fort Worth, which, along with schools of missions throughout the state, greatly forwarded the cause of missions. What was termed "a new miracle in stewardship" was reported. All but four of the 3,519 churches affiliating with the Convention in 1953–54 made a contribution to missions, and in 1954–55, of the 3,620 churches, all but half-a-dozen made contributions to missions. The year 1957 brought an enlarged program in missionary activity. Struggling state bodies in Arizona, Washington-Oregon, and Colorado were assisted financially in stabilizing their work. The Board also assisted in pioneer mission work in Wisconsin and Minnesota, and paid one-half of the salary of a professor at Southwestern Seminary to assist in training student pastors in rural work.

On May 1, 1957, in a reorganization of the administrative staff, Arthur B. Rutledge came from the First Baptist Church, Marshall, as first secretary of the Stewardship and Direct Missions Department. This Department emphasized the Cooperative Program ministries, the Forward Program of church finance, the 30,000 Movement, and the enrollment of churches in the Church Achievement Program.

Department of Evangelism. Under the leadership of C. Wade Freeman a strong program was developed in the period from 1953 through 1958. In 1953 Freeman pointed out that in the last five-year program of the Convention a total of 282,312 persons had been won and baptized, representing nearly twenty-five percent of the Baptist church membership in Texas. The regular state-wide conference in January of each year was continued year by year; approximately 1,000 churches had accepted the plan of the Church Council of Evangelism, which was designed to carry on a perennial effort. The Department personnel had conducted ninety meetings during 1953, gave direction to twenty associational crusades, and worked on college campuses, in encampments, and in various other rallies and meetings throughout the year. It was reported in 1954 that plans had been made to cooperate with the Home Mission Board in a nationwide simultaneous Revival Crusade in 1959. Every association in the state had agreed to cooperate in this revival effort.

Sunday School Department. It is difficult to summarize the widespread activities of the Sunday School Department during these five years under the leadership of Andrew Allen. Five-year goals were set for the number of Sunday schools (3,600 by 1958), Sunday school enrollment (1,200,000 by 1958), Training in Churches (2,200 by 1958), Training Awards (125,000 by 1958), Vacation Bible School's (3,500 by 1958), Vacation Bible School enrollment (500,000 by 1958), number of Group Training Schools (300 by 1958), and enrollment in Group Schools (100,000 by 1958). The calendar of the Sunday School Department was built around these activities during the next five years. An exciting program of individual and group training, leadership clinics, and intensive promotion through the state Sunday School Convention year by year reached many of the goals set in 1953. The Vacation Bible School statistics reported in 1958 showed that the goal for these schools was exceeded, although the enrollment did not quite reach the goal.

Department of Student Work. The many-sided ministries of the Department of Student Work made amazing progress in this five-year period. Efforts were made to enlist every Baptist student to participate in a college or community church during his days on the campus; to enter into the worship, prayer, and Bible study sessions to promote Christian growth; to engage in community mission projects in the college territory, Youth Revivals, summer missions, and personal witnessing; to develop supporting friendships and the creation of an atmosphere of a Christian community on the campuses; and to be maximum students in the total college experience, regardless of life-work plans. In 1953 there were sixty active Baptist Student Unions and Bible teaching for elective credit through seventeen Baptist Chairs of Bible in which more than two thousand students were enrolled. In that year there were ten permanent student centers and seven temporary student centers to serve the major non-Baptist campuses throughout the state.

In the summer of 1953 there were ninety-five department-directed meetings in Youth Revival. A program of ministerial student orientation on each of the seven Baptist college campuses in Texas involved more than 1200 ministerial students.

By 1958, Secretary W. F. Howard was able to report a total of twenty-three student centers adjacent to non-Baptist campuses throughout Texas; Bible courses taught by seventeen combination director-teachers, and three full-time teachers enrolling more than two thousand students; the use of nineteen students to carry on summer mission work around the world; the attendance of approximately 850 students from Texas at Glorieta and Ridgecrest during Student Weeks as well as large numbers at the Baptist Student Convention at Wichita Falls and the Spring Planning Conference at San Marcos; the journey of more than five hundred from Texas to attend the Baptist World Youth Conference at Toronto, Canada; the promotion of 135 revivals led by young people during the summer; two International Student Baptist Retreats sponsored jointly by the Home Mission Board and the State group; and the organization of seven new Baptist Student Unions during the year.

Training Union Department. The achievements of the Training Union Department during this five year program were remarkable.

In the first year the enrollment was 384,643. After showing substantial increases during the first three years, the membership decreased due to a number of circumstances. However, in 1958, at the end of the period, the Training Union enrollment was 461,338 with an average attendance of 223,092.

The basic Training Union objectives of increasing in the knowledge of the Scriptures, Christian growth, education in Baptist life, and Christian activity were forwarded by clinics for leaders, "M" Nights, training sessions at Glorieta and Ridgecrest, the state Training Union conventions, and vigorous leadership in the program on the part of the state workers. The great pioneer, T. C. Gardner, noted for his enthusiastic and intense leadership, retired in 1956 after more than forty years of service to Texas Baptists. The growth of the Training Union during his period as Secretary from a few hundred unions to over 16,500 mark him as a leader of the highest order. He was succeeded by R. H. Dilday.

Woman's Missionary Union. The work of the women developed steadily during these five years. During the first four years, Mrs. Clem Hardy was president; in 1958 she was succeeded by Mrs. R. L. Mathis. Miss Eula Mae Henderson was Executive Secretary-Treasurer during all of this period. The body grew from 10,147 organizations in 1954 to 11,425 organizations in 1958. Year by year the Woman's Missionary Union led in securing great mission offerings. In 1954 the Lottie Moon offering for foreign missions amounted to $1,298,680.11; the Annie Armstrong offering for home missions $234,725.97; the Mary Hill Davis offering for state missions $165,830.98; and for Ministerial Relief, $42,975.20. In 1958 it was reported that the Lottie Moon offering had increased to $1,717,373.90; the Annie Armstrong offering to $346,811.43; the Mary Hill Davis offering to $188,229.70; and the Ministerial Relief offering to $49,036.01.

In 1958 the Texas Woman's Missionary Union adopted goals in line with those set out by the Executive Board of Woman's Missionary Union, Southern Baptist Convention, in the Baptist Jubilee Advance, which in 1964 would celebrate one hundred and fifty years of Baptist cooperation and missionary emphasis in the United States.

Brotherhood Department. The five-year goals for the Brotherhood in Texas were quite challenging. For example, in 1954 the goal for new church Brotherhoods was 135, while 101 were organized. The goal for Laymen-Sponsored revivals was 75, while 30 were held. The goal for officers' clinics was 75, while 48 were held. The goal for new boys in Sunday schools by Brotherhoods was 200, while 151 was achieved. The goal for the Brotherhood *Journal* circulation was 14,000, while 12,719 was achieved. The goal for Brotherhood enrollment for 1954 was 61,000, while the actual achievement was 64,690. In 1958 it was reported that the number of Brotherhoods was 2,149 (compared with 1,780 in 1954). Total Brotherhood enrollment in 1958 reached 75,688. During these five years the influence of the Brotherhood was felt through a number of channels. There was major emphasis on evangelism in all Brotherhood groups; Officers' clinics were held in many of the associations; Royal Ambassador work under Robert B. Chapman was carried out extensively after the transfer of the Royal Ambassador sponsorship to the Brotherhood from the W. M. U.; Laymen-Sponsored revivals, Brotherhood encampments and rallies, Friendship Centers, the Man-and-Boy Movement, Texas laymen helping in revivals in other states, and many other ministries characterized the period.

The Executive Secretary of the state Brotherhood during this entire period was L. H. Tapscott. Brotherhood Presidents were T. Gordon Ryan (1953–54), Fred C. Hughes (1955–56), W. A. Stephenson (1956–57); and C. C. Kelly (1957–58).

Department of Church Music. Through conducting music schools, special conferences, special music programs, state music festivals, enlistment of qualified music workers, special emphasis on leadership training, and the distribution of tracts and other free literature, the program was strengthened year by year. In 1954, J. D. Riddle, who had been the first Secretary of the Church Music Department when it was founded on January 1, 1945, died, and on July 1, 1954, V. F. Forderhase came from the First Baptist Church, Arlington, to head this work.

Christian Life Commission. Under the leadership of Foy Valentine, this Commission was very active in these five years. The

Commission endeavored to lead Texas Baptists to apply the whole gospel of Christ to every area of life. Major attention was given to the five general areas of Family Life, Race Relations, Economics, Moral Issues, and Christian Citizenship. In 1955 the Convention adopted the recommendation of the Christian Life Commission to enter into a Southwide Crusade for Christian Morality to continue from 1955 to 1956. The Commission reported in 1956 that about 250,000 appropriate pamphlets on race relations, honesty, personal purity, Christian citizenship, and abstinence from alcohol had been distributed in Texas, and an additional 350,000 pamphlets had been sent out upon request to Texas Baptist people who had asked for such literature. Christian Life Commissions were organized on the associational level, seminary extension classes were begun for Negroes through Southwestern Baptist Theological Seminary, and a Christian Life Workshop was held. In 1958 it was reported that 550,000 pieces of literature had been distributed, most of them by specific requests. Sixty-six associational Christian Life committees were active throughout the Convention in 1958, compared to twenty-nine reported in 1957.

The Baptist Standard. The official Texas Baptist paper made excellent progress in the five years of this program. The subscription list numbered 268,441 at the beginning, and in 1958 reported a total of 342,141. The editor of the paper until 1954 was David M. Gardner. He was succeeded by E. S. James, who came from the pastorate of the First Baptist Church, Vernon.

When this second Five-Year Plan was completed in 1958, the Convention already had set out goals for the six year period from 1959 to 1964. The Southern Baptist Convention had chosen emphases for these years leading into 1964, the sesquicentennial of the first general organization by Baptists in America in 1814. T. A. Patterson was chairman of a committee to integrate the emphases in Texas with those of the southwide body. As a result, the Convention voted that evangelism through cooperative witnessing would be magnified in 1959; evangelism through teaching and training in 1960; evangelism through stewardship and enlistment in 1961; evangelism through church extension in 1962; evangelism through world missions in 1963; and in 1964, the celebration of the third jubilee. The committee suggested that 1958 be a year of prayer to prepare for the evangelistic effort in 1959.

At the Convention meeting in 1959, the Executive Board recommended an overall budget of $12,880,000.00 for the following year, the largest budget ever adopted by this or any other state convention in American Baptist life at that time. In every respect, the year 1959 was outstanding. Undesignated Cooperative Program receipts totalled $8,921,499.21, while designated receipts were $3,291,014.35. Each department reported excellent advance in its work.

The Survey Committee (1957–59). The year 1959 will be a landmark in Texas Baptist history. It was the occasion of the greatest organizational revision Texas Baptists have yet known. For over two decades Texas Baptist leadership had recognized the need for a careful study of the organizational structure of the Convention and its agencies. This was a continuing theme after Secretary Feezor took office. Year by year the departmental work showed new refinement and better articulation. For example, in 1957 a committee studied the relationship of the Convention to the various institutions sponsored by Texas Baptists; in 1958, as a means of protecting the Cooperative Program, special offerings were reduced to three only: the Lottie Moon Christmas Offering, the Annie Armstrong Home Missions Offering, and the Mary Hill Davis Offering for state missions; and in 1958 the Convention voted on constitutional amendments in an effort to match the functions of the structure with the best methods of doing its work.

However, the enlarging task and the increase in membership and giving during the 1950's brought calls for a thorough study of the organizational structure in order to make specific expansion plans for the years ahead. The Plans and Policies Committee of the Executive Board recommended the appointment of a large committee to make this study, assisted by the professional management consultant firm of Booz, Allen, and Hamilton. The committee was composed of Chairman T. A. Patterson, W. A. Criswell, Grady Metcalf, J. H. Landes, Charles Wellborn, W. M. Browning, Mrs. Clem Hardy, Lattimore Ewing, W. Fred Swank, A. J. Ballard, Mrs. Marie Mathis, Howard E. Butt, Jr., Orba Lee Malone, L. L.

Morriss, A. A. (Gus) Jackson, R. B. Smith, Groner Pitts, S. N. Reed, Elwin Skiles, W. L. Martin, W. M. Shamburger, C. E. Hereford, Vernon Elmore, Carroll B. Ray, and Rex Baker, Jr. Ex-officio members were Carl Bates (who was succeeded by M. B. Carroll when Bates left the state and was thus forced to resign as president of the Texas Convention) and E. Hermond Westmoreland. This Committee made a masterful analysis of the development of Baptist work in Texas and of probable future trends in Texas population. The organization of the Convention and all of its facets of work were then examined. Four major sections came under careful scrutiny: (1) the Convention itself, (2) Convention committees, (3) Convention institutions, and (4) the Executive Board.

The principal criticisms of the Convention organization as a whole were basic in making subsequent recommendations. These were:

> The organizational structure is not patterned after our basic objectives.
> The main streams of activity do not stand out.
> In many cases, the division of functions and responsibilities among different levels or among different groups at the same level is unclear.
> There is not a clear differentiation between policy decisions and action decisions. There is no body of consistent policy to guide planning and action decisions at all levels.[5]

There followed a thorough survey and criticism of the Convention, Convention committees, Convention institutions, and the Executive Board. After isolating the areas requiring attention, the Survey Committee made extensive organizational recommendations. It is not possible, of course, to list in detail the significant recommendations of the Committee, but recommendations relative to the Executive Board, which in essence constitutes the Convention functioning throughout the year, were the heart of the report. The Executive Board, said the Committee, should:

> Formulate and recommend to the convention the over-all objectives to be sought by the convention.

Appraise denominational needs and formulate objectives for the Convention in the following major program areas:

State missions

Education

Human welfare

Denominational newspaper and Foundation activities

Approve long-range plans for the orderly development of programs for each major program area.

One of the most fundamental responsibilities of the Executive Board should be to recommend Convention approval of objectives for the Convention's work. To meet this responsibility, the Executive Board should:

Determine the over-all objectives of the Convention in Texas.

Determine the needs of churches and church members that can best be served at the state-wide level.

Determine the denominational objectives in education.

Determine the denominational objectives in human welfare.

Determine the proper denominational roles of the "Baptist Standard" and the Baptist Foundation.

Once these basic determinations have been made by the Executive Board, it should:

Develop summary statements of objectives in each of these areas and present them to the Convention for approval.

Develop long-range plans for achievement of Convention-established objectives in each of the program areas.

Once objectives have been established, the Executive Board should develop the means for achieving them. It should, subsequently, appraise the progress made toward the accomplishment of objectives.

The Executive Board should confine its attention to matters of broad policy. Responsibility for operations should be delegated by the Board to the staff of the Board and to the commissions.[6]

The Committee then outlined in clear language a revised plan of organization and a description of the function of each part of the structure. Basically, the recommendations noted that the Executive Board was too large to become expert in all of its areas of function, and needed the advice and assistance of specialized committees, as well as the service of a highly competent staff to which the Board could delegate specific responsibilities. A Program Coordinating Committee should assist the Board in unifying all major program areas of the Convention; a Business Administration and Audit Committee should advise on matters of business; and a Public Relations Committee should assist the Director of Public Relations in his several tasks.

Three major Commissions, each with a Secretary and staff, were structured to provide the basic programs of the Convention: the State Missions Commission, the Christian Education Commission, and the Human Welfare Commission, the last-named to provide leadership in relation to hospitals and benevolent homes. The *Baptist Standard* and the Baptist Foundation were related to the Executive Board through the Program Coordinating Committee. The Christian Life Commission and the Church Loan Board were to be under the general administrative guidance of the State Missions Secretary between sessions of their own governing groups.

The Committee not only set out the structure, functions, and philosophy of the proposed revision, but also worded the proposed constitutional amendments and the action necessary to bring the new structure into existence. On November 4, 1959, with only a few minor amendments, the Convention approved this monumental structural revision.

In 1960, the final year before the retirement of Secretary Feezor, large strides were made toward implementing the recommendations of the Survey Committee. The Christian Education Commission was organized along the lines recommended by the Committee, and E. N. Jones, an experienced and dedicated school expert, was secured as its Secretary. A Human Welfare Commission was formed "to serve the Board in its ministry to hospitals, child-care homes, a facility for the aging, a haven for unwed mothers, and a ministry to boys and girls to prevent their delinquency." James Basden, a successful pastor and denominational leader, became the first Secretary of this Commission, which supervised eight hospitals, four children's homes, two homes for the aging, a boys' ranch, a facility for delinquent girls, and a haven for unwed mothers. J.

Woodrow Fuller, a veteran of the state office, became the Secretary of the reorganized State Missions Commission. The structure of the Christian Life Commission was modified to take the form described in the Committee recommendations, and Jimmy Allen was named as its Secretary, succeeding Foy Valentine, who had accepted a similar office with the Southern Baptist Convention during the year. James C. Cantrell, a Christian business man, was named Secretary of the Baptist Foundation, while A. B. White continued as Secretary of the Church Loan Board. The distinguished veteran of the Board, R. A. Springer, in his twenty-third year in the state office, headed the Business Administration and Audit Committee. Secretary Lloyd Wright continued as head of the Public Relations Department.

In every respect the report for the year 1960 was outstanding. Texas Baptists had 125 associations with 3,845 churches and 494 missions. Baptisms totalled 59,777. Membership had increased to 1,625,980. The Brotherhood enrollment was 107,204; W. M. U. enrollment, 201,444; Sunday school enrollment, 1,162,927; Training Union enrollment, 484,167; choir enrollment, 96,538. Mission gifts were $16,311,930.00, while Texas Baptists gave almost $89,000,000.00 for all purposes.

The Convention of 1960 approved several items of considerable significance. Following the enthusiastic vote of the Mexican Baptist Convention, the Baptist General Convention of Texas, in the same spirit, approved the unification of the two bodies, effective July 1, 1961. In addition, the charter of the Convention was altered to show that its Executive Board "shall be constituted by one hundred and eighty directors and the ex-officio members." A capital needs campaign of $28,000,000.00 in behalf of the colleges, universities, and the academy fostered by the Convention was approved.

In the report of Secretary Feezor for 1960, he said:

> Under the retirement policy of the Board, the current Secretary relinquishes the work on December 31. In its September meeting, the Board entered into the election of a new Secretary. After a prayer period of nearly an hour, the election proceeded by secret ballot. Dr. T. A. Patterson was chosen by a majority vote on the fourth ballot. He has given his acceptance and will assume his duties on January 1.

Dr. Patterson brings to the position a forceful and pleasing personality. Also, he brings a knowledge of the Board's work and a denominational loyalty not surpassed by any Secretary preceding him.[7]

Thomas A. Patterson (1961-present)

The words of Secretary Feezor introducing the new leader were well deserved. Patterson was an experienced pastor, a knowledgeable denominational leader, and an academic scholar holding the highest theological degree from Southwestern Seminary. He had been chairman of the important committee to structure the last five-year program for Texas Baptists, as well as chairman of the Survey Committee that had provided the radical revision in the state organizational structure in 1959.

The numerous activities developed or continued under Secretary Patterson by each Commission, Division, and Department of the staff, as reported in nine 500-page *Annuals,* can hardly be summarized. It is clear, however, that the new Secretary's grand design was to enlist all of the resources of all Texas Baptists in confronting all of the world with the gospel. The re-tooling of the organizational structure in 1959 provided a much more effective instrument for unifying all facets of the Board in the achievement of practical goals. The Program Coordinating Committee was able to translate the dreams and goals of the leadership into effective working programs by utilizing all of the capabilities of the staff without reference to organizational lines. The enlistment of all resources of all Texas Baptists for all of Christ's work has been attempted during this period through several program emphases.

Secretary Patterson had displayed his concern for an aggressive missionary outreach during his leadership in the Executive Board before he assumed the secretaryship. He played an important role in preparing the way for the unification of the Mexican Baptist Convention with the Baptist General Convention in 1961. The Survey Committee, which Patterson headed, underlined the challenge of the Mexican-Americans in Texas, estimating that by 1975 there would be possibly 3,700,000 of them in Texas. Some thought this estimate to be an exaggeration in 1959, but as a matter of fact, this total was reached by 1969. Patterson recognized that the Mexican-American population would increasingly make a fundamental impact upon the economic, social, and religious life of Texas, and that "God has moved a mission field to our door."

A concerted effort was begun to reach Mexican-Americans for Christ. The Valley Baptist Academy and the Mexican Baptist Institute, although educational institutions, were not placed under the supervision of the Christian Education Commission but were designed to aid in the mission thrust and were structured in the State Missions Commission. After thorough preparation, a Mexican New Life Crusade was launched in 1964, resulting in about 7,500 professions of faith and almost the same number of other decisions. Following the pattern of the Japan and Southeast Asia New Life Movement, the significant metropolitan areas were the first target, followed by an intensive campaign in all contiguous churches.

The Mexican crusade did not exhaust the plans for evangelizing this important segment, but was the beginning of a continuing program. Secretary Patterson and Director Charles P. McLaughlin of the State Missions Commission made a personal 900-mile tour down the Rio Grande River from El Paso to Brownsville, conferring with Baptist pastors and feeling the pulse of the Mexican-American people. The River Ministry program was begun in 1967, and Elmin K. Howell was secured as Coordinator. A film, *This is My Hand,* showing the needs of the people, aroused statewide interest. Since the Foreign Mission Board was working just across the imaginary line between Texas and Mexico, and the Home Mission Board on the Texas side of the line, a series of conferences was held between the executives of these two Southern Baptist Convention agencies and the Texas leaders to insure complete cooperation.

Every Division and Department of the Board has made its contribution to this ministry. The Evangelism Division, for example, has trained workers up-state for service in this area, planned and promoted the New Life crusade, and organized a Latin-American Evangelism Conference; the Church Training Department provided Latin-American conferences; Texas Baptist Men translated their Brotherhood program materials for use in Mexican Brotherhoods, and Woman's Missionary Union has actively supported the movement in service and offerings. The Missions Division, of course, has taken the lead through assistance in developing the several programs, helping in the building of churches in Latin-American communities, and the ministry of the Language Missions Department. The Mexican Baptist Institute and the Valley Baptist Academy have been used as rallying points for leadership training and inspirational conferences.

This same program of mission outreach has looked in other directions. A Japan and Southeast Asia New Life Movement was projected in 1963 after careful planning and liaison with other Southern Baptist agencies. Over 40,000 decisions were recorded, and hundreds of Texas Baptist workers were immeasurably blessed and in turn radiated that blessing to their churches and communities. Other crusades were held under the aegis of the Evangelism Division. In addition, an increasingly larger program of Pioneer Missions in the Minnesota-Wisconsin area was structured into the work of the Missions Division.

A second program emphasis of this period has been the effort to increase lay participation in contemporary witnessing for Christ. The New Life movements in the Orient and among the Mexican-Americans confirmed the belief that busy men and women could play a major part in missionary involvement if given the opportunity. A task force of 50,000 Texas Baptists was visualized, who could witness in formal campaigns or in daily activities. The California Encounter of 1968 utilized approximately 800 Texans in preaching and witnessing.

A third emphasis has looked toward tapping the material resources in the hands of Texas Baptists. Such films as *Decision at Friendship* and *A Train Goes Through Our Town,* and the publication, *Channels of Compassion,* have challenged Texas Baptists to be faithful in their stewardship. The last-named publication explored new ways of honoring God with material possessions. This did not visualize an endowed mission program, but contemplated what could be done if the regular gifts through the Cooperative Program were substantially supplemented with other resources.

Such supplementary giving has become increasingly a necessity for the support of benevolent institutions and the schools.

Adequate financial support for the schools, for example, has been a matter of great concern for Texas Baptists. The severe financial depression in Texas (which lasted from about 1923 to 1940), together with the growth in size and number of Texas Baptist schools, diminished the percentage of the total budget of the schools that has been provided by the Convention. Local trustees and administrators have been called upon to shoulder more of the burden of financial support. In 1960 the Convention fostered an intensive financial campaign to assist the schools, but it is likely that in the long run a much better contribution was made by the leadership of the Convention in assisting the schools to organize development programs of their own.

When O. D. Martin came to the Stewardship Division in 1962, only Baylor and Hardin-Simmons had structured any type of development program. Since that time, every Texas Baptist school has effective development programs by which they interest prospective donors, appeal to Foundations, approach corporations, and use other legitimate means to provide for their financial needs. Over $20,000,000.00 was secured by Texas Baptist schools in 1968 from developmental programs, earnings on endowment, etc. This achievement by the schools probably represents the brightest hope for the future of Baptist education in Texas.

Another emphasis of this period has been the probing of the nature and effectiveness of the denominational structures. What financial aid may the schools seek from the government? What limitation shall be placed upon hospitals and medical schools as they seek financial undergirding? What is the nature of the constitutional wall that separates church and state, and is there any point at which it may be breached? These and similar questions relative to the nature of the Convention and its agencies have occupied the attention of the messengers at many of the sessions. Perhaps as never before, the effectiveness of the structure has been scrutinized. Committees of various numbers—100, 300, etc., have made lengthy studies, resulting in an improved definition of the task, a better delegation of responsibilities, and an increased responsiveness of the organizational structures. The total involvement of the staff across organizational lines, for example, in the state mission thrust and work with young people, speaks well of the elasticity of the state structure. Similarly, the proposal of a vigorous ministry in the twenty-three metropolitan areas of Texas already has involved the utilization of the staff in many departments as they have planned together.

Without attempting to describe all of the activities of the staff during this period, an effort will be made to identify the personnel; to note the principal thrust of the four Commissions, as well as the supporting and related ministries of the Executive Board; to introduce the new Area Program; and to mention additional organizational and program refinements through the work of the Committee of One Hundred.

The Organizational Staff and Its Personnel. When Secretary Patterson began his work on January 1, 1961, there were six supporting and related ministries: (1) Treasurer, R. A. Springer, with Robert H. Bolen as Controller and Cecil G. Goff as Director of Statistical Services. (2) Public Relations, Lloyd Wright, Director. (3) Baptist Foundation, James C. Cantrell, Secretary. (4) The *Baptist Standard,* E. S. James, editor. (5) Church Loan Department, A. B. White, Executive Vice President. (6) Woman's Missionary Union, Mrs. Bert Black, President, and Miss Eula Mae Henderson, Executive Secretary.

The four Commissions, as developed under the constitutional revision of 1959, were staffed as follows: (1) Christian Life Commission, Jimmy R. Allen, Director. (2) Christian Education Commission, E. N. Jones, Secretary, with C. Eugene Kratz as Coordinator of Institutional Programs, and W. F. Howard as Director of Student Work. (3) Human Welfare Commission, James Basden, Secretary. (4) State Missions Commission, J. Woodrow Fuller, Secretary. There were four Divisions in this Commission. C. Wade Freeman was Director of the *Evangelism Division.* The *Missions Division,* Charles P. McLaughlin, Director, had three Departments: the Church Building Department, H. Taylor Pendley, Secretary; the Direct Missions Department, Roy A. Lambert, Secretary; and the Language Missions Department, Dallas P. Lee, Secretary. The *Church Services Division,* R. Hooper Dilday, Director, included four extensive departments: the Sunday School Department, W. R. Bumpas, Secretary, succeeding Andrew Q. Allen, who had died on January 14, 1960; the Training Union Department, Edward E. Laux, Secretary; the Brotherhood Department, L. H. Tapscott, Secretary; and the Church Music Department, V. F. Forderhase, Secretary. The *Stewardship Division* was at this time without a Secretary. This Division was created in 1960 as a part of the reorganization of the State Mission Commission. It had formerly been a part of the Direct Missions program. There were two departments in this Division: the Cooperative Program and Church Finance Section, Cecil A. Ray, Secretary; and the Endowment Department, Calvin B. Reeves, Secretary.

A surprisingly few number of major changes were made in the principal posts of leadership during this nine year period. Jay L. Skaggs succeeded Robert H. Bolen as controller in 1964; Richard T. McCartney succeeded Lloyd Wright in Public Relations in 1962, and was in turn succeeded by Billy R. Keith in 1968; A. B. White was succeeded by Don J. Singletary in the Church Loan Association in 1967; and E. S. James was succeeded by John Jeter Hurt as editor of the *Baptist Standard* in 1966. In the Christian Life Commission, James M. Dunn succeeded Jimmy R. Allen in 1968. In the Christian Education Commission, Woodson Armes succeeded E. N. Jones in 1968. In 1964 J. Woodrow Fuller resigned as Secretary of the State Missions Commission, and Charles P. McLaughlin succeeded him. In the Church Services Division, James Frost succeeded W. R. Bumpas in 1967. On December 31, 1963, L. H. Tapscott, who had served faithfully and effectively as Brotherhood Secretary since 1945, retired. He was followed by W. L. Smith, who was succeeded in 1969 by Robert E. Dixon. In 1967 the Brotherhood Department was restructured and placed in the category of a supporting and related ministry under the name Texas Baptist Men. In the Missions Division, Harold C. Bennett succeeded Charles P. McLaughlin in 1964, and in 1968 Charles Lee Williamson succeeded Bennett. In 1966 Darwin Farmer was named as head of the Direct Missions Department. In the Stewardship Division, O. D. Martin was named Director in 1962. He was succeeded in 1967 by Cecil A. Ray.

The Thrust of the Four Commissions. The increasing effectiveness of the four Commissions in the 1960's justified the architects of the new structure. Only a brief reference to the considerable activity of each one can be attempted here.

(1) The Christian Life Commission. Social, economic, and political patterns were changing rapidly in this decade. This Commission engaged in workshops, youth conferences, clinics, and general meetings of various sorts to lead Texas Baptists in the development of Christian attitudes and activity. A million tracts each year on various aspects of the Christian life were prepared and distributed. In 1968, under the leadership of Secretary Dunn and his associates, Phil D. Strickland and Charles Petty, the state convention adopted concise recommendations affecting lawlessness, narcotics traffic, alcohol and drugs, television, youth, race, planned parenthood, state legislation, traffic safety, church-state developments, war, and evangelism and ethics.

(2) The Christian Education Commission. During the early years of this period a campaign was instituted to raise $28,000,000.00 for Christian Education in Texas. The objectives, however, went beyond the financial aspect. They included recruitment, the enlistment of Baptist students in B. S. U. programs on non-Baptist campuses, vocational Christian service, and a general deepening of spiritual resources. The Commission was at the same time engaged in an intensive study of the Survey Committee recommendations, and in 1963 published a 150-page report which, it was hoped, would chart the direction Christian education should take among Texas Baptists. The Commission sponsored faculty retreats and workshops on inter-institutional cooperation, Academic accreditation for all Texas Baptist schools has been emphasized, and high scholastic standards have been encouraged. The Carden study of 1967–8 provided valuable data.

This Commission in 1968, under Secretary Woodson Armes, fostered nine colleges and one academy, as follows: Baylor University, Waco, Abner V. McCall, President; Dallas Baptist College,

Dallas, Charles P. Pitts, President (This school was formerly Decatur Baptist College, but was moved to Dallas in 1965, and in 1968 became a senior college); East Texas Baptist College, Howard C. Bennett, President; Hardin-Simmons University, Elwin L. Skiles, President; Houston Baptist College, William H. Hinton, President; Howard Payne College, Guy D. Newman, President; Mary Hardin-Baylor College, William G. Tanner, President; University of Corpus Christi, Kenneth Maroney, President; Wayland Baptist College, Roy C. McClung, President; and San Marcos Baptist Academy, Jack E. Byron, President.

In addition, through the Division of Student Work directed by W. F. Howard and his associates, Chester L. Reams and Jack Greever, this Commission supervised seventy-nine Baptist Student Unions in Baptist schools, tax supported colleges, and other private colleges and universities. In thirty-one of the tax supported schools there were Bible Chairs where Bible courses were taught by Baptist personnel as elective credit courses.

Baylor Medical School in Houston was disassociated from the Baptist General Convention of Texas in 1969, except for academic recognition.

(3) The Human Welfare Commission. At the opening of the period this Commission, under the leadership of Secretary James Basden, began the development of criteria for selecting trustees of human welfare institutions, formulated a statement of objectives for the human welfare program, and revised the charters of all institutions controlled by the Convention.

In 1962 the Amarillo Area Foundation, Inc. addressed a resolution to the Convention through this Commission offering to construct and equip a hospital in that area, without the use of federal assistance, if the Convention were willing to operate it. This proposal was accepted in 1962. The institution was named the High Plains Hospital and a Board of Trustees was elected by the Convention. Emmett Johnson was made Administrator effective November 15, 1963. The hospital was dedicated in February, 1968.

The scope of the ministry of this Commission was quite extensive in 1968. It supervised nine hospitals, as follows: Baptist Hospital of Southeast Texas, Beaumont, Guy H. Dalrymple, Administrator; Baptist Memorials Geriatric Center, San Angelo, Alton Pearson, Executive Director; Baptist Memorial Hospital, San Antonio, David A. Garrett, Administrator; Baylor University Medical Center, Dallas, Boone Powell, Executive Director; Hendrick Memorial Hospital, Abilene, E. M. Collier, Administrator; High Plains Baptist Hospital, Amarillo, Emmett R. Johnson, Administrator; Hillcrest Baptist Hospital, Waco, Julian H. Pace, Administrator; Memorial Baptist Hospital System, Houston, W. Wilson Turner, Executive Director; and Valley Baptist Hospital, Harlingen, T. H. Morrison, Jr., Administrator. Buckner Baptist Benevolences, R. C. Campbell, President and General Manager, included many types of benevolence, as follows: Buckner Child Care Services, Dallas, Bill J. Baker, Director; Buckner Baptist Children's Home, Dallas, Harold H. Hime, Administrator; Buckner Baptist Children's Home, Lubbock, A. L. Gatewood, Administrator; Buckner Baptist Boys Ranch, Burnet, B. Jack Whyburn, Administrator; Buckner Marriage and Family Counseling Center, Dallas, James L. Barber, Administrator; Buckner Baptist Maternity Home, San Antonio, Tom J. Drewett, Administrator; Buckner Baptist Maternity Home, Dallas, Bill J. Baker, Supervisor; Buckner Baptist Trew Home and Ryburn Home, Dallas, Robert L. Herring, Administrator; and Buckner Baptist Haven, Houston, Thomas E. Jackson, Administrator.

Three other children's homes were fostered by this Commission: Mexican Baptist Children's Home, San Antonio, J. Ivey Miller, Administrator; South Texas Children's Home, Beeville, J. M. Lunsford, Administrator; and Texas Baptist Children's Home, Round Rock, Charles I. Wright, Administrator.

(4) The State Missions Commission. In 1969 the general staff of this Commission, in addition to Secretary McLaughlin, included E. Eugene Greer, Program Planning Associate; Harry V. Hamblen, Coordinator of Area and Association Missions; and Elmin K. Howell, River Ministry Coordinator. The four Divisions of this Commission were Church Services, Evangelism, Missions, and Stewardship.

In the Church Services Division, headed by R. Hooper Dilday, with staff associates John R. McLaughlin and John LaNoue, were three departments: Church Music, Sunday School, and Church Training (Training Union).

The Church Music Department, headed by V. F. Forderhase, with associates S. W. Prestidge, Jr. and Jack Terrell, developed a constantly enlarging ministry during this period. Typical of the work of each year was the report for 1968, when 32,082 participated in the church music festivals; 6,625 participated in the choral, vocal, and hymn-playing clinics; 7,867 participated in the state junior choir festivals and clinics; choir enrollment was 155,178, an increase of 10,380 over the previous year; 911 enrolled in the approved worker program; 307 participated in the Latin-American program of music schools; and a special church music program study was held in the Plains-Caprock Area.

The Sunday School Department, led by Secretary James E. Frost (who has since moved to a similar post in Florida), and associates Karl Bozeman, Cecil Roenfeldt, Richard Sims, and Ed Browning, continued its intensive program. In addition to the work generally identified with this department, such as Vacation Bible Schools and clinics, Sunday school Bible conferences, workshops, and enlargement campaigns, the cross-department activity of the staff was illustrated by cooperation with the Evangelism Division in holding almost three dozen evangelism-Sunday school associational conferences, and six one-night workshops provided for the Minnesota-Wisconsin Pioneer area.

Similarly, the work of the Church Training Department included training conferences in the Minnesota-Wisconsin area, as well as conferences for Mexican-Americans, in addition to their regular clinics, workshops, leadership conferences, etc. Secretary Edward E. Laux was assisted by R. Clyde Hall, Jr., Tommy Dixon, and Bill D. King.

The Evangelism Division, of course, played an active part in the Japan and Southeast Asia New Life Movement of 1963, the Mexican New Life Crusade in 1964, the Puerto Rico Crusade in 1966, and the Dayton, Ohio, crusade in 1967. Encounter-California provided 800 Texas preachers and laymen to witness on the West Coast. In Texas the evangelism seminars, crusades, and institutes were supplemented by the statewide Evangelism Conference, the

Youth Evangelism Conference, and the Latin-American Evangelism Congress. Director Wade Freeman had as his associates Theron V. Farris, Carlos Paredes (who succeeded Rudy Hernandez), James E. Hester, Gil Stricklin (who succeeded Ralph W. Neighbors), and O. Byron Richardson.

The Missions Division was the focal point of the state mission outreach. Charles Lee Williamson became its Director on July 15, 1968. It consisted of three departments: Church Building and Pioneer Missions, H. Taylor Pendley, Secretary, with Ed L. Clark, Frank B. Burress, Warren Littleford, and Robert B. Chapman, associates; Direct Missions, Darwin Farmer, Secretary, with Lloyd Henderson, Clinton Watson, and J. V. Thomas, associates; and Language Missions, Dallas P. Lee, Secretary, with Daniel G. Aleman, George B. Joslin, and Roberto Garcia (who replaced Abraham B. Smith), associates. This Division specifically worked through Texas Baptist men to forward the emphasis of lay participation in the mission outreach. In addition, it supervised the Mexican Baptist Bible Institute, H. B. Ramsour, President, and Valley Baptist Academy, Howard E. Gary, President. The former school enrolled 90 in 1968, while the latter enrolled 135.

Reflections of the involvement of this Division in the principal emphases of the period were seen in the extensive assistance given Mexican-American Baptists in church building, church extension, the River Ministry through the Language Missions Department in particular, and the operation of the two educational institutions. Increasing assistance has also been provided to the Minnesota-Wisconsin Pioneer area, as well as a vital ministry to the deaf, Orientals, and Indians. One interesting aspect of the Church Building and Pioneer Missions Department has been the work of men like E. O. Hartwell. He and others of the same selfless spirit dedicated themselves to the task of building church edifices. The pattern was for Hartwell, for example, to accept the pastorate of a little struggling church that needed a building, then to serve as contractor-builder and with other members of the congregation, erect a building for worship and training. These men have built literally hundreds of church buildings like this since the 1950's.

Texas Baptist Men, Robert E. Dixon, Executive Secretary-Treasurer, with Cameron Byler as associate, has worked closely with the Missions Division. In 1968 their Prisoner Rehabilitation Conference, regional Brother training institute, regional Royal Ambassador rallies, schools of missions (reaching almost 85,000), church staff training camp, and their ministry to Latin-American Brotherhoods through translating Brotherhood program material, forwarded their work with men and boys.

The Stewardship Division, Cecil A. Ray, Director, was restructured in 1968 to include three departments: Church Stewardship Department, Douglas C. Brown, Secretary, and Johnny M. Smith, associate; Estate Stewardship Department, W. F. Vanderburg, Secretary (who died on December 27, 1969), and Harry Truelove, associate; and the Development Department, Bob Longshore, Secretary. This Division actively promoted Christian stewardship through the churches, challenged individuals to use their possessions in a Christian way, and appealed to individuals qualified to do so to provide financial support for churches, institutions, and missions. Through stewardship conferences, printed materials, state and national meetings, film strips, and church and associational clinics, this Division has had a part in the remarkable financial growth of this period. In 1965 the Executive Board approved the Faith in Action Movement, which represented a church-centered approach to long-range planning. This Division helped in the development and promotion of that movement. In 1968, led by Convention President Gordon Clinard, B. J. Martin, and Ed Brooks Bowles, nineteen area rallies magnifying stewardship were conducted across the state.

The Supporting and Related Ministries. In 1968 Treasurer R. A. Springer completed thirty years of effective service as the financial officer of Texas Baptists, during which time the annual receipts have increased from $634,000.00 to over $19,000,000.00. In addition to many other duties, Springer has played a large part in the preservation of Texas Baptist history. Working closely with the Historical Commission of the Southern Baptist Convention and with Southwestern Seminary, he has long kept an eye on safeguarding historical records. Under his leadership a Texas Baptist historical center and museum have been developed at Independence, the site of the first missionary Baptist church in the state. In 1951 the congregation of the little church there, faced with increasing financial obligations and diminishing revenues, voted to give this property to the Convention. It is the only church owned by the state body. The ruins of old Baylor, nearby, were deeded to the Convention by the school on September 18, 1965. Earl Allen was called by the church as pastor, and with assistance from the Convention he and his gifted wife served as curators of the Texas Baptist Museum, which was dedicated on March 26, 1967.

Controller and Assistant Treasurer Jay L. Skaggs served as office manager, purchasing agent, and supervisor of the accounting and building staff, and in other ways provided for an efficient operation.

In connection with the close relationship between the Annuity Board of the Southern Baptist Convention and the Convention, H. H. McBride has served jointly for the two bodies in the promotion of plans offered by the Annuity Board in Texas.

Statistical Secretary Cecil G. Goff handled the difficult assignment of securing and providing accurate statistics. As a means of observing progress made during the period from 1961 to 1969, some of his figures are included, as follows:

	1961	1969
No. of Churches	3,889	3,897
Church Membership	1,660,449	1,868,235
Baptisms	60,541	56,407
Sunday School Enrollment	1,171,321	1,132,219
Training Union Enrollment	482,300	412,281
Choir Enrollment	106,226	161,617
W. M. U. Enrollment	201,729	161,451
Baptist Men Enrollment	105,659	60,754
Mission Gifts	$16,592,891.00	$21,475,020.00
Total Receipts	$91,746,841.00	$141,039,327.00

It will be noted that like Baptists in other states and like other denominations, Texas Baptists incurred losses in some of their study and training programs, although impressive gains were made in many important categories.

Baptist Foundation. Associated with Executive Secretary J. C. Cantrell in 1968 were George L. Shearin, Glenn L. Sybert, and

Gordon L. Bowers. It reported assets of $81,231,034.00. In the previous seven months (the figures are not shown for twelve months due to a change from the fiscal to the calendar year), the Foundation paid $2,341,535.00 to Baptist institutions and agencies, and $338,145.00 to individuals who had placed funds with the Foundation on an annuity basis.

The *Baptist Standard*. The able editor of the paper in 1969 was John Jeter Hurt, assisted by Donald T. McGregor and John A. Welch. The circulation increased from 365,220 in 1961 to 367,000 in 1968. Its ministries are many. It has served as a "camera lens" to help Texas Baptists focus on their state, the homeland, and the world in order to inform and inspire them for "their greatest possible activity in evangelism, missions, Christian education and benevolent work."

Public Relations. In the never-ending task of interpreting and reporting Texas Baptist activity for themselves and others, this department has provided news, graphics, audio visuals, and many technical services. The Director, Billy R. Keith, was assisted by Robert O'Brien in the Press section, Lynn Yarbrough and Lurae Biffer in the Art section, and Bob Russell, Technical Director.

Church Loans. President Don J. Singletary reported in 1968 that the Church Loan Association and the Baptist Church Loan Corporation had made loans amounting to $31,090,984.00 in the relatively brief time they had been in existence. Combined capital assets had reached $3,415,521.00, with total resources of $12,650,-708.00.

Woman's Missionary Union. During all of this period the women, led by Executive Secretary Eula Mae Henderson, continued their energetic program with local societies, the Young Woman's Auxiliary, the Girls' Auxiliary, and the Sunbeams. In 1969 her staff associates were Katharine Bryan and Mrs. Joyce Kelsay. The familiar format of state and district workshops, conferences, House Parties, conventions, Queens' Courts, and clinics provided information and inspiration. Each year brought special emphases. The year 1961–62 was one of preparation for the Seventy-Fifth anniversary of Woman's Missionary Union and the Fiftieth anniversary of Girls' Auxiliary. An enlarged program in

1962–63 celebrated these anniversaries. The following year stressed "enlistment, training and involvement in missions." In 1965 the spirit of a prayer retreat for state workers lingered throughout the activities of the year. Emphasis on camp leadership, Latin-American witnessing (especially through the River Ministry program), and literacy workshops was given in the following year. Training in methods and interpretations of the new organizational structure made 1967 and 1968 busy years—years of meetings and years of change. Between 1961 and 1969 the Lottie Moon Christmas Offerings increased from $1,912,433.45 to $3,407,267.87; the Annie Armstrong Offerings from $462,735.97 to $870,113.92; and the Mary Hill Davis State Mission Offerings from $168,146.36 to $629,694.60.

The Area Program. In 1963 the Executive Board appointed a large Missions Study Committee under the leadership of W. E. Denham to examine the geographical divisions in the sub-structure of Texas Baptist organizational life. This committee reported to the Convention in 1963 that there was an imbalance in the "District" structure that had been developed about thirty years before. The Convention adopted their recommendation that associations group themselves into smaller units called Areas (one to four associations to an Area) with from fifty to one hundred churches in each Area (except in larger cities) and a resident membership of from 12,000 to 18,000 per Area. A missionary would be secured for each Area. The Convention noted that this plan would have to be developed over a period of several years, depending on the needs and initiative of the individual associations. It was agreed that the State Board would continue its financial policies with all association and districts as long as these groups so desired or until the Area plan was adopted by a given Area or until there was a vacancy in personnel.[8]

In 1964 it was reported to the Convention that the State Missions Commission had been working to implement the changeover from the District plan to the Area plan. In 1968 there were thirty-nine functioning Areas, each with a missionary, constituting over eighty-five percent of the Baptist churches in Texas.

The Committee of One Hundred. In 1966 the Convention noted that the 1959 reorganization had greatly increased the participation of Baptist laymen on the Boards, Commissions, and Committees of the Convention, and desiring to encourage this, as well as to make other refinements in the organizational structure, the Convention authorized the appointment of a committee of one hundred pastors and laymen to review and evaluate the work of the Convention and its agencies, and to explore ways to enlist the total resources of Texas Baptists in the implementation of their task. This committee, headed by E. Hermond Westmoreland, reported in 1967, saying that

> the recommendations of the 1959 Survey Report have been implemented and in most instances are proving highly effective in their results. The reports also reveal that Texas Baptists for the most part are fortunate in the dedicated leadership that serves the denomination and the churches of our convention. The intervening years since the adoption of the Survey Report have been characterized by continuous progress and fruitful results.[9]

A number of detailed recommendations involving changes in structure and function were made, most of them being adopted or referred to the same committee for further study. In 1968 the Committee made its second and final report, including fifty-nine recommendations, most of which passed without emendation.[10]

What Hath God Wrought!

After one has recited this story of Texas Baptists during the past one hundred and fifty years, he surely must close by thanking God and taking courage. It is not possible to know the dimensions of the vision of Z. N. Morrell when he preached his sermon at Nacogdoches in 1836 that suggested the theme of Texas Baptist history —that the desert would blossom as a rose. In his *Flowers and Fruits* he marvelled at the progress made during his lifetime. He seemed to feel that he had lived long enough to see the fulfilment of his vision of almost fifty years before. Could he possibly have conceived of a day when Texas Baptists would number almost two million and would make gifts to the Lord's work of over $140,000,000.00?

But the vision of faith must always recede. As great things are achieved, the vision must advance far beyond the grasp in order to inspire and lead God's people onward. What noble Baptist people have achieved already must simply become the place of departure for their sons and daughters.

> And we who follow in their wake
> Mark well the price they paid.
> His mantle lies upon us now,
> But we are not afraid
> If God be with us: This we cry
> "The light of Jesus shall not die
> 'Till earth's remotest corner knows
> And the deserts blossom as a rose."

DOCUMENTATION

CHAPTER ONE

1. Z. N. Morrell, *Flowers and Fruits in the Wilderness* (Dallas, 1886), 4th rev. ed., pp. 46–48.
2. Sybil Leonard Armes, in the *Baptist Standard* (Dallas, Texas), Vol. 60, No. 46, for Nov. 11, 1948. Used by permission.

CHAPTER TWO

1. Stephen F. Austin, "Austin to Friends, May 28, 1823," Eugene C. Barker, ed., *The Austin Papers* (Washington, 1924), 3 vols.
2. *Ibid.*, "Austin to Public, October 30, 1823."
3. *Ibid.*, Letter of December 17, 1824.
4. Quoted by J. M. Carroll, *A History of Texas Baptists* (Dallas, 1923), p. 42.
5. Louis W. Newton and Herbert T. Gambrell, *A Social and Political History of Texas* (Dallas, 1935), p. 98.
6. William S. Red, *The Texas Colonists and Religion, 1821–1836* (Austin, 1924), p. 87.
7. John Bond, comp., *History of the Baptist Concord Association of Middle Tennessee and North Alabama* (Nashville, Tenn., 1860), p. 26.
8. J. M. Carroll, *op. cit.*, p. 116.

CHAPTER THREE

1. Z. N. Morrell, *op. cit.*, p. 67.
1a. While the records show eight members in this Washington church at the time of its organization, the two letters sent to the missionary societies make reference to *nine* members. Perhaps this included Ellis.
2. Z. N. Morrell, *op. cit.*, pp. 75–77.
3. For the text of the home mission appeal, see the *Southwestern Religious Luminary*, Jan., 1838, p. 20; for the foreign mission appeal, see the *Christian Index*, February 22, 1838.

4. For a summary of this entire story, see W. W. Barnes, "Dr. Jesse Mercer," in the *Chronicle*, January, 1953, pp. 43–45.

5. See the *Baptist Advocate* (New York), September 11, 1841, p. 1.

6. See A. J. Holt, "A Brief History of Union Baptist Church, Nacogdoches County, Texas, 1836–1911, Compiled from Original Records of the Church, December 8, 1911." Manuscript copy in Fleming Library, Southwestern Baptist Theological Seminary, Fort Worth, Texas. The original records of the church were destroyed by fire after Holt prepared this material. See also William Tellis Parmer, *Seventy-Five Years in Nacogdoches—A History of the First Baptist Church 1884–1959* (Dallas, 1959), pp. 39ff.

7. Z. N. Morrell, *op. cit.,* p. 188.

8. *Ibid.,* p. 108.

9. *Ibid.,* pp. 108–9.

10. *Ibid.,* pp. 110–12.

11. *Ibid.,* p. 81.

12. J. M. Carroll, *op. cit.,* p. 195n.

13. *Ibid.,* p. 156.

14. Letter from James Huckins to Corresponding Secretary Benjamin M. Hill, American Baptist Home Mission Society, New York, dated November 14, 1841, published in the *Baptist Advocate* (New York), December 18, 1841, p. 1.

15. Letter from William Tryon to Corresponding Secretary Benjamin M. Hill, American Baptist Home Mission Society, New York, dated July 1, 1841, published in the *Baptist Advocate* (New York), September 18, 1841, p. 1.

16. Z. N. Morrell, *op. cit.,* pp. 110–12.

17. Letter of R. E. B. Baylor to J. H. Stribling, dated April 13, 1871, from Holly Oak. Original in Library, Baylor University, Waco, Texas. No pagination.

18. See letter of James Huckins to Hill, *op. cit.,* p. 1.

19. See letter of P. B. Chandler, missionary at La Grange, in *Southern Baptist Missionary Journal,* Vol. II, No. 5, for October, 1847, p. 121.

20. R. E. B. Baylor to Stribling, *op. cit.,* n.p.

21. See *Minutes of the Good Hope Baptist Church* (now First Baptist Church), Talladega, Alabama, showing that in March, 1840, a letter was granted to Baylor through Brother Chilton (Thomas J., a cousin of Baylor).

22. See letter of P. B. Chandler, *op. cit.,* p. 121.

23. J. S. Newman, *A History of the Primitive Baptists of Texas, Oklahoma and Indian Territories* (Tioga: Baptist Trumpet, 1906), Vol. I, p. 42.

CHAPTER FOUR

1. Letter of R. E. B. Baylor to Stribling, *op. cit.*, n.p.
2. Z. N. Morrell, *op. cit.*, pp. 134–35.
3. J. M. Carroll, *op. cit.*, p. 86.
4. Letter in the *Baptist Advocate* (New York), December 7, 1839, p. 1.
5. *Ibid.*, December 28, 1839, p. 1.
6. *Ibid.*, February 8, 1840, p. 1.
7. *Ibid.*, March 14, 1840, p. 1.
8. J. M. Carroll, *op. cit.*, p. 144.
9. Letter in the *Baptist Advocate* (New York), June 27, 1840, p. 1.
10. See the *Baptist Advocate* (New York), for December 5, 1840, p. 1. Notice the date of the farewell in Carroll is later than the diary that follows it.
11. *The Baptist Advocate* (New York), February 20, 1841, p. 1.
12. *Ibid.*, September 25, 1841, p. 1.
13. Not November 10, as shown in Carroll, *ibid.*, p. 163.
14. The *Baptist Advocate* (New York), September 11, 1841, p. 1.
15. *Ibid.*, September 18, 1841, p. 1.
16. *Ibid.*, December 25, 1841, p. 1.
17. Z. N. Morrell, *op. cit.*, p. 183.
18. *Ibid.*, pp. 195–96.
19. *Ibid.*, p. 198.
20. *Ibid.*, pp. 233–38.
21. *Southern Baptist Missionary Journal*, Vol. I, No. 10, March, 1847, p. 236.
22. Z. N. Morrell, *op. cit.*, p. 238.
23. Letter of James Huckins dated November 14, 1841, in the *Baptist Advocate* (New York) for December 18, 1841, p. 1.
24. Letter from Baylor to Stribling, *op. cit.*, n.p.
25. Z. N. Morrell, *op. cit.*, p. 277.

CHAPTER FIVE

1. Z. N. Morrell, *op. cit.*, p. 132.
2. *The Union Baptist Association Centennial History*, D. R. Pevoto, comp., (no place of pub., n. d.), p. 9.
3. See Robert A. Baker, *A Baptist Source Book* With Particular Reference to Southern Baptists (Nashville, 1966), pp. 70–78.
4 R. E. B. Baylor, *op. cit.*, n.p.
5. Z. N. Morrell, *op. cit.*, p. 144f.
6. See letter of James Huckins, *op. cit.*, dated November 14, 1841.

7. Z. N. Morrell, *op. cit.*, pp. 146–47.

8. *Minutes of the Good Hope Baptist Church,* Talladega, Alabama; entries for the December term, 1838, and March term, 1841.

9. J. B. Link, *Texas Historical and Biographical Magazine* (Austin, 1891–92), Two Volumes, Vol. I, pp. 38–50.

10. See *Southern Baptist Missionary Journal,* Vol. II, No. 2, for July, 1847, p. 49.

11. See the *Baptist Advocate* (New York), for December 18, 1841, p. 1.

12. *Ibid.*

13. Georgia J. Burleson, *The Life and Writings of Rufus C. Burleson* (no place of pub., 1901), p. 101.

14. Z. N. Morrell, *op. cit.*, p. 138.

15. J. B. Link, *op cit.,* Vol. II, p. 158.

16. R. E. B. Baylor, *op. cit.*, n.p.

17. J. B. Link, *op. cit.*, Vol. I, p. 150.

18. R. E. B. Baylor, *op. cit.*, n.p.

19. *Southern Baptist Missionary Journal,* Vol. II, No. 4, for September, 1847, pp. 98–100.

20. J. M. Carroll, *op. cit.*, p. 230.

21. See story of Gillette by Arthur A. Grusendorf, "Henry F. Gillette—Baylor's First Teacher," in *The Baylor Line* (Waco), Vol. XXX, No. 2, for March–April, 1968, pp. 26–27.

CHAPTER SIX

1. Letter of Noah Hill to his brother-in-law from Wharton, Texas, dated October 1, 1854. Original is now in my possession, preserved by Walter S. Adams, Cartersville, Georgia, a descendant of Hill.

2. B. F. Riley, *History of the Baptists of Texas* (Dallas, 1907), p. 137.

3. R. N. Richardson, *Texas the Lone Star State* (Englewood Cliffs, New Jersey, 1958—2nd ed.), p. 156.

4. D. R. Pevoto, comp., *op. cit.*, p. 17.

5. *Southern Baptist Missionary Journal,* Vol. IV, No. 5, p. 137.

6. *Ibid.*, Vol. III, No. 12, p. 202.

7. *Ibid.*, Vol. IV, No. 5, p. 137.

8. J. B. Link, *op. cit.*, Vol. I, p. 279.

9. J. M. Carroll, *op. cit.*, p. 264.

10. *Ibid.*, p. 265.

11. *Ibid.*, p. 265.

12. See D. R. Pevoto, comp., *op. cit.*, p. 24.

13. Louis W. Newton and Herbert T. Gambrell, *op. cit.*, p. 282.

14. *Southern Baptist Missionary Journal,* Vol. III, No. 1, p. 17.

CHAPTER SEVEN

1. J. B. Link, *op. cit.*, Vol. II, p. 532.
2. Louis W. Newton and Herbert T. Gambrell, *op. cit.*, p. 301.
3. *Minutes of the Eighteenth Annual Session of the Baptist State Convention of Texas*, 1865, p. 7.
4. *Minutes of the Colorado Baptist Association*, 1854, p. 4.
5. *Minutes of the Union Baptist Association*, 1855, p. 23.
6. *Proceedings of the Baptist State Convention of Texas*, 1857, p. 16.
7. J. M. Carroll, *op. cit.*, pp. 337–38.
8. *Ibid.*, p. 338.
9. *Ibid.*, p. 342.
10. *Ibid.*, p. 354.
11. See report of *Missionary Baptist General Convention of Texas* (Galveston, 1914), pp. 54–55.

CHAPTER EIGHT

1. J. M. Carroll, *op. cit.*, pp. 515–16.
2. *Ibid.*, p. 518.
3. Robert A. Baker, *Relations Between Northern and Southern Baptists* (Seminary Hill, 1948), p. 101.
4. *Home Mission Monthly* (New York: American Baptist Home Mission Society), Vol. VII, pp. 12–13.
5. *Proceedings of the Seventeenth Annual Session of the Baptist General Association of Texas*, 1884, p. 28.
6. J. M. Carroll, *Op. cit.*, p. 524.
7. *Ibid.*, p. 629.

CHAPTER NINE

1. J. M. Carroll, *op. cit.*, p. 722.
2. *Proceedings, Forty-Eighth Annual Session of the Baptist General Convention of Texas*, 1896, p. 23.
3. *Ibid.*, 1895, p. 36.
4. B. F. Fuller, *History of Texas Baptists* (Louisville, Ky.: Baptist Book Concern, 1900), pp. 437–66.
5. *Proceedings of the Baptist General Convention of Texas*, 1893, p. 8.
6. *Ibid.*, p. 21.
7. *Ibid.*, 1887, p. 22.
8. L. R. Elliott, ed., *Centennial Story of Texas Baptists* (Chicago: Hammond Press, 1936), p. 161.
9. J. M. Carroll, *Op. cit.*, p. 820.

10. *Proceedings, Sixty-Second Annual Session of the Baptist General Convention of Texas,* 1910, p. 105.
11. *Annual of the Baptist General Convention of Texas,* 1913, p. 139.

CHAPTER TEN

1. *Annual of the Baptist General Convention of Texas,* 1915, pp. 65–66.
2. Article V, Sections 3–4 of the revised constitution.
3. *Annual of the Baptist General Convention of Texas,* 1922, pp. 15–16.
4. *Ibid.,* 1927, pp. 22ff.
5. *Ibid.,* 1924, pp. 177ff.
6. *Ibid.,* 1929, pp. 129ff.

CHAPTER ELEVEN

1. *Annual of the Baptist General Convention of Texas,* 1942, pp. 69ff.
2. *Ibid.,* 1943, p. 62.

CHAPTER TWELVE

1. *Annual of the Baptist General Convention of Texas,* 1946, p. 65.
2. *Ibid.,* 1950, p. 200.
3. *Ibid.,* 1953, p. 42.
4. *Ibid.,* 1949, p. 56.
5. *Ibid.,* 1959, p. 16 of Survey Committee Report.
6. *Ibid.,* p. 38.
7. *Ibid.,* 1960, p. 65.
8. *Ibid.,* 1963, p. 92.
9. *Ibid.,* 1967, p. 57.
10. *Ibid.,* 1968, pp. 36ff.

INDEX

271

272 ☆

Religious freedom p. 17-18
Lord's Supper p. 43
pastors pay, never enough — p. 66
Controversy, among Baptists p 97, 105 f
Sunday School, function; benefits from p 109 f